Praise for *The Animal Manifesto*

"*The Animal Manifesto* is Marc Bekoff's gentle challenge that we all go
a little further in extending the boundaries of our compassion toward
nonhuman animals. I found it hard to resist the call of a work so brim-
ming with awe, insight, and optimism concerning the creatures who
share our world. You will too."
— Wayne Pacelle, president and CEO of
the Humane Society of the United States

"We need books like this. We need writers like Marc Bekoff to remind
us of the emotional lives of animals and of our mismanagement of the
wild. We need to be reminded that we share this world with other animals, that we do not own it, that we do not even run it. We ignore all
of this not only at our peril, but to our great loss."
— Martha Grimes, bestselling author of *Dakota* and *The Blue Last*

"For more than thirty years, Marc Bekoff has occupied a unique niche in
the social movement to advance moral concern for animals, functioning as a fearless scientist relentlessly pressing the scientific community
to recognize the reality of animal thought, feeling, and emotion; as a
philosopher articulating the grounds for an expanded moral vision of
animals; and as a tireless advocate for justice for all creatures. In *The
Animal Manifesto*, he has distilled his knowledge and efforts into a document that should inspire all of us to 'expand our compassion footprint' in thought and action. Bekoff is incapable of writing a boring
paragraph, and his text is peppered with unforgettable anecdotes as
well as fascinating scientific data. I strongly recommend this book."
— Bernard E. Rollin,
bioethicist and professor of philosophy, animal sciences,
and biomedical sciences at Colorado State University

"Marc Bekoff at his best! He enhances our respect and understanding of animals using the science of ethology and philosophical inquiry to explain their behavior, and in the process awakens our compassionate concern for all creatures great and small."

— Dr. Michael W. Fox, veterinarian, syndicated columnist, and author of *Dog Body, Dog Mind* and *Cat Body, Cat Mind*

"Proof that animals are wistful, altruistic, tender, jealous, and conversational. But are these interesting facts to use to enliven a cocktail party, or do human obligations ensue when we realize that the intelligent life forms we seek in space are all around us here on earth? Marc Bekoff's challenge to humanity to relate to those on the plate — and in other places no sentient being deserves to be — is riveting reading that may occupy your thoughts long after the last page is turned and the lights are out."

— Ingrid E. Newkirk, founder of People for the Ethical Treatment of Animals (PETA)

"As a humane educator, I am always searching for books about pressing global issues that teach through critical thinking and inspire us to deeply embody our values. Marc Bekoff has written a superb book, with a gentle voice, one that will make each reader a better person and will go far to creating a more compassionate world for animals. He offers us crucial knowledge about animals, ignites our curiosity, and fosters our reverence, respect, and responsibility. I've never read a more convincing and powerful call for compassion. You will be changed by this book. It will be required reading for my students."

— Zoe Weil, president of the Institute for Humane Education and author of *Most Good, Least Harm; Above All, Be Kind*; and *The Power and Promise of Humane Education*

# THE
# ANIMAL
# MANIFESTO

# ANIMAL MANIFESTO

## Six Reasons for Expanding Our Compassion Footprint

## MARC BEKOFF

New World Library
Novato, California

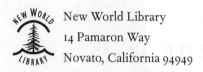

New World Library
14 Pamaron Way
Novato, California 94949

Text design by Mary Ann Casler

Library of Congress Cataloging-in-Publication Data
Bekoff, Marc.
The animal manifesto : six reasons for expanding our compassion footprint / Marc Bekoff.
   p.   cm.
Includes bibliographical references and index.
ISBN 978-1-57731-649-7 (pbk. : alk. paper)
1. Emotions in animals. 2. Human-animal relationships. 3. Animal behavior. I. Title.
QL785.27.B448 2010
179 .3—dc22                                2009043833

First printing, February 2010
ISBN 978-1-57731-649-7
Printed in Canada on 100% postconsumer-waste recycled paper

g New World Library is a proud member of the Green Press Initiative.

10 9 8 7 6 5 4 3 2 1

*In October 2008, when I was visiting the Moon Bear Rescue Centre outside of Chengdu, China, I met seven dogs to whom I dedicate this book: Henry, Matilde, Stevie, Lady Lobster, Butch, Tremor (aka Rambo), and Richter.*

*I also dedicate this book to the billions of anonymous animals who are in dire need of our support, and to all the wonderful people worldwide who are working hard to better the lives of animals, who dearly need our kindness, compassion, empathy, and love.*

*And also to Sarah for her unwavering passion.*

# CONTENTS

# INTRODUCTION

## *Our Common Bonds of Compassion*

"Anyone who says that life matters less to animals than it does to us has not held in his hands an animal fighting for its life. The whole of the being of the animal is thrown into that fight, without reserve."

— Elizabeth Costello, in *The Lives of Animals* by J. M. Coetzee

ANIMALS ARE CONSTANTLY ASKING US in their own ways to treat them better or leave them alone. This book is their manifesto. In it, I explain what they want and need from us and why they are fully justified in making these requests. We must stop ignoring their gaze and closing our hearts to their pleas. We can easily do what they ask — to stop causing them unnecessary pain, suffering, loneliness, sadness, and death, even extinction. It's a matter of making different choices: about how we conduct research to learn about the natural world and to develop human medicine, about how we entertain ourselves, about what we buy, where we live, who we eat, who we wear, and even family planning. Please join me. The animals need us, and just as importantly, we need them. This manifesto presents a much-needed revolution — a paradigm shift in what we feel and what we do regarding animals — that has to happen now because the current paradigm doesn't work. The status quo has wreaked havoc on animals and Earth. Denial and apathy must be replaced by urgency. If we all work to improve the lives of animals, we will improve our lives as well.

Of course, it's hard to speak for the animals, but because they share so much with us, it's not presumptuous to believe that what they want isn't so different from what we want: to avoid pain, to be healthy, to feel love. Their feelings are as important to them as our feelings are to us. Even further, many living beings seem wired to do good and to make others feel good. The central theme of *The Animal Manifesto* is that animals, including humans, are basically kind, empathic, and compassionate beings. As fellow animals sharing a single world, humans can, and increasingly must, do more to act on behalf of our kindred beings. That's a good part of why I'm an optimist. Goodness, kindness, empathy, and compassion come naturally, and they allow us to do what needs to be done, whether healing our conflicts with other animals or among ourselves. Despite enormous problems, there are some very promising trends that show that most people really do care. Goodness, kindness, empathy, and compassion are leading people all over the globe to talk about ways to treat animals with more respect and dignity and to lighten our carbon footprint, knowing that humanity's fate — or rather, the planet's fate and that of all the species on it — hangs in the balance and depends on our acting proactively now.

When it comes to protecting animals, we must think of expanding our compassion footprint, and then do something to make this happen. We lessen our negative impact on animals when we increase our compassion for them and strive to make the planet a peaceful, sustaining place for all beings. There are always trade-offs — some things work and some don't — but if we put an animal's well-being first, we can arrive eventually at the right decision. As with the environment, some of this involves society-wide changes. But expanding our compassion footprint is also a lot about the small decisions we as individuals make every day; bit by bit, we can continually work toward making things better. Will this require doing things that take us out of our comfort zone? Probably. But this really isn't asking too much, since humans are constantly making impositions on animals and taking them out of their comfort zones.

Polls show that just as green awareness is blossoming across the planet, so too is a new understanding of our relationship with other species. The Green Movement is a concept actively supported by more than 90 percent of child-rearing families in America. To support a cause they care about, 66 percent of adults in one study said they would switch brands, and 62 percent said they would switch retailers. This shift in thinking includes animals. A 2006 study conducted by Lake Research Partners revealed that nine out of ten Americans believe "strongly" that "we have a moral obligation to protect the animals in our care." The Best Friends Animal Society used this poll to develop its first Kindness Index, and noted that Americans are also "adamant about passing these values on to their children." Best Friends said that most people were ready to help, but "we simply have to create the opportunities." When those opportunities appear, people act. A 2008 Gallup Environmental

Poll found that, over the previous five years, 55 percent of Americans said they had made at least " 'minor [lifestyle] changes' to protect the environment" and 28 percent said they had made " 'major changes' in their lifestyle." In the same study, 65 percent of children aged six to twelve embraced the idea of linking a brand with helping to ensure the survival of endangered animals, and 78 percent of adults said they were more likely to buy a product that is associated with a cause they care about.

These polls confirm a society-wide trend that I've noticed in my own life with the strangers I meet. Often when I'm flying, or waiting in an airport, someone will strike up a conversation, and I'm always amazed and pleased at how interested they invariably are in animals and our impact on them. On one flight I happened to be sitting next to a woman who worked for a major software company. I was writing and spell-checking a manuscript, and she asked what program I used. I told her and said I was working on a book on animal emotions and that I wished that word-processing software would stop asking me to change the words "who" and "whom" to "that" or "which" when I refer to animals — because animals aren't objects but subjects. At first she didn't get it, but eventually she did, and she said she'd talk to the people at her company about changing their software. Whether she followed through or not, I was glad that she was open to seeing animals differently and that she recognized that the language we use affects our attitudes. Perhaps the next generation of spell-checking software will reverse its presumptions, prompting writers to refer to animals as "he" or "she," not "it."

Indeed, most people are simply accustomed to thinking and doing things the way they always have, without considering the effects of their actions, but when you call attention to them, and explain the facts in a nice, polite way, people often listen. Quite frequently, people are astounded to learn what really happens on the way to, and at, slaughterhouses; they simply don't know. Likewise, many people don't know what happens behind closed doors at laboratories and at sporting events. When what is hidden is exposed, it can become headline news. In May 2008, I was flying home from the World Forum for Animals in Barcelona when the story about the racehorse Eight Belles appeared in newspapers worldwide. Eight Belles broke her front ankles while running during the 134th Kentucky Derby, and this abused filly had to be euthanized — or killed — right in front of spectators on the racetrack at Churchill Downs, not off in some private stable. In the name of money, racehorses are often mistreated and pushed beyond their limits until they are injured, sometimes to the point that they must be killed, but the mistreatment and death of Eight Belles was so disturbingly public it couldn't be ignored. On the plane, the guy sitting next to me agreed how horrible this was, and we had a great chat about animal sentience and animal abuse of all kinds. The man didn't know the facts about racehorses, or much about animal abuse in general, but he said he wanted to raise his children in a kind and compassionate world, and the incident and our conversation led him to feel he needed to change some of his ways. Good for him.

Perhaps because I live at high altitude in what some people call "The People's Republic of Boulder" — twenty-five square miles in Colorado surrounded by reality — some people regard my embrace of the compassionate and caring side of human nature as merely "wishful thinking fluff." But as we'll see, solid science backs my belief. In *Wild Justice: The Moral*

*Lives of Animals*, Jessica Pierce and I argue that the same is true for animals — they have the cognitive and emotional capacities to make moral decisions and show kindness, compassion, and empathy — and we can learn a lot about ourselves by studying how animals negotiate their challenging and changing social worlds. *The Animal Manifesto* is a natural descendant of my books *Wild Justice* and *The Emotional Lives of Animals*, where I also discuss the "nice" side of animals. This "manifesto" takes what we've learned about the amazing animals with whom we share Earth and asks: What does that mean for us? And what should we do?

## This Manifesto Isn't Radical

Like any good manifesto, *The Animal Manifesto* is a call for action. I take the facts that have been established about animal sentience and emotions and look at how they affect our society's current value system. In other words, I freely mix science with ethics, morality, and emotion. This call to action addresses a variety of groups, ranging from the general public to policy makers to those who live in ivory towers, from humane and conservation organizations to grassroots groups and individuals, and from those who make their living studying, displaying, raising, or processing animals to those working to make their lives better. We all need to raise our consciousness about the lives of our fellow animals and change the current paradigm, in which those who work on behalf of animals and the environment are seen as "radicals" or "extremists." No one should be an apologist for passion and no one should be shamed for feeling.

Do we know everything there is to know about the minds and emotions of other animals? Certainly not, but we know enough to change our ways. Some scientists remain skeptical about the emotional lives of animals — but this view, which was once predominant, is dwindling rapidly. As we will see, it's simply impossible to ignore the growing amount of solid science concerning animal sentience. We need to take the skeptics to task and switch the burden of proof, so that skeptics have to "prove" that animals don't have rich emotional lives rather than others having to prove that they do. This is also part of the paradigm shift I argue for, in which the most "radical" stance becomes doubt.

Nevertheless, it's important to address these doubts head on. Some say life is too short to mess with skeptics, but I feel that life is too long for the misleading skeptical view of animal sentience to continue because it allows for far too much animal suffering and abuse. Often the skeptics raise the ante so high that most *humans* wouldn't qualify as feeling beings. For instance, some scientists dismiss anecdotes as valid proof (in any context), but I agree with my close friend philosopher Dale Jamieson that the plural of anecdote is data. Narrative ethology (a term coined by my colleague Jessica Pierce) is a perfectly good way to learn about the lives of animals. After I published my own observations of a magpie funeral ceremony — in which individual magpies paid tribute to their dead friend by standing silently around her, touching the corpse lightly, and flying off and bringing back grass that was laid down by the body — I had a slew of emails from people who had seen the same type of ritual in other birds in the corvid family: magpies, crows, and ravens. These stories, even from nonresearchers, are indeed data, and they challenge science to prove or disprove them. More than ever, controlled scientific studies are validating what our eyes clearly see.

Is it radical, then, to draw ethical conclusions from these facts? In 2009, when President Barack Obama nominated Harvard University law professor Cass Sunstein to run the Office of Information and Regulatory Affairs (which oversees the implementation of consumer, health, and environmental regulation), this was considered by some to be a radical move. As described in a January 2009 article in *Mother Jones* magazine, the Center for Consumer Freedom claimed that Sunstein is "an extremist" because, among other reasons, he once wrote, "There should be extensive regulation of the use of animals in entertainment, scientific experiments, and agriculture." Sunstein also believes that "hunting for 'sport and fun' — not for food — should be 'against the law' and that greyhound racing, cosmetic testing on animals, and the eating of meat raised in inhumane conditions ought to be eliminated." However, while Sunstein argues for extensive regulation of animal use and against sport hunting, he also "eats meat and has no secret plan to force vegetarianism on the American people," and he has written that "it is excessive to ban experiments that impose a degree of suffering on rats or mice if the consequence of those experiments is to produce significant medical advances for human beings." Is this a truly radical overall approach, to try to protect animals and their homes from unnecessary harm while not unduly burdening or endangering humans in the process?

More to the point, if animals can think and feel, what do they think and feel about the ways humans treat them? What would they say to us, and what would they *ask* of us, if they could speak a human language? Here is what I believe their manifesto would consist of:

1. All animals share the Earth and we must coexist.
2. Animals think and feel.
3. Animals have and deserve compassion.
4. Connection breeds caring, alienation breeds disrespect.
5. Our world is not compassionate to animals.
6. Acting compassionately helps all beings and our world.

Is such a manifesto radical? I think it's common sense. These six items are also the six "reasons" we can use to expand our compassion footprint; they are an extension of the ideas about which Jane Goodall and I wrote in our book *The Ten Trusts*. Yet, even though these ideas reflect common sense, I think that they are often denied or resisted because people intuitively understand that following them — respecting what we see before our own eyes — would lead to radical changes in how we live and what we do. This is hard, but it's not impossible, and we've done it before. It's important to remember that people who are at first considered "on the fringe" and radical aren't always wrong, nor is taking nature seriously sentimental, fluffy thinking. At first, hardcore scientists ridiculed Rachel Carson after she published *Silent Spring*, but her evidence and predictions about the horrible effects of pesticides and environmental toxins unfortunately proved to be true; since then, we've made major changes in our lives to help protect our environment. Many researchers criticized Jane Goodall when she first named the chimpanzees she studied; they didn't believe she'd seen David Graybeard use a blade of grass as a tool for fishing out termites until she showed them a video of this groundbreaking discovery. In the early 1960s, the ideas that an animal had an individual personality (warranting a name) and could make and use a tool (which only humans were thought capable of ) were heretical, crazy. Both are now commonplace, self-evident.

I have good company in arguing that animals, humans included, are basically good. University of California at Berkeley psychologist Dacher Keltner (who also lives in a city frequently associated with fluffy thinking), in his book *Born to Be Good*, also shows that the competitive, survival-of-the-fittest mentality is not who we really are or have to be to have a good life. It's not really a dog-eat-dog world because dogs don't eat other dogs. Being kind and good includes embracing cultural pluralism, which is a necessity in the diverse and often tough world in which we live.

We also know that we are influenced by the actions of others. If we see compassion, we are more likely to adopt it — compassion begets compassion, virtuous acts beget virtuous acts. Further, we receive what we give. If we employ compassionate proactive activism using humility, heart, and love, it can spread contagiously, and we will have a good chance of pulling ourselves out of the deep holes we've been digging for our fellow animals, ourselves, and Earth's highly compromised ecosystems.

We also know that it feels good to be nice. We're often filled with warm feelings when we cooperate. Recent neural imaging research on humans by James Rilling and his colleagues shows that mutual cooperation is associated with activation of the brain's reward processing centers, the dopamine system. Our brain releases dopamine when we cooperate, giving us instant pleasurable feedback and reinforcing the behavior. This is significant research, for it posits that being nice is rewarding in social interactions and might in itself be a stimulus fostering cooperation and fairness.

Surely, humans and other animals can be mean to one another. Nonetheless, cooperation and compassion are central to our own existence and to coexistence with other beings. It is for this reason that I remain optimistic that with hard work and patience we will be able to make the lives of other animals better as we expand our compassion footprint. Dacher Keltner uses the Confucian concept of *jen*, which refers to "kindness, humanity, and reverence" to discuss our "good nature," and he offers the concept of the *jen* ratio to "look at the relative balance of good and uplifting versus bad and cynical in life." This ratio is one way to measure our compassion footprint.

I hope academics, activists, and people interested in making the world a more peaceful and compassionate place will find this book to be of interest and inspire them to go out and do more for animals and Earth. I hope you find that my agenda isn't radical. To this end I weave in the latest science from academic journals with anecdotes taken from the popular media, the people I've met, and my own life to make the case that we all need to do more to care for animals and the habitats in which they live. In the three years since my book *The Emotional Lives of Animals* was published, we've learned an incredible amount about animal sentience and emotions, and I want to share that. I also want to appeal to people who don't agree with me, rather than preach to the converted, because that is where change occurs. Yet for all of us, the real challenge is living and realizing our beliefs in our actions; every day, we must try to do so, even in small ways, and even when it forces us to move outside of our comfort zone.

I've been thinking about animal minds — what they're like and what's in them — for many years, and I've really been writing this manifesto for decades. I have conducted a lot of research and engaged in a good deal of on-the-ground activism. My parents tell me that I've "minded" animals since I was about three years old. I intuitively knew as a child that animals are smart and passionate; it took decades of laborious scientific inquiry to learn how correct I was. Science is still trying to catch up with what so many of us already understand. It turns out that our intuitions are disarmingly correct, and we ought to give ourselves credit for this.

It's also a matter of simply paying better attention. I well remember waking up one morning and deciding to put a window in my office that looked straight out at a tree. Now, twenty years later, I'm so happy I did this. At the time, my friend Tim, who put the window in for me, thought I was nuts. But my window doesn't just look on a gorgeous tree. As I type, small lizards often walk up the bark, staring at me and doing pushup displays as if to say "this is my territory," while beautiful blue Steller's jays squawk telling me that this also is their home. Red foxes come by and pee on the tree, saying this is theirs. And chipmunks scamper up, stop, peer in, and continue on their merry way. What a gift to see them all.

HEADLINE NEWS:
### The Good, the Bad, and the Ugly

Any argument for change is predicated on an evaluation and understanding of the way things are, and this I provide throughout. Every day I try to keep track of what's happening in our world regarding animal welfare, scientific research, and everyday stories that illustrate the amazing intellectual skills of animals and their deep and rich emotional and moral lives. These I share with you, though I have to admit, it's impossible to keep up with them all. For instance, within a few days in early 2009 I saw stories on the BBC news that at once showed the good, the bad, and the ugly of our current interactions with animals. I learned that the number of mountain gorillas in the Democratic Republic of Congo's Virunga National Park had increased, that emperor penguins face extinction, and that global warming seems irreversible.

In June 2008 I had a similar good news/bad news experience. First I read about how the U.S. Forest Service was designating the first wildlife migration corridor through the Greater Yellowstone ecosystem to preserve an ancient pathway for pronghorn. Here was concrete evidence of humans "making room" for animals, letting them travel their established route instead of forcing them to search for alternatives. Shortly afterward, though, I read about a study of primates that found that 303 species — almost half the world's primate species — are under threat of extinction because they are being eaten or having their homes destroyed by humans.

Within one week of March 2009 I learned that imperiled right whales seem to be recovering, and that for the first time since the 1600s, it appears that not one North Atlantic right whale died because of human activity. Plus I discovered that Russian authorities fully banned the hunt for baby seals less than one year of age. Then I read that fully one-third of bird species in the United States are endangered, and Africa's first bird extinction is likely by 2013 (the Sidamo lark).

The ups and downs of what's happening with the world's species are sometimes confusing and emotionally draining.

With global warming showing its dramatic influence all over the world, it's hard not to feel pessimistic about the fate of animals who have evolved to fit the Earth's many delicate habitats. For example, sheep living on the remote island of Hirta off the coast of Scotland have been shrinking in size, and researchers have discovered that the most likely cause is warmer winters that allow the smaller sheep to survive. Climate change is also affecting charismatic large mammals. In January 2009 it was estimated that about three times as many polar bears are in a fasting state compared with twenty years ago due to melting ice. In August 2008, ten polar bears were seen swimming in open water off the northern coast of Alaska, an unusually large number. In June 2008, a polar bear who swam a hundred miles in near freezing water was shot dead on his arrival in Skagafjordur, Iceland, because he was supposedly a threat to people.

I can feel the anxiety and fear a polar bear feels as she, and perhaps her offspring, slowly drown while wondering, "Where's the ice?" I can also imagine what is going through the mind of an elephant being relentlessly pursued by people with automatic rifles in a truck, a coyote being pursued by shooters in an airplane, or a wolf writhing on the ground after being trapped — waiting to be shot or to starve to death, or waiting to be used as bait to lure other wolves in so that they too may be killed.

When we face the prospect of these species disappearing, the world stands to lose a lot. As author Richard Nelson writes about polar bears: "I looked toward her and away, careful to avoid what might seem like an aggressive stare. And I wondered: What does this polar bear know that I could never fathom — about traveling on the ice, living through storms, meeting others of her kind, nursing cubs in a snow cave, stalking walruses on the summer floes, and waiting for seals at their breathing holes? What understanding of the Arctic world is woven through the pathways of her mind? What could I learn in a lifetime of tracking polar bears across the ice, as generations of Inupiaq hunters have done? And what secrets could she reveal to us about this land now in peril?"

Focusing on what works and on our capacity for compassion is the best way forward. Part of what can drive that compassion is a new understanding of our close bonds with animals: they are compassionate, too, with rich emotional lives. Popular media regularly feature how smart and emotional animals are. For example, a May 2007 issue of *Newsweek* contained an essay about the emotional lives of elephants and how they deserve far more respect than we currently give them. We now know, from innumerable stories and research, that elephants suffer from post-traumatic stress disorder (PTSD), but wolves also can suffer from PTSD. Wildlife biologists Jay Mallonée and Paul Joslin described unique changes in the behavior of Tenino, a wild female wolf, who was darted twice from a helicopter and put in captivity because she'd preyed on livestock. Tenino became hypervigilant, was easy to startle, and showed generalized fear, avoidance, and arousal, whereas the other wolves with whom she was kept did not show these patterns of behavior. We also now know that fish have distinct personalities; birds plan future meals and are more sophisticated in making and using tools than chimpanzees; whales have spindle neurons that are important in processing emotions; turtles mourn the loss of their friends; and mice feel the pain of other mice. Research also has shown that fish, lobsters, and even insects feel pain. In 2007, the *New York Times* published obituaries for two famous animals whose language abilities startled the world: Washoe, a "chimpanzee of many words"; and Alex, an African gray parrot who mastered English and could count and recognize different shapes and colors.

The mainstream media are also deeply concerned about what we're doing for and to animals. As one example, in October 2008, the *New York Times Magazine* published a major piece of investigative journalism about the plight of farm animals, focusing on the horrible conditions at the Westland/Hallmark Meat Company and Proposition 2, a bill then pending on the ballot in California that was designed to phase out some of the most restrictive animal confinement systems. At Westland/Hallmark, workers were videotaped using chains to drag sick and injured cows and jabbing them with electrical prods. As a result of this undercover work, the San Bernardino district attorney shut down the plant. In November 2008, the California proposition passed with 63 percent of voters saying, "Yes, let's improve the welfare of factory farm animals." This law now phases out some of the most restrictive confinement systems used by factory farms — gestation crates for breeding pigs, veal crates for calves, and battery cages for egg-laying hens — which affect 20 million farm animals in the state. Simply put, the law now grants them space to stand up, stretch their limbs, turn around, and lie down comfortably. Before the vote a *New York Times* editorial supported Proposition 2, saying: "To a California voter still undecided on Proposition 2, we say simply, imagine being confined in the voting booth for life. Would you vote for the right to be able to sit down and turn around and raise your arms?"

It's impossible to follow all the news, new science, and evolving legislation that emerges, and I can't survey it all in this short book. As a rule, I have chosen to mention stories and scientific data that are readily accessible to the general public and that speak to the big picture: who animals are; how and why we must understand, appreciate, and respect their amazing lives; and what, in fact, they want from us. While I can only provide snippets of these stories, by following the weblinks and publication information in this book's endnotes, readers can find the originals for themselves to learn more. Information about animal behavior, animal cognition and emotions, conservation, and environmental ethics is appearing everywhere these days. On occasion, I must confess, even I find it overwhelming, while at the same time I'm pleased that so much is happening.

## Each Animal Matters, Each Individual Counts

Human beings have a natural tendency toward kindness, but we also need awareness, education, honesty, and courage in order to translate that tendency into concrete action. Humans will act with kindness toward animals when we understand and respect what animals want, feel, and need, and when we believe that *all* animals matter, not only our close relatives. Humans will act on behalf of animal welfare when we expand our moral circle to include them at all times, not just when it's convenient, and when we honestly assess our own actions.

Usually, our own needs are our main concern whenever we consider how we influence — that is, manage and control — the lives of billions of animals. It's easy to think this way because we have, or think we have, more power, and it seems as if we can control and dominate other forms of life and landscapes as we want. In reality, as global climate change has made clear, we are less in control than we'd like to believe. But also, we sometimes mask the truth of what we are doing in bland euphemisms; often the words "manage" and "control" really just mean killing. One morning as I was riding my bicycle back into Boulder I saw a truck that was advertising "wildlife management," and when I asked the man behind the wheel what he did, he chuckled and said, "I go to houses and kill whatever animals the people want me to kill." I asked him, "Is that your idea of wildlife management?" He responded, "Whatever works is fine with me, and killing gets rid of the problem."

What allows us to do the things that we do? How can we sit back and watch animals die? Sometimes good people do bad things to animals simply through a lack of awareness. Our alienation from other creatures allows us to treat them as objects. Those who stop to look and see animals differently are often transformed. When that happens, we can see all sorts of ways that we can act with more kindness toward animals within the context of our daily lives.

I wrote this book in cars, planes, trains, on boats, and even as I rode my indoor bicycle. I traveled to more than a dozen countries around the world, where I met amazing people doing incredible things for animals, often in very difficult circumstances. I'll introduce you to many of these inspirational people who are doing what they do because they love to make a positive difference for individual animals and because they know that more compassion for animals also means more compassion for people.

The adage "Act locally and think globally" certainly applies to activism on behalf of animals. In Denver, Colorado, not far from my hometown of Boulder, I learned in 2007 that the University of Colorado at Denver Health Sciences Center had killed at least 18 dogs and 191 pigs during sales "training" for Boulder-based Valleylab. This appalling form of vivisection was not for legitimate research. Local activists were led by Rita Anderson — a grandmother whose passion for animal activism influenced her grandchildren, who I once recruited to protest the proposed killing of prairie dogs on their school grounds — and they were instrumental in bringing this abuse to light and putting an end to it. It's easy to feel overwhelmed when the issues facing animals are so huge, pervasive, and difficult to change. By carefully choosing where we put our energy, we can be more effective in creating change without burning out. However, even the smallest changes, those involving only one person and one animal, are still constructive positive steps toward a kinder world for all animals.

## Our Compassion Footprint

This manifesto is a journey through six reasons why all animals matter, why we need to do better, and why we need to expand our compassion footprint. I thought of the phrase "compassion footprint" while cycling around Boulder. I'd been having a discussion with some friends about the notion of the carbon footprint and how that phrase had taken on a life of its own. I've actually heard people use the terms "carbon footprint" and "carbon credit" in tiny remote towns in India, Kenya, and China. It's become a powerful global catchphrase for trying to measure the impact of our lifestyles on Earth.

As teacher and writer Todd Nelson has pointed out, "a 'footprint' is a good metaphor for our individual impact on the social or natural environment. It's personal, tactile, organic, and immediately comprehensible. It's elementary: we're bipeds; we all walk and leave tracks." Nelson writes about what he calls a "civility footprint." He used to think that civility just meant being nice, as Mom used to say. As it turns out there's a lot more to it — a more global consideration of being nice, attentive, focused, generous, humble, and thoughtful. Meanwhile, the Animal Welfare Institute calculates a "compassion index" for politicians, which they post on their website.

So, like our civility footprint, and unlike our carbon footprint, our compassion footprint is something we can try to make bigger. It's a lens for evaluating our daily decisions. We can all make more humane and compassionate choices for animals. It's typically pretty simple. For example, an eight-year-old boy humbly reminded me that when we buy something, we're essentially saying, "It's okay for the store to carry it," and "It's okay for the manufacturer to make whatever it is we buy." Everything we purchase is a vote for more of that thing. As we'll see, it's easy to make changes in how we spend our money, which always sends out a ripple effect and influences the choices of others. Amirtharaj Christy Williams, a biologist with the World Wildlife Fund's Asian elephant and rhino program, notes that "intelligent buying by western consumers, and informed policies from governments in areas where elephants occur" really do help in relieving tension between humans and elephants.

Coexisting compassionately with animals will make us better human beings and make our lives easier. Compassion can lead to justice for all. Compassion begets more compassion and unifies diverse peoples. The bottom line is that we can all do more in evaluating the choices we make. If we make ethical choices, then we can change the way business is done, because money talks. And of course, we should err on the side of the animals and take into account their best interests.

Some people ask, "Why are you working for animals when there are so many people who need help?" The answer is simple: Many people around the world who work for animals also work selflessly for people. Caring for animals doesn't mean caring less for humans. Indeed, a major message of this book is that compassion begets compassion. When we learn to be compassionate to all animals, that includes humanity. Compassion easily crosses species lines.

I hope that if you're ready to throw up your hands in frustration and quit working for animals or making choices that benefit them, that you'll reconsider — animals need everyone to do what they can. It is essential that we realize that we are making a difference by helping one individual at a time. Eventually, step by step, we can create a world where ethical choices are commonplace and compassion is the name of the game, rather than a world where we ignore the welfare of our fellow animals.

So let's move forward and expand our compassion footprint. Let's place animals squarely in the agenda of people all over the world. Now is the time to tap into our innate goodness and kindness to make the world a better place for all beings. This paradigm shift will bring hope and life to our dreams for a more compassionate and peaceful planet.

We are wired to be good, we are wired to be kind, and we are wired to be compassionate. Let's allow our children to retain and exercise these tendencies. The mistreatment of animals must not be allowed to continue. The beginning is now.

# All Animals Share the Earth and We Must Coexist

THE LATE THEOLOGIAN THOMAS BERRY stressed that our relationship with Nature should be one of *awe*, not one of *use*. Individuals have inherent or intrinsic value because they exist, and this alone mandates that we coexist with them. All animals, including humans, have a right to lives of dignity and respect, without forced intrusions. We need to accept all beings as and for who they are.

Any manifesto on behalf of animals must begin with this essential proposition, from which everything else flows. All animals, all beings, deserve respectful consideration simply for the fact that they exist. Whether animals think and feel, and what they know, is irrelevant. Reverence and awe for creation should guide human actions, along with a humble acknowledgment that humans have limited knowledge about the mysteries of our own existence. However, that animals do think, feel, and know only makes what humans often do to them worse.

If we humans acted with just this simple idea foremost in mind, our coexistence with animals would look a lot different. I'm constantly pleased to receive emails and the occasional letter from people who just love watching animals with the attitude of awe that Berry recommends. In July 2008, Ted Groszkiewicz of Berkeley, California, shared this story with me about his trip to Rocky Mountain National Park in Colorado, where I studied coyotes in the mid-1970s. Ted wrote:

> My wife and I have been coming here every summer for the past twenty years, and we had a singular experience this morning. We were driving to the park, traveling westward along the Big Thompson, when I noticed a line of oncoming traffic traveling very slowly. Odd at this time of the morning, I thought. And then I noticed that there was an animal in front of the lead car; first glance said, fawn.... But right away I could see that wasn't right; this animal was much more graceful. Ah, coyote! I stopped my car to watch the oncoming parade. What a happy beast, prancing in front of all those cars. Head held high this coyote wove back and forth across the lane of traffic at a slow trot. The coyote smiled and looked me straight in the eye as it came level with our car. And, still weaving back and forth across the lane like a highway patrol motorcycle cop running a traffic break, the bouncing tail receded into the east leading a procession of at least ten cars. I would have given a tidy sum to share the mind of that coyote!

Me too! I've learned firsthand that the worlds of our fellow animals are laden with magic and wonder. I've been extremely fortunate, having had numerous personal experiences around the world with both animals and people working on their behalf. I've seen lions, leopards, and spotted hyenas in Kenya, helped to rescue dogs and rehabilitate moon bears in China, observed dolphins off the coast of Adelaide, Australia, been confronted by an angry baboon in the Masai Mara, collected yellow snow in Boulder and elephant poop in Northern Kenya, and been nipped in the butt by a mother coyote who thought I was getting too close to her youngsters. I've also studied a wide range of animals over the past forty years, from domestic dogs, coyotes, wolves, and foxes to archer fish who catch prey by spitting water at them; from Adélie penguins living at Cape Crozier near the Ross Ice Shelf to Steller's jays and western evening grosbeaks living around my home.

The key to all these encounters, as Ted discovered, is slowing down or stopping in order to "share the road." Coexistence is a two-way street; it requires accommodations by all parties, not all parties but one.

Further, just as we exclaim "Wow" when we marvel over the mysterious lives of animals, I would not be surprised if animals say "Wow" in their own ways as they experience the ups and downs of their daily lives and the grandeur and magic of the environs in which they live. Look at their eyes — gleaming with joy when they are happy. How strange and marvelous must we sometimes appear to them?

## Overcoming Speciesism

The attitude that allows us to mistreat animals and habitually fail to consider their needs is speciesism. Speciesism is also behind our failure to consider ourselves as part of nature, as if humans were somehow separate from nature and exempt from the basic principles by which all species live and die. For example, overpopulation and overconsumption can lead to our own extinction just as they have caused the extinction of many other species that overwhelmed their environment. Our arrogance and denial of who we are — big-brained mammals with enormous potential, and power, to both improve and destroy the world we live in — is self-destructive in the long run. Indeed, we're failing now in so many areas that we should be ashamed of ourselves.

For instance, through a combination of habitat loss, overconsumption, overpopulation, spread of invasive species, and climate change, Earth is in the midst of its sixth great extinction of species. Researchers agree that humans are the major cause of this incredible loss of biodiversity, and they have coined the term "anthropocene" to highlight humanity's significant anthropogenic impact on Earth's ecosystems and climate.

Speciesism results in animals being classified hierarchically as "lower" and "higher," with humans on the top rung of the ladder. This anthropocentric view not only leads humans to ignore the welfare of animals, but it is really bad biology. The *Oxford English Dictionary* defines speciesism as "discrimination against or exploitation of certain animal species by human beings, based on an assumption of mankind's superiority." Terry Tempest Williams, in *Finding Beauty in a Broken World*, poignantly notes: "To regard any animal as something lesser than we are, not equal to our own vitality and adaptation as a species, is to begin a deadly descent into the dark abyss of arrogance where cruelty is nurtured in the corners of certitude. Daily acts of destruction and brutality are committed because

we fail to see the dignity of Other." Truth be told, the obliteration of animal dignity happens more than daily — every second
of every day a mouse or a rat is used in research, and a nonhuman primate is used about every seven and a half minutes.

Regardless of the differences among species, how we treat
our fellow animals always comes down to individuals. In his
book *Created from Animals: The Moral Implications of Darwinism*, the late philosopher James Rachels presents the important
notion of moral individualism, which is based on the following
argument: "If A is to be treated differently from B, the justification must be in terms of A's individual characteristics and
B's individual characteristics. Treating them differently cannot be justified by pointing out that one or the other is a member of some preferred group, not even the 'group' of human
beings." According to this view, careful attention must be paid
to individual variations in behavior within species. It is individuals who personally feel pain and suffer, not species.

Even further, leaving aside morality and simply peering
into the biological mirror, the reflection shows that it's misleading to separate humans from other animals in an "us" versus "them" framework. Our reactions to animals are often
contradictory: we are attracted to them, and wonder if we see
thoughtful sentience in their behavior, while at the same time
we push them away and emphasize our differences as a way
to establish our superiority. When describing a deplorable
act, how often have you heard someone say that the person
"acted like an animal"? However, variations among species
don't arrange themselves into a neat self-evident hierarchy
from dumb to smart, from vicious to kind. Variations among
species should be embraced and cherished rather than used to
justify human dominance. If we instead focus on the numerous

similarities among species, we see clearly that "we" are "them" and "they" are "us" in many ways. The borders are indeed blurred. Tool use, consciousness, rationality, morality, humor, language, culture, and art are shared among animal species to varying degrees and can no longer be used as the defining difference between humans and other animals.

Many of the differences between other animals and humans are differences in degree rather than differences in kind. Charles Darwin stressed this in his theory of natural selection in which he discovered evolutionary continuity in the anatomy, behavior, and mental lives — including thinking, consciousness, and emotions — of a wide variety of animals. Species that at first and superficial glance seem to be radically different from our own are actually not so different after all. This surely isn't a radical notion — if humans possess some skill or attribute, more than likely, other animals must possess it, too. If not, where did our intelligence, sentience, emotions, and morality come from?

Not only is the notion of a hierarchy of species used to justify our inhumane treatment of other animals, it is practically meaningless when comparing other species. For example, when chimpanzees do something that birds don't do, such as using joysticks and computers to negotiate mazes, people say, "See, chimpanzees are smarter than birds." However, when birds make and use more complex tools than chimpanzees, few if any say, "See, birds are smarter than chimpanzees." We really don't learn much when we try to establish that one species is smarter than another; instead, members of a given species do what they need to do to survive and to be card-carrying members of their species. Rather than refer to some real, verifiable continuum of intelligence, we tend to simply claim that species that are closer to us in the great chain of being, or species that look more like us, are more intelligent than species that are more distantly related to us or don't look like us.

Speciesism is lazy thinking. It's what allows us to abuse and kill animals "in the name of science," but what this really means is "in the name of humans." Once we declare we are special and better and more valuable than our animal kin, we close the door on their lives. We shut down our senses and our hearts to their pain, and we refuse to hear their pleas to be respected for who they are and not made into what we want them to be to justify our narrow anthropocentric view of the world. Who, after all, benefits from the invasive research on animals that scientists and others argue is often necessary, even required? Invariably humans. Rarely if ever are there any benefits for the relatives of the animals being used.

## What Our Laws Say about Animals

Throughout the world animals have little to no legal standing. They're merely property or things, like backpacks or bicycles, and humans are their owners. Animals can legally be abused, disenfranchised, moved, bartered, harmed, and killed. Often this happens in the name of education, science, entertainment, decoration, clothing, or food, which amounts to in the name of humans. Yet this legal philosophy betrays our fundamental human understanding of animals. Even young children know that animals aren't merely property. Noah Williams, a second-grade activist in Connecticut, wrote, "Animals should not be called things because they are beings, not things.... If you loved someone, would you call them a thing? ... A rug or something is a thing, but not an animal." Another youngster once asked me, "How can we hug a dog and cook a cow or pig?" Good question. Our relationships with animals are indeed confused.

Our laws betray the contradictions and ambivalence we have regarding animals. In his book *Animals and the Moral Community*, Bucknell University philosopher Gary Steiner argues that there is strong and enduring historical prejudice and momentum against animals. More people and organizations than ever before are interested in animal well-being, yet there is also more abuse. Our attitudes and practices are full of contradictions and ambivalence. It's as if we suffer from moral schizophrenia. Animal advocate and lawyer Gary Francione noted in an email to me, "We claim to accept the principle that we should not inflict suffering or death on nonhumans unless it is 'necessary' to do so, but we do so in situations in which 99.99999999% of the suffering and death cannot be justified under any plausible notion of coherence." On the one hand animals are revered, worshipped, and form an indispensable part of the tapestry of our own well-being — they make us whole, they shape us, and they make us feel good. On the other hand animals are used and abused in a morally repugnant array of human-centered activities.

## Companions in Our Home

Overall, our relationship with our fellow animals may be complicated, frustrating, ambiguous, and paradoxical, but we typically feel no ambivalence at all when it comes to the domestic animals who share our lives and our homes — that is, our pets. We have come to love our pets so much that Cornell University historian Dominick LaCapra claims this is now the "century of the animal." Children in the United States are more likely to grow up with a companion animal than with a sibling or both parents. City University of New York psychologist William Crain reports, "Recent research has revealed that animals are so important to young children that they routinely dream about them. In fact, 3- to 5-year-olds dream more frequently about animals than about people or any other topic, and animal dreams continue to be prominent at least until the age of 7 years."

The only problem, it seems, is that sometimes we are accused of loving our domestic companions too much, such as when people leave tons of money in their will to their dogs. When she died, Leona Helmsley left $12 million in a trust to care for Trouble, her pint-sized Maltese dog, and many people were outraged. Trouble even received death threats. Eventually, as has happened with similar bequests, Ms. Helmsley's wishes were overturned in February 2009. Would people have been more accepting if Trouble were a racehorse?

Though few people could, or might, leave such a fortune to their companion animal, most pet owners (aka guardians) understand the devotion behind such a gesture. Many people embrace their pets like family, and they spend as freely on the care of their animals as they do on themselves. In the months before my late companion dog Jethro died, I arranged for him to have a massage once a week; I'm sure he loved it and felt loved, and I'm equally sure he would have done the same for me if our situations, and species, were reversed. When domestic animals share our lives, we feel their caring, gratitude, and love for us directly, and it inspires humans to respond in kind. Pet owners across the United States spent $16.1 billion on their dogs' veterinary bills in 2006, up from the $4.9 billion spent in 1991, according to the American Veterinary Medical Association. Cat owners spent $7 billion in 2006, up from the $2 billion spent in 1991. While paying for veterinary care is standard and expected, 27 percent of pet owners buy birthday gifts for their dogs, according to the American Pet Products Manufacturers Association. In 2004, U.S. pet owners spent $34.4 billion on their pets, making the pet industry larger than the toy industry (with sales of $20 billion).

Companion animals are also growing ever more popular. In 1988, according to the American Pet Products Manufacturers Association, 56 percent of American households had a pet. By 2006, that figure had climbed to 63 percent, which works out to a national pet census of 88 million cats, 75 million dogs, 16 million birds, 14 million horses, 142 million fish, plus assorted small mammals and the occasional leopard or Madagascan hissing cockroach. And these are just the numbers for America. Taken altogether, this represents an enormous number of humans who have intimate, emotional relationships with animals, and who feel duty bound to care for and love them.

The number of stories that could be told to illustrate this is nearly endless. Take horses, for example. While racehorses often suffer abuse, they can also be extremely well cared for. Consider the extended care that the thoroughbred Barbaro received after shattering a leg in the 2006 Preakness Stakes. There's also the story of Molly, a gray speckled pony who was abandoned by her owners when Hurricane Katrina hit Louisiana in 2005. After weeks on her own, she was finally rescued and taken to a farm holding abandoned animals. While there, she almost died after being attacked by a pit bull terrier. When her injured right front leg became infected, her vet sought help at Louisiana State University, where surgeon

Rustin Moore agreed that, rather than euthanize her, he would fit her with a prosthesis; Moore removed her leg below the knee and fashioned an artificial limb. Today, Molly can walk and run, but she has a new job — she goes to shelters, hospitals, nursing homes, and rehabilitation centers, inspiring people with her perseverance. Wherever Molly goes, she offers hope to people who are struggling.

The question is, if so much human care and feeling can be generated in relation to one horse, why don't we foster it with all animals?

## Living with the Wild

Today, particularly in wealthy countries, "wilderness" is almost by definition every place that is not civilization. For millennia, humans have domesticated nature to build cities and towns, suburbs and farms, and whatever is wild is meant to remain outside, at the border. However, inevitably and without fail, conflicts arise because wild animals are curious, or hungry, and they don't necessarily recognize the boundaries we put up; once they enter our domestic arena, wild animals are often considered dangerous "problems" or "pests" for whom the only solution is death. Conflicts also arise whenever humans themselves seek to live in or "manage" wilderness, arranging the furniture in what is, in reality, someone else's home.

In other words, it's very easy for humans to love domestic animals, who have learned to live and play by human rules, but it's much harder to coexist with the majority of animal species who don't. Those of us who live in wealthy countries make up a small fraction of the world's population, and we are incredibly fortunate to live with an amazing array of animals and plants. We should never take this for granted because it may not always be so. In theory, when humans make conservation and environmental decisions regarding nature, most people agree that animals must be factored in; they are part of the equation. Yet when push comes to shove — when profits are compromised or people's lives are impacted or threatened — the welfare of our fellow animals seems to count for nothing.

Thus, any manifesto on behalf of animals would demand that animals be granted their own homes and allowed their own ways of life. Animals deserve land free from human interference and intrusion. Coexistence means not only that animals must accommodate human society, which they already do (sometimes to the point of extinction), but that humans must accommodate, and make room for, animal societies. Ironically, often the very characteristics of animals that draw us to them, or to the land where they live, become the source of conflicts and the reasons we decide we don't like them anymore. Often people like to brag that they live in the woods among wild animals, but they're only happy as long as the animals behave as humans want them to, not as the beings they are. We misunderstand wild animals, or provoke them unwittingly, then blame and punish them for our own mistakes.

This is seen most dramatically, and usually tragically, whenever wild animals enter our towns. In January 2009 a coyote in a town near Boulder supposedly attacked a woman who had been playing Frisbee with her dog. The question is, did the coyote aggressively "attack" the woman or was the animal just trying to join the game? When I played fetch with my late companion dog Jethro, the local red foxes would on occasion try to play with us; whenever this happened, I stopped the game, because I don't want foxes to feel *that* comfortable around us. Wild animals can be unpredictable; we don't speak their language or understand all their signals. As an expert in animal behavior, I know an animal's motivation isn't always obvious or self-evident. People often label an animal as "aggressive" when in fact he or she is merely curious. Nonetheless, the Colorado Division of Wildlife (CDOW) immediately went out to kill the coyotes who had been "harassing" the woman. A group of us protested this because, first, they couldn't identify exactly who the coyotes were, and second, it was far from clear that they had been aggressive. As it turned out, CDOW killed a coyote who *didn't* nip the woman! Then, a few weeks later, CDOW killed five more coyotes in what they called a precautionary measure. Wildlife officials had no idea if any of the coyotes were involved in the incident, but afterward, simply being a coyote apparently warranted a death sentence.

### The Bear Who Came to Dinner

In July 2008 the lives and unnecessary deaths of two black bears entered into the hearts of people around the world. In my hometown of Boulder, Colorado, representatives of the Colorado Division of Wildlife killed a mother bear when she supposedly posed a danger to humans in the neighborhood. But did she? It was discovered this female was simply looking for her child, who'd been electrocuted after she touched an electrical wire. It was possible but unknown whether the mother was the same bear who'd been in the neighborhood before because people living there had fed her. So, even at worst, the bear was guilty of looking for her child and accepting an invitation to a meal. What a double-cross. She was killed because Colorado has a "two strikes and you're dead" policy for wild animals who venture into human environs, but in this case, it was an inhumane "no strike and you're dead" policy.

Human safety surely is important, but so too is human responsibility. Why aren't there consequences for the people who invite bears by feeding them? Why couldn't the bear have been moved to a remote area where she could live out her life away from humans? A representative from the Colorado Division of Wildlife told me, "I absolutely agree that it's not the bear's fault." Nonetheless the bear had to be "tranquilized and put down," which is simply a euphemism for ruthlessly killing. One of the inmates in the Roots & Shoots course that I teach at the Boulder County Jail wrote, "The mother searching for her dead cub was destroyed for doing the most natural thing in the world." Others agreed that killing innocent wildlife sets a terrible example for children and others who must learn to co-exist with our wild neighbors.

Soon after the Boulder incident, the Minnesota Department of Natural Resources (DNR) killed a male bear who had gotten his entire head stuck in a plastic jar. The poor animal couldn't eat or drink and had become emaciated and dehydrated. To quote Rob Naplin, a local wildlife supervisor, "When it got into town, our main concern was public safety." Again, a bear was killed ostensibly to protect humans. People were outraged and wrote to the DNR in Minnesota. Why didn't they tranquilize the bear, remove the jar, treat him, and relocate him, rather than kill him? What's especially disturbing was that people were able to get close enough to take pictures of this bear with his head stuck in the jar and that there was time enough to choose how to handle the situation. After I inquired as to why the bear had to be killed, a representative from the Minnesota Division of Natural Resources wrote to me:

"Euthanizing the animal was not the DNR's first choice. It became the only choice when the bear's physical condition deteriorated and its presence in Frazee posed a public safety risk." They also said that a suitable veterinarian couldn't be found, one who had experience tranquilizing a large mammal. In other words, human trash threatened the bear's life, and it was too inconvenient for us to do anything other than finish the job. How hard did the DNR consider tranquilizing the animal? After the bear was killed I received an email from a local veterinarian who could have done it.

Of course, wild animals sometimes become truly aggressive and pose mortal danger to humans. In extremely rare cases, killing the animal might be necessary, and if so, it must be done humanely. Yet the default reaction, as these incidents make clear, is that wild animals are always dangerous and the only or preferred option is killing them. This is lazy thinking. Further, humans almost never acknowledge or accept their responsibility for creating these situations, and they sugarcoat their actions in high-sounding language. For instance, euthanasia literally means a "good death" or painless mercy killing. But in these incidents, neither bear had to be killed; mercy required just the opposite. Simply put, the bears were killed because it was the easy thing to do; guns were handy, tranquilizers were not. There was no evidence the bears posed a danger; this was just assumed. What a regrettable model for coexistence.

The stories of these unfortunate bears raise numerous issues about the ways in which humans *choose* to interact with other animals: What are our responsibilities? What value do we place on life? Who do we think animals are? Whose land is it? To what degree should we amend our lives, or change our habits, to make room for other species? Is it okay to trump their interests in living a good life with our interests in living a good life? I say "choose" because we do indeed make choices about how we treat our fellow animals, and we are responsible for the decisions we make.

### Taming the Wild: Betraying Travis

"Wild" is itself a loaded term, implying out of control. Yet, animal species are only "wild" in relation to humans. It would be more accurate to say certain species are beyond human control; they have norms of behavior that have nothing to do with us. As close as we might feel to them, as much as we might be able to communicate with and understand them, many species will never be able to be integrated into human society the way domesticated cats, dogs, chickens, and pigs are. A very good example of how difficult our relationships with animals can be centers on the keeping of exotic animals as our household companions or pets. In February 2009 a chimpanzee named Travis, who had lived in a human home for years, attacked and maimed a close friend of his female human companion. As a result, Travis's longtime friend had to stab him to stop the attack, and ultimately a policeman killed Travis.

Numerous people were saddened by this tragedy and outraged that Travis had been kept as if he were a dog or a cat. This terrible situation could easily have been avoided if Travis had been living at a sanctuary, rather than in a private home being treated as if he were a human. Travis had been allowed to drink wine and brush his teeth with his human companion. Needless to say, chimpanzees don't typically drink wine or brush their teeth with a Water Pik. In an Associated Press story, Travis was called a "domesticated chimpanzee," which is a complete misrepresentation of who he was. Domestication is an evolutionary process that results in animals such as our companion dogs and cats undergoing substantial behavioral, anatomical, physiological, and genetic changes. Travis was an imperfectly *socialized* chimpanzee — an exotic pet — who usually got along with humans, but he was not a domesticated being. He still had his wild genes, just as do wolves, tigers, and bears — all species that sometimes live with humans in situations that can lead to tragedies whenever humans forget these remain wild animals.

Many people were surprised by what seemed to be an unprovoked attack. But to say there was no known provocation for the attack is to ignore the basic fact that Travis was still genetically a wild chimpanzee. Wild animals do not belong in human homes, since what may provoke an attack can be almost impossible for humans to predict — yet if we could ask another chimpanzee, he or she would no doubt tell us easily why Travis did what he did. Just consider the other attacks by famous animals on their longtime handlers, who otherwise knew their companions well. Wild animals should be allowed to live at sanctuaries that are dedicated to respecting their lives while minimizing human contact. I hope that this tragic situation serves to stimulate people to send the wild friends who share their homes to places that are safe for all. In response, an editorial in the local Connecticut paper *The Advocate* called for a ban on the keeping of wild animals as pets. Then, on February 24, 2009, the U.S. House of Representatives moved to ban the transport of monkeys and apes across state lines for the purpose of selling them as pets.

We observe animals, gawk at them in wonder, experiment on them, eat them, wear them, write about them, draw, paint, and photograph them, move them from here to there as we redecorate nature, make decisions for them without their consent, and represent them in many varied ways. Yet we often dispassionately ignore who they are and what they want and need.

## Taming the Wild: Managing Nature

It's almost too obvious to say, but animals do not need our help to live in nature. Whenever humans seek to "manage" nature, creating parks and artificial boundaries, it is always only for the benefit of humans. Perhaps, to the degree to which animals are left alone within these parks, it might be said that animals benefit, that they have been protected from humans. Otherwise, most of what passes for "wildlife management" looks like nothing so much as a direct attack on wildlife itself, bent on destroying homes and killing indiscriminately.

From an animal's perspective, it's hard to see how the U.S. government is working with their best interests in mind, nor how the federal Wildlife Services — formerly called Animal Damage Control, ADC — is their friend. Consider their conflict of interest: many divisions of wildlife and state and federal parks support themselves by the sale of hunting and fishing licenses. Their essential mandate is to preserve animals so that some can be killed. Hunting is promoted as a source of income and as a "culture" to be preserved; to get more kids involved, in June 2009 Wisconsin lawmakers moved to lower the legal hunting age from twelve years of age to ten. State Representative Scott Gunderson noted, "It's important for us to include young people in the activities that a lot of us hold near and dear.... This is about our heritage." The Colorado Division of Wildlife claims that they keep Colorado wild by managing and protecting all wildlife. Clearly they don't, for they support the killing of innumerable fish and other sentient beings using methods that cause great pain, suffering, and death. Would humans put up with such a trade-off in their own communities, in which some folks are sacrificed so that others might live?

Sport hunting and fishing are only one aspect of "management," however. Typically, Wildlife Services has spent about $100 million a year to actively kill more than one million animals, of which about 120,000 are carnivores, but these numbers have spiked recently. Of course, though they maintain official counts, they can't keep track of all the individuals they kill. Wildlife Services shoots, traps, and snares animals, and uses a panoply of dangerous toxicants that harm a wide variety of species, not only the target species, for the benefit of the agricultural industry. Between 2004 and 2007, by their own records, Wildlife Services killed 8,378,412 animals. The numbers of mammals killed overall has increased recently. In 2004, for example, the agency killed 179,251 mammals compared with 207,341 in 2006. Wildlife Services has increased the number of endangered species it has killed as well, for a total of almost 2,500 individuals, primarily gray wolves, since 1996. The average number of endangered species killed annually between 1996 and 2004 was 177.5, while the average between 2005 and 2007 was 294.3. This represents a 66 percent increase in the numbers of endangered species killed in the past three years (2005–2007) as compared to the previous nine (1996–2004). As one employee of Wildlife Services was quoted as saying, "No one wants you to see this shit.... It's a killing floor."

The numbers are staggering, sickening, and increasing. In the fiscal year 2007, people working for Wildlife Services killed 2.4 million animals representing 319 species and spent $117 million doing so. This included a total of 196,369 mammals, of which 340 were gray wolves, 90,326 coyotes, and 19,584 feral hogs. Along with the larger trend, the number of carnivores killed has been steadily rising, and these numbers do not include youngsters who die after their mothers or other caregiving adults are killed. In 2008, Wildlife Services killed nearly five million wild animals and pets, a record number and a 125 percent increase from the number killed in 2007.

Invariably, the "wildest" places need the most "management," resulting in more killing. In Wyoming alone during the fiscal year 2007, Wildlife Services gunned down, snared, trapped, and poisoned 10,914 coyotes, 2,054 more than were killed the previous fiscal year. During the summer of 2008, the Alaska Board of Game approved the killing of all wolves in an area near Cold Bay, and state officials illegally killed fourteen wolf pups after gunning down their mothers — yet another grisly chapter in Alaska's out-of-control wolf slaughter.

Nontarget species are also killed for being in the wrong place at the wrong time. During the fiscal year 2006, at least 400 river otters were killed by accident, as were about 700 turtles. Not even humans are safe. Airplanes are used to track and kill animals as part of their aerial slaughter program, and Wildlife Services had twenty-four accidents with seven fatalities between 1989 and 2006.

Wildlife Services was established for "creating a balance that allows people and wildlife to exist peacefully." Not even the most strident utilitarian could come up with a cost/benefit analysis that would make any sense of this slaughter. Where is the balance and peace in a situation that requires so much death to maintain? For many decades this has been humanity's answer to the "problem" of wild animals intruding on our farms, ranches, and communities — or of predators who "compete" with hunters for elk and deer — and by the simple standard of effectiveness, it should be clear by now that killing does not work. We must figure out new ways of coexisting with our fellow animals. Indeed, the data show that in fact poor husbandry and disease have a larger impact on food animals than predation by wild animals.

Killing wildlife in the name of peaceful coexistence is not restricted to America; it occurs worldwide. There has been ongoing debate about whether or not elephants in certain areas of Africa have to be culled, or killed, to solve problems that occur when they intrude into human habitat. Not everyone agrees that killing elephants is the best answer. For example, John Skinner, the former head of the Mammal Research Institute at Pretoria University, said there was not a shred of evidence that the elephants in Kruger National Park or elsewhere adversely affected ecosystems. Other researchers, including Ian Raper, president of the South African Association for the Advancement of Science, also are opposed to culling. Raper notes, "Based on studies from across Africa we conclude that science does not provide satisfactory evidence that elephants have a lasting negative effect on either animals or plants. It's not true that culling reduces numbers. So what purpose does it serve?"

Meanwhile, elephants are already struggling to survive without being directly targeted by humans. Psychologist Gay Bradshaw notes in an essay in my *Encyclopedia of Animal Rights and Animal Welfare*:

> The threat of elephant extinction is very real in terms of pure numbers and in consideration of the degree to

which land and animals are pressed to change. And there is something more dire. In Kenya, heart of elephant lands, the human population has jumped from 8.6 million in 1962 to over 30 million in 2004, and between 1973 and 1989 elephant numbers plummeted from 167,000 to 16,000. As a result, there are no places in Africa or Asia that can claim elephant herds even remotely resembling those of two centuries ago.... Infants are largely reared by inexperienced, highly stressed, single mothers without the detailed knowledge of local plant ecology, leadership, and support that a matriarch and all mothers provide. Disoriented teenage mothers raise families on their own without the backbone of elephant society to guide them.... Parks... offer no sanctuary from marauding soldiers and villagers hungry for ivory and machine gun sport. Like the majority of remaining elephant habitat in Africa, in all of Asia, the total population is estimated as low as 35,000 and dwindling fast.

Without deliberately meaning to, humans have unbalanced nature, and then take it as their right to preserve and enforce this imbalance through "wildlife management."

## How We Unbalance Nature

The fact is, we influence the lives of animals in myriad ways, most often without any knowledge that we're doing so. Our impact on animals and the unbalancing of nature has often occurred very subtly, over the long term, and in unexpected and surprising ways. For example, birds in different locations are known to mimic ambulance sirens, car alarms, and cell phone rings, and they show changes in behavior due to the inundation of these unnatural sounds. Researchers from England's University of Sheffield have reported that robins in urban areas are singing at night because it is too noisy during the day — not necessarily because streetlights trick the birds into thinking it's daytime. But light pollution affects wildlife in other ways. Strong polarized light from glass buildings and roads can confuse animals and change their feeding and breeding habits because the intense visual cues attract them to areas where they won't find the food or habitat they are looking for. In another example, baby sea turtles rely on the direction of starlight and moonlight reflected off the water's surface to help them find the ocean when they emerge from their nests, but in urbanized areas, they may move toward bright buildings and street lamps instead and never find the sea.

Human-created noise in the ocean disrupts communication among whales, dolphins, and other marine mammals, and high-energy sonar causes mass strandings and deaths of various whale species. Sonar might also disrupt diving so that cetaceans suffer the equivalent of the "bends" that humans get when they surface too rapidly. Despite this, in November 2008, the U.S. Supreme Court deferred to military pressure and lifted the restrictions on the use of sonar off the coast of California. As noted in the *New York Times*, "Most disturbing was the majority's strong statements of deference to the professional judgments of military officers. A district court and appeals court in California had shown much more willingness to probe behind the military's claims. They concluded that the navy could effectively train its strike groups even under the two restrictions it most vigorously opposed: that sonar be shut down if marine mammals were spotted within 2,200 yards and pow-ered down during certain rare sea conditions."

Of course, humans impact fish and sea creatures more di-rectly, through both recreational and commercial fishing. Here, too, unintended negative consequences and imbalance are the rule, not the exception. Simply put, we're overfishing. In Feb-ruary 2006, the Food and Agriculture Organization of the United Nations noted that their "most recent global assessment of wild fish stocks found that out of the almost 600 major commercial species groups monitored by the Organization, 52 percent are fully exploited while 25 percent are either over-exploited (17%), depleted (7%) or recovering from depletion (1%). Twenty percent are moderately exploited, with just three percent ranked as underexploited." Meanwhile, nontarget species are getting literally caught in the net. For example, in 1990, about 42 million marine mammals and sea birds were caught in drift nets as squid and tuna were being harvested. About 129,000 Olive Ridley turtles have died over the past thirteen years because they suffocate in the nets of fishing boats not using mandatory turtle-excluder devices. Experts know the movement of giant ships and artificial illumination will put the turtles in even deeper trouble in the years ahead. Whales are also nontarget victims of fishing nets. In 2003 the World Wildlife Fund reported that nearly a thousand whales, dolphins, and porpoises drowned daily after becoming entangled in fish-ing nets and other equipment. Annually, more than 300,000 of these animals may perish because of fishing activities.

Finally, there is human-induced climate change. With this, all of nature is unbalanced, and it's important to remember, when studying animal behavior, that its effects might be influencing our fellow creatures in unanticipated ways. For example, it's been shown that local changes in climate are responsible for an increase in tiger attacks in India's Sundarban Islands; the tigers have lost 28 percent of their habitat in the last forty years and dwindling prey causes tigers to enter villages looking for food. The migration patterns of Pacific brants, a sea goose, are changing, with warmer Alaskan winters leading an increasing number not to migrate south at all (a potential disaster for them if a harsh winter hits). Also, recent studies have found that polar bears are getting smaller, most likely as a result of pollution and a reduction in sea ice (which means bears must work harder to catch food). While polar bears have become the iconic species for the threat posed by global climate change, biologist William Laurance argues that other less charismatic species, such as lemoroid possums and animals living in the tropics, may actually be more vulnerable.

## The Difficult Dance of Coexistence

"When human beings lose their connection to Nature, to heaven and earth, then they do not know how to nurture their environment or how to rule their world — which is saying the same thing. Human beings destroy their ecology at the same time they destroy one another. From that perspective, healing our society goes hand in hand with healing our personal elemental connection with the phenomenal world."

— Chögyam Trungpa, *Shambhala: The Sacred Path of the Warrior*

On February 1, 2007, a cold, snowy day in Boulder, I went out to my car to scrape the windshield. As I focused on the frozen car, I felt what Rupert Sheldrake calls "the sense of being stared at." I turned around to see three large mule deer staring at me from about three feet away. The fog of their breath in the cold almost touched me, and I really might have been able to reach out and touch them physically. They didn't move for about three minutes, as I stood there telling them how beautiful they were and how lucky I felt to be able to share their land and their presence. Eventually, I turned around to continue scraping, and they remained where they were. I got goose bumps being so close to them. They knew they were safe. After I walked down to my house, I looked back at them and thanked these trusting and generous deer.

In the hustle-bustle of our days, it's so easy to dismiss this sort of encounter. It's easy to forget that, globally speaking, we've intruded into the homes and lives of our fellow animals and that this incessant and unrelenting trespassing will only continue as humans grow in numbers and available habitat dwindles. Getting out into nature reminds us how lucky we are to see and feel the presence of animals, and it can remind us that this land is their land, too. So is the air they breathe and on which they soar and the water in which they feed and frolic. We need to make room for other animals. I like what author Terry Tempest Williams wrote in *Finding Beauty in a Broken World* as she reflected on watching black-tailed prairie dogs: "They are teaching me what it means to live in community."

We know we need to coexist. But coexistence involves many intricate, difficult ethical choices. We can't even agree among ourselves if there are right or wrong answers to certain questions, such as: Should we kill nonnative red foxes to save endangered native birds? Should we shoot feral goats whose grazing threatens certain plants with extinction? To what degree should we make environmental changes that benefit us but are a detriment to individuals, or to a particular species? To what degree should we limit human society so that animals or a species can thrive? How do we value animals and nature?

Expanding our compassion footprint means thinking of animal welfare in our smallest routine decisions. John Hadidian, author of *Wild Neighbors: The Humane Approach to Living with Wildlife* and the director of urban wildlife programs for the U.S. Humane Society, believes we can always do more to form a community and coexist with our wild neighbors. Many of the things we can do are really simple. For example, raccoons tend to go for corn when it ripens. Rather than trap or kill the raccoon, Hadidian suggests leaving a radio "tuned to an all-night talk show" out in the garden on the nights just before harvest. He reminds gardeners that the Migratory Bird Treaty Act protects most species of birds; killing birds to protect a garden may be breaking the law even as it fails to solve the problem. Woodchucks are a classic case; if you don't alter the burrow system or protect against reinvasion, others will come back.

We must all accept that our living space encroaches on that of other animals; we should expect to see animals, and learn to recognize and address potential conflicts with them before they happen. Where I live encroaches on the terrain of mountain lions and many other carnivores, including coyotes, red foxes, and black bears. The likelihood of my meeting one of these beasts is fairly high, but in my many years living in the foothills above Boulder, none of these wild, and potentially dangerous, animals has ever caused me harm. The animals allow me to come and go as I please. Indeed, recent studies of mountain lions living around Thousand Oaks, California, show that "lions, which feed primarily on mule deer, are posing no threat to people or to their pets and show no desire to be 'urbanized.'

... They are doing the best they can to stay out of the way.... Mountain lions see people more than people see them."

Much happens in the complex lives of our animal kin to which we're not privy, but when we're fortunate to see animals at work, how splendid it is. Red foxes entertain me regularly by playing outside of my office or on my deck. When it's hot and dry, they queue up on my deck to drink any water that has collected in indentations after a storm. One morning when I was riding my bicycle up Flagstaff Mountain near my house, a young fox ran alongside me and playfully nipped at my heels. Foxes and other animals seem extremely comfortable sharing my home range with me, having habituated to my presence over the years. And really I was the one who moved into *their* home. Somebody had redecorated and disrupted their habitat by building my house in the middle of their living and dining rooms.

I've also been lucky. Nature doesn't hold court at our convenience, and I've survived a series of unplanned encounters with various animals. I once had a young male black bear casually stroll onto my deck and try to swat open the screen door that leads to my dining room, where I happened to be eating dinner at the time. He stepped back when he couldn't get the door to open, looked at me, and just hung out until I went to the door and asked him what he thought he was doing. He continued to look at me, shrugged as if he couldn't care less about my being there, and wandered down the hill to rest under my neighbor's hammock.

On July 1, 2008, as I was preparing for a long trip to Budapest, Hungary, I opened my front door and heard some loud footsteps on my deck. I knew that it wasn't the usual entourage of foxes who show up around five o'clock to take a drink out of the water bucket and then look for an inattentive mouse who might be caught unawares. I was right. I confronted a large black bear. Perhaps he'd come to say good morning and now was hanging out, waiting for what I'm not sure. He just sat and looked as happy as could be. I know better than to toss food over my porch or to leave garbage outside. To get to my car, I have to walk about a hundred feet up a hill, but I really couldn't with the bear right there, so I waited until he meandered off to see what treats my neighbor might have. Ten days later, when I returned home from my trip around midnight, I stepped in a pile of fresh bear poop left right at my front door. Welcome home!

Mountain lions have also visited my home with little or no hesitation. Or, more accurately, after someone built a house in the middle of where they live, they have become extremely comfortable sharing their home range with me. Lions and I truly are close neighbors, so it's not surprising that I've had some very close encounters with them. Once, in fact, I almost fell over a huge male as I walked backward to warn some of my neighbors of his presence.

Sometimes we don't know just how lucky we are that other animals have allowed us to live in their homes and allowed us to coexist with them. We ought to pay them the same favor and make room for them in our own lives. This land is their land, too.

# REASON 2

## *Animals Think and Feel*

"It is remarkable how often the sounds that birds make suggest the emotions that we might feel in similar circumstances: soft notes like lullabies while calmly warming their eggs or nestlings; mournful cries while helplessly watching an intruder at their nests; harsh or grating sounds while threatening or attacking an enemy.... Birds so frequently respond to events in tones such as we might use that we suspect their emotions are similar to our own."

— Alexander Skutch, *The Minds of Birds*

IF ANIMALS COULD CONVINCE HUMANS of only one thing with their manifesto, it would be that they think and feel. Animals are sentient, and they care about what happens to them. In their various ways, animals are passionate, deliberate, logical, self-aware, and have individual personalities.

Animals are, in other words, a lot like humans, even if they are not the same as humans. The emotions of our fellow animals are not necessarily identical to ours, and there's no reason to think they should be. Their hearts and stomachs and kidneys differ from ours, and those of one species differ from those of another species, but this doesn't stop us from recognizing that animals have hearts, stomachs, and kidneys that serve the same functions as ours. There's dog-joy and chimpanzee-joy and pig-joy, and dog-grief, chimpanzee-grief, and pig-grief. Just because other animals feel differently does not mean that those animals don't feel.

At a meeting in Palermo, Italy, a biologist told me about his dog, who for twelve years was friends with a mule. After the mule died, the dog followed the cart in which the corpse was being carried, and when the mule was buried, the dog slowly walked over to the grave of his friend and wailed. The biologist had never seen his dog do this before. The biologist told me that before my lecture on animal emotions, he'd been hesitant to tell this story. After all, how could he know what his dog's behavior meant, if anything? But after hearing stories of animals ranging from turtles to magpies to elephants who displayed grief, he was now certain his dog had also grieved the loss of his longtime friend.

## Anthropomorphism: Are We Just Making It Up?

*Anthropomorphism* is attributing human characteristics to animals and inanimate objects. Is this what we're doing when we sense that animals are expressing sadness, anger, or joy? Are we just projecting human emotions onto them? It's a valid concern. Humans have a history of solipsism, seeing anger in a hot wind and malice in shark attacks. We have a way of making everything about us.

In this case, though, we more often make the opposite mistake: we prefer to discount what is right before our eyes and consistently underestimate what animals know, do, think, and feel. Consider, for instance, that our human likes and dislikes are in fact useful; they help us make successful choices and move through the world, and animals have the same type of emotional compass. Further, animal feelings aren't private, hidden, or secret. The emotional lives of animals are very public. Animals display exactly how they feel about what is happening to them. Instead of recognizing this for what it is, scientists especially have argued that we can't "know" what animals think and feel. Yet today, this is no longer simply a conservative interpretation of the scientific data; it is an excuse to retain the status quo and prop up the idea of human superiority. Historically, humans have differentiated themselves as higher than other animals in large part based on the special quality of our feelings and thoughts. However, denying animal emotions now flies in the face of a growing mountain of solid, challenging, and exciting scientific research — more of which is appearing almost every day.

For example, mammals share the same brain structures that are important in processing emotions; this alone suggests that they serve a similar function. Interestingly, as we rehabilitate animals who have experienced trauma in zoos or through habitat encroachment, we are finding that many psychological treatments for humans also can work for animals, precisely because of our shared neural structures. In a 2008 essay in the *New York Times*, James Vlahos wrote about "pill-popping pets." He noted that we give the same pills to animals that we give to ourselves to relieve their psychological distress and trauma, such as abuse, aggression, separation anxiety, depression, and obsessive-compulsive disorder. Vlahos asks: "If the strict mechanistic Cartesian view were true — that animals are essentially flesh-and-blood automatons, lacking anything resembling human emotion, memory and consciousness — then why do animals develop mental illnesses that eerily resemble human ones and that respond to the same medications? What can behavioral pharmacology teach us about animal minds and, ultimately, our own?"

Birds are quickly being recognized as equal to mammals in terms of cognitive ability. Magpies have a sense of self and some birds plan future meals. Burrowing owls attract their favorite beetle meals by placing mammal dung around their homes, and New Caledonian crows are better than chimpanzees at making and using tools. We know that all birds have a similar version of what is called the language gene, FOXP2. In the zebra finch, its protein is 98 percent identical to ours, differing by just eight amino acids. Constance Scharff at the Max Planck Institute for Molecular Genetics in Berlin, Germany, discovered that levels of FOXP2 expression are highest during early life, which is when most of their song learning occurs. In canaries, birds who learn songs throughout their lives, levels of this protein increase annually and reach their peak during the late summer months, when they rework their songs.

We're trained to think our personal impressions are too subjective, and therefore must not be right, but when it comes to animal emotions, this assumption is wrong. Extensive research by ethologist Françoise Wemelsfelder and her colleagues has shown that even regular folks (as opposed to trained scientists) do a consistently accurate job of identifying animal emotions. Research by Audrey Schwartz Rivers, who runs animal-assisted programs for at-risk youth, agrees with Wemelsfelder, and other researchers have come to the same conclusion — whether people are observing wolves, dogs, or cats, they discern emotions nearly as well as trained researchers. This means that animal emotions really aren't well hidden and that humans have a natural ability to discern emotions in other species.

Animals aren't emotional beings because we want them to be but because they must be for their own survival — just like us. And what is so interesting is that our intuitions are being strongly supported by scientific research — science is finally catching up with what we've sensed all along.

### HEADLINE NEWS:
### Monkeys Teach! Whales Steal! Goldfish Remember!

There's so much going on right now in the field of cognitive ethology — or the study of animal minds — that it's hard to keep up. Did you know that monkeys teach their kids to floss their teeth? That magpies recognize their reflection? That bees display consciousness, and crabs don't just feel pain but remember it? Each of these discoveries is exciting on its own, but taken together, they drive home the truth that animals think and feel, just in their own various, distinctive, marvelous, surprising ways.

However, it's worth remembering that it's only for humans that this remains headline news. Animals, if they could, would no doubt tell us much more about their abilities, and humans have had ample evidence for a long time. Consider, for instance, the ability of cormorants to count: since the 1930s, certain Chinese fishermen have used cormorants to catch fish for them. This cooperative arrangement is striking in itself, but in the 1970s, a researcher discovered that some fishermen rewarded their birds by allowing them to eat a fish after every seventh fish caught. Once each cormorant had caught his or her quota, the bird would not fish again or even move till he or she was fed the fish. As the researcher noted, "One is forced to conclude that these highly intelligent birds can count up to seven."

Here is only a small sampling of recent findings:

### Crabs "Sense and Remember Pain"
*BBC News*, March 27, 2009

"Queen's University says new research it conducted shows crabs not only suffer pain but retain a memory of it. The study ...looked at the reactions of hermit crabs to small electric shocks.... The crabs reacted adversely to the shocks but also seemed to try to avoid future shocks, suggesting that they recalled the past ones....

"Professor Elwood, who previously carried out a study showing that prawns endure pain, said: 'There has been a long debate about whether crustaceans including crabs, prawns and lobsters feel pain. We know from previous research that they can detect harmful stimuli and withdraw from the source of the stimuli but that could be a simple reflex without the inner "feeling" of unpleasantness that we associate with pain.

"'This research demonstrates that it is not a simple reflex but that crabs trade-off their need for a quality shell with the need to avoid the harmful stimulus.'"

### Dolphin Woos with Wood and Grass
*BBC News*, March 26, 2008

"A South American river dolphin uses branches, weeds and lumps of clay to woo the opposite sex and frighten off rivals, scientists have discovered. Researchers observed adult male botos carrying these objects while surrounded by females, and thrashing them on the water surface aggressively.... They say such behaviour has never before been seen in any marine mammal."

## What a Rodent Can Do With a Rake in Its Paw
*New York Times*, March 26, 2008

"Degus are highly social, intelligent rodents native to the highlands of Chile. They adorn the openings of their burrows with piles of sticks and stones, have bubbly personalities and like to play games. But in a laboratory setting, degus can do much more than play hide-and-seek.... They can learn to use tools.

"Specifically, degus have been trained to reach through a fence, grab hold of a tiny rake and pull their favorite food, half a peeled sunflower seed, close enough to reach with their mouths. After two months of practice, researchers say, the degus can move the rake as smoothly and efficiently as croupiers in any Las Vegas casino.

"This is [the] first time rodents have been trained to wield tools, said Atshushi Iriki, a neuroscientist, who led the experiments.... But other species may soon join them."

## The Secret Language of Cuttlefish
*New Scientist*, April 26, 2008

"Recent research shows that cuttlefish can do things that are way beyond most molluscs and only rarely seen in mammals. Their response to an approaching predator is tailor-made for the carnivore in question, for example. Not only that, they have also developed a secret communications system that could be the marine equivalent of invisible ink."

## Wild Dolphins Tail-walk on Water
*BBC News*, August 19, 2008

"A wild dolphin is apparently teaching other members of her group to walk on their tails, a behavior usually seen only after training in captivity...."

"Scientists say tail-walk tuition has not been seen before, and suggest the habit may emerge as a form of 'culture' among this group. 'We can't for the life of us work out why they do it,' said Mike Bossley from the Whale and Dolphin Conservation Society (WDCS), one of the scientists who have been monitoring the group on the Port River estuary."

[I was fortunate to see these dolphins off the coast of Adelaide, Australia, along with Mike when I visited him in March 2008.]

## Schoolboy Explodes Goldfish Memory Myth
*The Age*, February 18, 2008

"A 15-year-old South Australian school student has busted the myth that goldfish have a three second memory.

" 'We are told that a goldfish has a memory span of less than three seconds and that no matter how small its tank is, it will always discover new places and objects,' Rory [Stokes] said. 'I wanted to challenge this theory as I believe it is a myth intended to make us feel less guilty about keeping fish in small tanks. . . . My results strongly showed that goldfish can retain knowledge for at least six days. . . . They can retain that knowledge indefinitely if they use it regularly.' "

[Rory's discovery has since been supported by more research, as reported in *The Daily Mail*, January 7, 2009, "Three-Second Memory Myth."]

## Exploring Consciousness through the Study of Bees
*Scientific American*, December 2008

"Bees display a remarkable range of talents — abilities that in a mammal such as a dog we would associate with consciousness.

...[Scientists] trained free-flying bees, using sugar water as a reward, in a variety of complex learning tasks.... Although bees can't be expected to push levers, they can be trained to take either the left or the right exit inside a cylinder.... [The bees] even generalize to a situation they have never previously encountered.

"Although these experiments do not tell us that bees are conscious, they caution us that we have no principled reason at this point to reject this assertion."

### Ants "Get Aggressive with Cheats"
*BBC News*, January 10, 2009

"Worker ants in colonies with a queen are physically attacked by their peers if they try to reproduce.... This 'reproductive policing' plays an important role in maintaining harmony in the ant world.... 'The idea that social harmony is dependent on strict systems to prevent and punish cheating individuals seems to apply to most successful societies,' [researchers] said."

### Monkeys "Teach Infants to Floss"
*BBC News*, March 12, 2009

"Female monkeys in Thailand have been observed showing their young how to floss their teeth — using human hair. Researchers from Japan said they watched seven long-tailed macaques cleaning the spaces between their teeth in the same manner as humans.

"They spent double the amount of time flossing when they were being watched by their infants, the team said. This suggests the mothers were deliberately teaching their young how to floss, Professor Nobuo Masataka of Kyoto University's

Primate Research Institute said. 'I was surprised because teaching techniques on using tools properly to a third party are said to be an activity carried out only by humans.' "

### Chimps Craft Ultimate Fishing Rod
*BBC News*, March 4, 2009

"Scientists believe they have solved the mystery of why some chimpanzees are so good at catching termites. A team working in the Republic of Congo discovered that the chimps are crafting brush-tipped 'fishing rods' to scoop the insects out of their nests....

"[One scientist] said: 'The chimps seem to understand the function of the tool and its importance in gathering termites.'

"So far, the team have only found this behaviour in chimps in the Goualougo Triangle. The apparent absence of this in populations in eastern and western Africa suggests that it is not an innate skill found in all chimpanzees. Instead it seems that the Goualougo primates are learning the crafting techniques from other chimps."

### Hungry Whales Steal Birds' Dinner
*BBC News*, March 17, 2009

"Humpback whales have come up with a novel way for getting an easy snack — stealing birds' dinners. A BBC crew filmed seabirds carefully corralling unwieldy shoals of herring into tightly packed 'bait balls' from which the fish are easy to pluck.

"But they discovered that passing whales would wait for the birds to complete their hard graft before devouring the ball of fish in a single gulp. The team said this was the first time they had seen this behaviour.

"[The producer] said: 'It was like the whales had noticed what the birds were doing, and let the birds do all the hard work of creating the balls of fish so they could then come in to scoop them up....

" 'You have to take your hat off to them — it is when you see them doing things like that, you realise that they are really very very clever and that they are aware of their environment and what is going on.' "

## For the Tough Nuts, Capuchin Monkeys
## Select the Right Stones
*New York Times*, January 16, 2009

"Researchers have found that bearded capuchin monkeys in the wild will select the most effective stone for use in cracking nuts, rejecting those that are too light or crumbly....

"Other than in humans, such tool selectivity had been shown only in chimpanzees, which are closely related to humans. Capuchins are much more distant relatives. 'Here we showed that a species removed from humans 35 million years ago is capable of being extremely selective in terms of tool use,' [one researcher] said. 'I'm far from arguing that this is extremely special and unique. Perhaps it is simpler than we expected.' "

## Monkeys Have Regrets Just Like Humans —
## At Least When They're Playing Deal or No Deal
*Daily Mail*, May 15, 2009

"Monkeys can feel regret too — at least when playing a version of Deal Or No Deal. When given a task similar to the popular Channel 4 show, their brains registered missed opportunities.... Just as contestants on Deal Or No Deal wonder what might have been, the monkeys became wistful when realising their error.

"[One researcher] said: 'This is the first evidence that monkeys, like people, have "would-have, could-have, should-have" thoughts.'"

### Grumpy Mules "Highly Intelligent"
*BBC News*, September 3, 2008

"The legendary 'bad temper' of mules is because they are intelligent animals who are mentally understimulated, claim researchers studying them. Academics who carried out research at a donkey sanctuary in Devon found that mules were smarter than horses or donkeys. The animals are hybrids of male donkeys and female horses.

"[One researcher] said: 'The mules' performance was significantly better than that of either of the parent species and got faster over a period of time.'"

### Magpie "Can Recognise Reflection"
*BBC News*, August 19, 2008

"Magpies can recognise themselves in a mirror, scientists have found — the first time self-recognition has been observed in a non-mammal. Until relatively recently, humans were thought to be uniquely self-aware. Scientists now know that most chimpanzees and orangutans can recognise their own reflections.... "'We do not claim that the findings demonstrate a level of self-consciousness or self-reflection typical of humans,' the researchers wrote.... 'The findings do, however, show that magpies respond in the mirror...in a manner so far only clearly found in apes, and, at least suggestively, in dolphins and elephants.

" 'This is a remarkable capability that is at least a prerequisite of self-recognition and might play a role in perspective taking.' "

### Dolphin "Chef" Follows Cuttlefish Recipe
*National Geographic News*, January 28, 2009

"A wild dolphin has been observed following a specific recipe for preparing a mollusk meal, even stripping the animal of its internal shell and beating it free of ink, a new study says. The female Indo-Pacific bottlenose dolphin was seen repeatedly catching, killing, and preparing giant cuttlefish, which are relatives of octopuses and squid.

" 'It's an example of quite sophisticated behavior,' said [the study coauthor, who noted that] despite their lack of limbs, dolphins have developed clever ways to use their snouts. 'A dolphin is like a genius trapped in the body of a fish.' "

### Sperm Whales Use Babysitters for Young
*The Telegraph*, June 13, 2009

"Sperm whales are one of the deepest diving whales on the planet and make dives of more than 2000ft below the ocean's surface lasting up to an hour while they search for the squid they feed on. The calves, however, cannot make these dives and have to remain at the surface. This leaves the calves vulnerable to killer whales which often follow pods of sperm whales to prey upon the youngsters.

"Scientists...have now discovered the whales use the equivalent of a babysitting pool to ensure mothers can feed without endangering their young.... In larger groups the babysitting tended to be reciprocal.

"[One researcher said,] 'It is not unreasonable to suggest that the need to protect vulnerable offspring could have been an important evolutionary driver of cooperation among sperm whales, just as it may have been in humans.'"

### Turtle Love Goes Beyond the Grave
CNN, July 24, 2008

"Dozens of people flocked the shoreline at Laniakea Beach, hoping to get a glimpse of the Hawaiian sea turtle. News of the slaughtering of Honey Girl, a frequent visitor to Turtle Beach, has generated even more interest in the threatened species. But what happened Monday afternoon tugs at your heart even more. A large male, known as Kuhina, suddenly appeared on the shore and quietly made his way to a memorial that volunteers had set up for Honey Girl.

"[One woman said,] 'They had to move the ropes aside so he could come straight up through and just came up and put his head right near the memorial, right near the picture and just stayed.... It was almost like he was coming to say goodbye.'

"Kuhina stayed for hours. Volunteers say it appeared as if he never took his eyes off her picture."

### A Mother's Grief:
### Heartbroken Gorilla Cradles Her Dead Baby
*Daily News*, August 18, 2008

"Eleven-year-old gorilla Gana was holding her three-month-old baby in her arms on Saturday in her compound at the zoo in Munster, northern Germany, when it suddenly died. Initially puzzled, Gana stared at the body, bewildered by its lifelessness. For hours the distraught mother gently shook and stroked the child, vainly seeking to restore movement to his lolling head and limp arms. Visitors to the zoo openly wept as they witnessed her actions.

"Hours passed, during which Gana continually prodded and caressed the dead child, to no effect. But still she refused to give up hope. Gently placing it on her back and slowly walking around the compound, she stopped every few paces to look back and see if her much-loved son had returned to life....

"Gorillas usually have a strong attachment to their own kind. Like other apes with a well-developed social structure, gorillas mourn the death of loved ones. They exhibit both care for the dead and sadness at their passing — even keeping the body close until it begins decomposing. On occasion, gorillas have also been known to 'bury' their dead, by covering the body with leaves."

## The Observer Effect: The Truth about Octopi

How we study animals influences what we find — this is the observer effect. Too often, scientists take animals out of their natural environments and communities, place them in sterile cages or labs (where they may be held in isolation for years), and come up with all sorts of misleading conclusions about their cognitive and emotional capacities. A world-renowned primatologist who conducts laboratory and field research told me, "There is an interesting, but unreported fact about captive primates: after years of testing, they burn out, bored by material, and thus, generally unresponsive.... so we constantly have to shift the paradigms to trick them into thinking it is new."

By studying octopi in the wild, we're learning they are incredibly complex creatures, and we are reaching very different conclusions about them than we did when studying them in captivity. Christine Huffard, a graduate student at the University of California at Berkeley and now at the Monterey Bay Aquarium Research Institute, discovered that octopi engage in complex mating behavior, such as fighting over conquests, flirtatious color displays, and careful partner selection. "Until you see an animal in its natural habitat, everything you think about it is really a best guess," Huffard said. "And our best guesses about octopus mating were actually not correct."

Huffard continued, "Each day in the water, we learned something new about octopus behavior, probably like what ornithologists must have gone through after the invention of binoculars. We quickly realized that *Abdopus aculeatus* broke all the 'rules' — doing the near opposite of every hypothesis we'd formed based on aquarium studies."

Personal experiences with animals are essential for coming to terms with who they are. Consider the reflections of George Schaller, one of the world's preeminent field biologists:

When you're isolated in a different culture, a different country, you have to have an emotional attachment to what you do. You have to like the people, the country, and the animals. Without emotion you have a dead study. How can you possibly sit for months and look at something you don't particularly like, that you see simply as an object? You're dealing with individual beings who have their own feelings, desires and fears. To understand them is very difficult and you cannot do it unless you try to have some emotional contact and

intuition. Some scientists will say they are wholly objective, but I think that's impossible. Laboratory scientists wasted years putting rats in mazes to show they
were learning. They never got close enough to a rat to
realise that they were not going by sight and learning,
they were following the scent trails of previous rats.
By overlooking this simple fact they wasted years of
science.

Perhaps researchers and others who deny animals their intelligence and rich emotional lives do so because they haven't
taken the time to watch animals in situations where they can display their full repertoire of behavior. Or they do so because their
acceptance of the fact that animals have rich emotional lives —
that they have a point of view and don't like being subjected to
pain and suffering — might impede their research. Surely, a few
mice living in an impoverished cage alone or with a few other
mice cannot display the full array of mouse behavior or demonstrate behavioral variability. If the mice were born in the lab,
perhaps their brains aren't as well developed as their wild relatives, and this affects their behavior by making it less nuanced
and less elaborate. Researcher James Burns and his colleagues
reported in the prestigious journal *Ethology* that laboratory-
reared guppies have smaller brains than wild-caught individuals.
They concluded, "Any deficiencies in brain size of lab-reared
fish may hinder our ability to understand the basic mechanisms
of cognition and how it has been shaped by natural selection."

In other words, just because an animal doesn't do something in one setting does not mean that they cannot do it in
another context. Also, just because an animal doesn't express
something does not mean that they're not feeling something.

Of course, the same can be said about humans. Masking emotions can be a very important social skill, and both nonhumans and humans hide their feelings in various social situations.

Clearly, we already know a lot about the lives of diverse species and what they want, more than we often give ourselves credit for. The more we look, the more we see. As Nobel laureate and discoverer of bee language Karl von Frisch once said, "The life of bees is like a magic well. The more you draw from it, the more there is to draw."

## Revenge Is Sweet: Are Pissed-off Elephants Striking Back?

A natural question, given what we know about the depth of feeling and intelligence of our fellow animals, is: What do they think of humans? As we study them, they are assuredly, in their own ways, studying us.

In fact, there's a flurry of interest lately in the intriguing question of whether animals take revenge on humans when they're pissed off at being mistreated. Revenge is a complex cognitive reaction, involving memory, self-awareness, logic, hurt, justice, blame, and more. Anecdotal evidence is that some animals can and do take revenge. In China in December 2008, a trio of monkeys attacked their trainer during a public performance. When one of the monkeys refused to ride a mini-bicycle, the trainer hit the monkey with a stick; the other two monkeys got upset and came to their fellow's aide. One monkey twisted his trainer's ears, and another pulled out his hair and bit his neck; when the trainer dropped the cane, one of the monkeys picked it up and started hitting him in the head until the stick broke. In another incident, a male chimpanzee at the Kolkata Zoo in India apparently retaliated at visitors — after a few people began teasing him and throwing pieces of brick — by throwing stones into the crowd and injuring a mother and her daughter.

Elephants are highly social, highly emotional sentient giants who have also demonstrated that they don't like being mistreated, and revenge seems to have played a factor in some attacks by elephants on humans in some locales. Elephants surely have the cognitive and emotional capacities to remember who treated them unkindly and to bear grudges. In addition, the frequency of angry elephant-human encounters has increased. Elephant expert Iain Douglas-Hamilton wrote to me in a recent email: "I think what has happened is that the interface of human elephant conflict has increased as people expand into elephant range all across Africa, and there is also more reporting of what goes on."

We're certainly learning more about the extraordinary emotional capacity of elephants every day. We know that African elephants can actually form expectations about the locations of out-of-sight family members, and they can recognize up to seventeen females and possibly up to thirty family members from cues present in the urine-earth mix. They can also keep track of the location of these individuals in relation to themselves. Scientists are tapping into the phenomenal way in which elephants communicate over long distances using low-frequency infrasounds that travel through the ground. And there's a practical application of this discovery. By using the low rumble sound of a female in heat, researchers in Namibia's Etosha National Park are luring bull males away from adjacent farms (and those farmers' guns).

Elephants and other animals also grieve the loss of friends and family. For instance, consider this moving account of a funeral service for a baby who was mauled to death by a lioness:

> On safari in Botswana, Peter Jackson came across a lioness that had mauled a baby elephant to death. As he watched the lioness and her cubs feast on its remains, he witnessed the rare spectacle of 100 elephants turning up to stage a funeral. On they came, until they began to assemble around the bloody remains of the baby elephant, some stamping their feet and snorting in the direction of the lion family they knew still to be near. But most would lightly touch and sniff the body with their trunks and then move to a respectable distance, standing in silent groups. Still more elephants arrived until there were at least 100 in all, the latecomers filtering their way to the body, seemingly paying their respects, then moving to the rear of the congregation.

Researchers have observed elephants mourning a black rhinoceros who had been killed by poachers, as well as elephant bulls grieving the loss of other bulls. Given all this, how much of a stretch is it to imagine that elephants might target humans whom they know have killed or injured one of their relatives?

Some have even gone so far as to speculate about whether what we're seeing are more premeditated, intentional acts of generalized animal revenge spanning the globe and widely separated habitats. This "conspiracy theory" seems unlikely, but it's quite possible that individual animals can and will respond to violence with violence of their own. We receive what we give. Douglas-Hamilton told me: "Simply put, if you treat elephants nastily, they are likely to be nasty in return. There is nothing new about this or particularly unique to elephants. If you are kind to elephants, they will respond in kind. The same is true for a huge range of mammals, from Cape Buffalo to dogs."

Elephants are an excellent example that animals are more than we give them credit for, which necessitates a change in how we interact with them. The effects of early elephantine trauma are devastating and long lasting. Some individuals cannot be rehabilitated after a decade of attempts to get them out of their misery and depression. I met some of these traumatized elephants at the David Sheldrick Wildlife Trust outside of Nairobi, Kenya, and saw the marvelous work that was being done there to rehabilitate individuals so that they could be returned to the wild. I also witnessed elephants who suffered from flashbacks and were unable to forget what they'd experienced years before.

Some zoo administrators are beginning to recognize that elephants are extremely sensitive beings and that zoos can't satisfy their social, emotional, or physical needs. Thus, five major zoos in the United States are phasing out their elephant exhibits despite the fact that they're moneymakers. Elephants in zoos also die younger than their wild relatives. Despite the absence of predators and the availability of veterinary care, captive elephants, especially Asians, don't do very well compared to wild relatives. A review of survivorship in Asian and African zoo elephants, written by six eminent biologists and published in the prestigious journal *Science* in December 2008, concluded: "Overall, bringing elephants into zoos profoundly impairs their viability. The effects of early experience, interzoo transfer, and possibly maternal loss, plus the health and reproductive problems recorded in zoo elephants...suggest stress and/or obesity as likely causes."

## Doubt, and Deciding What We "Know"

As we saw under "Headline News," a fifteen-year-old boy, Rory Stokes, believed that goldfish are mistreated when confined to small fish tanks or bowls, but to convince others, he had to demonstrate that goldfish can remember for longer than three seconds. Indeed, when he did this, proving that goldfish have a much longer memory than previously thought, it became worldwide news. Only afterward did adult scientists from Israel conduct similar experiments to determine that, yes, this teenage boy was correct.

Those of us who study and live with animals already know a great deal about the mental capabilities and emotions of animals, even if science hasn't yet proven beyond a shadow of a doubt that we're correct. But waiting for science to confirm what we already know about animals can be disastrous. Skepticism is an important trait for a scientist, but doubt can also be its own excuse, a way to avoid coping with the consequences of what we're doing to our fellow beings. For scientists, doubt is especially useful as a way to avoid the truth of what is done to the very individuals being studied. Let's consider two studies, one on empathy in mice and one on "muskrat love," in which individuals were abused and killed, all in the name of confirming what many of us already know.

First, do you believe mice are capable of empathy? If you've lived with mice, you're more likely to say yes, because you've probably seen it firsthand, but either way, up until a few years ago, "the science" hadn't been done to prove or disprove this, so it was considered a controversial claim. Then, in June 2006, researchers reported in the journal *Science* the first unequivocal evidence for empathy between adult, nonprimate mammals, that is, mice. What experiment do you think they devised?

Dale Langford, of McGill University, and her colleagues demonstrated that mice feel empathy by showing that they suffer distress when they watch a cage-mate experience pain. Langford and her team injected one or both members of a pair of adult mice with acetic acid, which causes a severely painful burning sensation. The researchers discovered that mice who watched their cage-mates in pain were more sensitive to pain themselves. A mouse injected with acid writhed more violently if his or her partner had also been injected and was writhing in pain. Not only did the mice who watched cage-mates in distress become more sensitive to the same painful stimuli, they became generally more sensitive to pain, showing a heightened reaction, for example, to heat under their paws.

One of the researchers suggested that an opaque barrier be used to separate mice so that they can't know what's happening to another mouse because mice who observe each other during experiments may be "contaminating" the data; the mice, in other words, were being too empathetic. It's difficult to believe that he really meant this, but it's a good example of a scientist shirking his responsibility to provide the animals he uses with the very best care possible. Of course, according to U.S. law, mice, voles, rats and other rodents, birds, rabbits, and fish aren't protected from invasive research in the United States. Yet this very study shows why this law is inadequate.

In a study of "muskrat love," researchers separated nine male voles from their partners to see how they coped with this stress. They then killed the voles and discovered elevated levels of a chemical called cortico-tropin-releasing factor (CRF) that is known to play a role in depression. An article about the study in the *Los Angeles Times* began: "Scientists have confirmed what poets have long known: Absence makes the heart grow fonder."

By that logic, does death make the heart grow fonder still? And what does it say about humans that they devised an experiment in which they killed animals to prove those animals can love? If animals wrote a manifesto, surely one of their demands would be that humans trust their instincts concerning them first. Then, if the humans have any lingering doubts, that they satisfy those doubts in ways that, in hindsight, don't accept cruelty as the price for knowledge.

## Anthropomorphism Is Alive and Well, as It Should Be

The more we learn about animals' cognitive abilities, the more these capabilities compel us to rethink how we treat them. Our fellow animals not only think, but they feel — deeply. Animals live and move through the world with likes and dislikes and preferences just like we do. This is not being anthropomorphic. We're not inserting something human into them that they don't have. It doesn't matter whether their thoughts and emotions are exactly the same as our thoughts and emotions. Both their feelings and ours are essential for a meaningful life. We know that there are individual differences among humans, so that what I think and feel, the pain I experience, might not be the same as someone else, but this obviously *doesn't* mean that either of us doesn't think, feel, and experience pain.

Critics who complain about anthropomorphism fail to notice their own anthropomorphism. The same zoo officials who accuse activists of being anthropomorphic when they call a captive elephant unhappy turn around and freely describe the same elephant as perfectly happy. Renowned philosopher Mary Midgley points out in *Animals and Why They Matter*, what's truly anthropomorphic is to assume that animals don't think or feel. Terry Tempest Williams calls this the "ultimate act of solipsism." It's important that we get over the issue of anthropomorphism and move on — there's important work to be done.

It's also important to remember that solid biological theory and a rapidly growing database of scientific research supports the claim that animals have their own sorts of pain and emotions and that what they feel matters to them. (See this book's bibliography and notes section for ample citations, scientific papers, and research, as well as my books *The Emotional Lives of Animals* and *Animals Matter*.) Anna Sewell notes in *Black Beauty*, "We call them dumb animals, and so they are, for they cannot tell us how they feel, but they do not suffer less because they have no words." Of course, while animals cannot tell us what they feel in words, they do clearly let us know what they're feeling using a wide variety of behaviors, sounds, and scents.

For the few remaining skeptics, it is unacceptable to only study animals in cages or in unnatural groups in which they can't display their natural repertoire of behavior — and their ability to change their behavior when there are variations in their social and physical environments. As we've seen, when we study animals in captivity, we can reach completely incorrect and limited conclusions.

Science is catching up with what many lay observers already know from living with animals every day. This growing understanding can help us see and relate to animals as fellow subjective beings rather than as objects. I like what Australian Bradley Trevor Greive writes in his book *Priceless: The Vanishing Beauty of a Fragile Planet*: "For endangered species we are both their greatest enemy and their only hope. These wonderful creatures will not argue their case. They will not put up a fight. They will not beg for reprieve. They will not say goodbye. They will not cry out. They will just vanish. And after they are gone, there will be silence. And there will be stillness. And there will be empty places. And nothing you can say will change this. Nothing you can do will bring them back. With so many lives hanging in the balance, the paths we choose today will decide the fate of the world. So it's up to us. It's up to you and me to decide who lives and who dies." I read these words as part of a "blessing of the animals" service at the Minding Animals conference in Newcastle, Australia, in July 2009, and the audience was stilled by their simplicity and compassionate call to action, a major message of this book.

I'm sure that the next decade is going to be a boon in terms of what we learn about animal emotions and beastly passions. Indeed, it's what animals feel and share that draws us to them. When we don't have these connections, we become alienated from life and other beings, and this is what allows us to abuse others. Empathy and compassion, then, lead us to the next item in this manifesto.

# REASON 3

## *Animals Have and Deserve Compassion*

"The satisfaction that washes over us as we watch our pets sleep is the ancient reminder that when all is well in their world, all is well in ours."

— Meg Daley Olmert, *Made For Each Other*

IN THEIR MANIFESTO, animals would surely seek to highlight the many areas in which all species are similar rather than focus on differences. Surely, a dolphin, a raven, and a human don't look the same, move the same, or perhaps even think the same, but these differences are minor compared to what these animals share: for instance, many of the same senses and organs, the ability to think and feel, and essential roles to play in maintaining the health of the world's ecosystems, large and small. In area after area, humans are in fact discovering that there isn't a great divide between other animals and us.

Further, animals would argue that different doesn't mean better or worse. Each animal has evolved for his or her own needs; an animal does whatever is necessary to be a card-carrying member of his or her species. Yes, some animals are better at using tools than others, and some don't need them; some animals have more highly developed senses than others, and some run faster or swim deeper. But this doesn't make them higher or lower, better or worse, on the evolutionary scale; it just means different. Should mice consider themselves better than people because they have a more highly developed sense of smell? Should bats pat themselves on the back as more intelligent than us because they use ultrasound and we can't?

Humans have a long history, particularly among themselves, of establishing hierarchies that place their own clan or race or species at the top. Yet invariably, these hierarchies rest on definitions that mistakenly equate surface differences with intrinsic ones and that undervalue similarities or discount them altogether. Philosopher Lynne Sharpe points this out in her book *Creatures Like Us*, when she says that the way we regard and value the similarities and differences among animals typically depends on how we define ourselves. She writes, "Those who define 'us' by our ability to introspect give a distorted view of what is important to and about human beings and ignore the fact that many creatures are like us in more significant ways in that we all share the vulnerability, the pains, the fears, and the joys that are the life of social animals."

Given this, an animal manifesto would demand that every species, and every individual within every species, deserves respect and compassion. No animal, humans included, is less deserving of empathy and kindness simply for being different. In addition, their manifesto would insist that animals are capable of acting compassionately. Still today, animals suffer under the unfair, baseless notion that they are inherently competitive and cruel to one another; that nature is "red in tooth and claw." On the contrary, lots of scientific research and anecdotal evidence is emerging that shows that animals — rather than being inherently cruel — instead have a natural inclination to work cooperatively and to respond with compassion and empathy. Faced with the pain of others, animals act in ways that display empathy, caring, a moral intelligence, and even a sense of justice.

Expanding our compassion footprint is first and foremost about acting with compassion at all times when we see others in pain or being harmed. In a way, this truly begins when we accept that animals, humans included, are born to be good.

HEADLINE NEWS:
Dog Saves Kangaroo! Birds Feed Fish!
Whale Rescues Diver!

I constantly receive stories about animals helping other animals, animals helping people, and people helping animals — and, of course, of people helping other people. The most intriguing stories are the ones that demonstrate cross-species empathy. That walruses would help fellow walruses is significant, but then again, we might assume that members of the same species would be inclined to help one another; that at least benefits one's own species. However, what would drive one species to help an entirely different species, one they have no particular need for or relationship with? Indeed, one they might even compete with or, in different circumstances, prey upon? Here are a few news stories that show that compassion comes naturally to many species, and that humans are not the only animals who will help other species and even risk their own lives to save someone else.

## Who Is the Walrus?
*New York Times*, May 28, 2008

"Scientists are gathering evidence that [walruses are] the most cognitively and socially sophisticated of all pinnipeds.... Evidence suggests that the bonds between walruses are exceptionally strong: the animals share food, come to one another's aid when under attack and nurse one another's young, a particularly noteworthy behavior given the cost in energy of synthesizing a pinniped's calorically rich, fatty milk."

## Best Mates, the Baby Kangaroo and the Wonder Dog That Saved It
*Daily Mail*, March 31, 2008

"By all accounts the baby kangaroo should have not survived the road accident that claimed its mother . . . but then along came Rex the wonder dog. The pointer discovered the baby roo, known as a joey, alive in the mother's pouch and took it back to his owner....

"The four-month-old joey's mother was killed by a car . . . in Torquay, Victoria, Australia. Amazingly, the 10-year-old dog — a cross between a German shorthaired and wirehaired pointer — had been so tender with the joey that it was both calm and unmarked.

"'The joey was snuggling up to him, jumping up to him and Rex was sniffing and licking him — it was quite cute,' [the owner] said.

"The joey...is now being cared for at Jirrahlinga Wildlife Sanctuary....Director Tehree Gordon said she was amazed by the trusting bond between the two animals....'That Rex was so careful and knew to bring the baby to his owners, and that the joey was so relaxed and didn't see Rex as a predator, is quite remarkable.' "

## Podmates Aided Dying Whale in Its Last Days
*Honolulu Advertiser*, May 27, 2009

"A pygmy killer whale that beached itself on Maui this month had been escorted for three weeks by a pod of pygmy killer whales, giving marine biologists a rare peek into how the cetaceans cared for one of their own before its death.

"Four or five pygmy killer whales had surrounded their 300-pound, seven- to eight-foot, male podmate and appeared to be flipping on their sides and backs to support the struggling mammal, scientists said.

"When it grew weaker and came closer to McGregor's Beach, the pygmy killer whales broke off one by one over the next several days and headed back out to the open ocean, where they live year-round in deep Hawaiian waters. . . . It was the first time that marine biologists had documented such 'pre-stranding, milling behavior' in pygmy killer whales around Hawai'i.

" 'We don't know so much about pygmy killer whales,' [one scientist] said. 'So it was very interesting for us to see this very highly evolved social behavior surrounding the care of this one individual by the other whales.' "

## The Amazing Moment Mila the Beluga Whale
## Saved a Stricken Diver's Life
*Daily Mail*, July 29, 2009

"It looks like a moment of terror — a diver finds her leg clamped in the jaws of a beluga whale. In fact, it was a stunning example of an animal coming to the rescue of a human life.

"Yang Yun, 26, was taking part in a free diving contest without breathing equipment among the whales in a tank of water more than 20ft deep and chilled to Arctic temperatures. She says that when she tried to return to the surface, she found her legs crippled by cramp from the freezing cold. At that point Mila the beluga took a hand, or rather a flipper.

" 'We suddenly saw the girl being pushed to the top of the pool with her leg in Mila's mouth,' said an official at Polar Land in Harbin, northeast China. 'She's a sensitive animal who works closely with humans and I think this girl owes Mila her life.' "

### Hero Dog Risks Life to Save Kittens from Fire
Reuters, October 26, 2008

"In a case which gives the lie to the saying about 'fighting like cats and dogs,' the terrier cross named Leo had to be revived with oxygen and heart massage after his ordeal. Fire broke out overnight at the house in Australia's southern city of Melbourne, [and] fire fighters who revived Leo said he refused to leave the building and was found by them alongside the litter of kittens, despite thick smoke."

### Stray Pit Bull Saves Woman, Child from Attacker
*Zootoo Pet News*, November 5, 2008

"The wandering 65-pound Pit Bull mix,...which authorities think is lost and not a stray, successfully thwarted a robbery attack on a mother and her 2-year-old son, who were held at knifepoint Monday afternoon. The Florida woman...was leaving a playground with her toddler son in Port Charlotte when a man approached her in the parking lot with a knife and told her not to make any noise or sudden movements.

"[The woman] didn't have to do either to protect herself and her child — a dog mysteriously ran to the scene and charged the man, who quickly fled.

" 'I don't think the dog physically attacked the man, but he went at him and was showing signs of aggression, just baring his teeth and growling and barking. It was clear he was trying to defend this woman,' [an animal control officer said].

"The exceptional part of the story... is that the dog had never met or even seen the people it quickly jumped to defend. 'You hear about family dogs protecting their owners, but this dog had nothing to do with this woman or her kid,' [the officers] said."

### Man Dives In to Save Dog from Florida Shark Attack
MSNBC, September 30, 2008

"A dog is recovering after a Florida Keys carpenter dove in to save his pet from a shark. [The man] said he took his 14-pound rat terrier Jake for a daily swim at a marina last Friday. The five-foot shark suddenly surfaced and grabbed nearly the entire dog in its mouth.

"[The owner] said he yelled, then balled up his fists and dove headfirst into the water off a pier.... 'I couldn't see the shark when I dived in... so I just put my fist together...but my hands landed solidly against the back of the shark.'

"Man and dog made it safely back to shore. The dog suffered bite wounds but was not critically injured."

### An Unusual Relationship Between Birds and Fishes
*Spluch* (Blog), August 30, 2007

"A local security guard recently discovered a peculiar scene where black swans can be seen feeding goldfish near the shore of a lake located in Hangzhou, China. According to the guard, nine black swans will climb onto a raft and start feeding the goldfish with their beaks at 10 AM every morning. The goldfish can always be seen following the swans closely after that. Locals were astonished to find such an affectionate tie existing between the two creatures."

### New Zealand Dolphin Rescues Beached Whales
*BBC News*, March 12, 2008

"A dolphin has come to the rescue of two whales which had become stranded on a beach in New Zealand. Conservation officer Malcolm Smith told the BBC that he and a group of other people had tried in vain for an hour and a half to get the whales to sea. The pygmy sperm whales had repeatedly beached, and both they and the humans were tired and set to give up, he said. But then the dolphin appeared, communicated with the whales, and led them to safety. . . .

" 'I don't speak whale and I don't speak dolphin,' Mr Smith told the BBC, 'but there was obviously something that went on because the two whales changed their attitude from being quite distressed to following the dolphin quite willingly and directly along the beach and straight out to sea.'

"He added: 'The dolphin did what we had failed to do. It was all over in a matter of minutes.' "

[Cetacean expert Philippa Brakes told me later it is certainly within the capacity of these intelligent animals to be able to communicate their distress to the dolphin and for the dolphin to empathize with that distress and lead them to safety.]

## Argentine Dog Saves Abandoned Baby

*BBC News*, August 23, 2008

"An eight-year-old dog has touched the hearts of Argentines by saving the life of an abandoned baby, placing him safely alongside her own new puppies. . . .

"[The baby] was born prematurely to a 14-year-old girl in a shanty town outside the capital, Buenos Aires. She is said to have panicked and abandoned the boy in a field, surrounded by wooden boxes and rubbish.

"Then along came La China, reports say, the dog which somehow picked up the baby and carried him 50m to place him alongside her own puppies. The dog's owner reported hearing the child crying and finding him covered with a rag.

"The baby, weighing [8lb 13oz], had some slight injuries, but no bite marks."

## Amazing Rescue by a Mother Duck
## Who Went the Extra Mile

*Daily Mail*, June 17, 2008

"Trapped in a dark sewer, the six little mallard ducklings found themselves cut off and facing an uncertain future. Their only hope of seeing daylight again lay with their mother — who they had last seen more than a mile away as they were sucked into a drain.

"Rescue seemed impossible. Yet somehow the mother duck had managed to follow her offspring for more than a mile, apparently listening to their cheeps of distress at manhole covers as they were swept along below ground. Her incredible journey took her across a busy roundabout, countless roads, a metro rail line, a housing estate, two school playing fields and hospital grounds.

"The trail finally ended when she waddled on to Barras-ford Close in Gosforth, Newcastle upon Tyne, where her chicks suddenly stopped. And it was there, standing over an-other man-hole cover, that the mother remained for the next four hours until local residents heard chirping coming from down below.

"They in turn launched a rescue operation, removing the manhole cover and using a child's fishing net to scoop all six from the sewer one by one and reuniting them with their mother in a paddling pool."

### Bear Rescued from Bridge after Nearly Falling Off
MSNBC, October 1, 2007

"A 250-pound bear stranded under a bridge near Lake Tahoe was saved by an army of rescuers, a tranquilizer dart and a nylon net bought at an Army surplus store....

"[The bear] was walking across the span on Highway 40 near Donner Summit in the Sierra Nevada when at least two oncoming cars spooked it, causing it to jump over the railing. At one point it was dangling over the edge of the 80-foot-high bridge, but it caught a ledge and pulled itself onto a concrete girder beneath the bridge.

"Officials initially decided nothing could be done, but when they returned the next morning and found it sleeping on the ledge, they decided to take action....

" 'I've been on a lot of bear rescues,' [one rescuer] said, 'and this is the most intense bear call that I've been on.' "

## Moral Intelligence and Wild Justice

Put simply, animals display moral behavior, or what Jessica Pierce and I call wild justice. They know right from wrong. When beings are in need, animals will go out of their way to help them, to keep them from harm, or to teach them how to successfully solve a problem. They can act unselfishly in ways that demonstrate empathy and compassion.

Consider these scenarios. A teenage female elephant was once nursing an injured leg and was knocked over by a rambunctious hormone-laden teenage male. An older female elephant saw this happen, chased the male away, and went back to the younger female and touched her sore leg with her trunk. Eleven elephants once rescued a group of captive antelope in KwaZula-Natal: the matriarch undid all of the latches on the gates of their enclosure with her trunk and let the gate swing open so the antelopes could escape. After Christina Germeni, who lives in Athens, Greece, read an article about my research in a Greek newspaper, she emailed me about seeing a male buffalo in the Okavango Delta in Botswana attack a lioness who was attacking his friend, forcing the lioness to give up the fight and saving his buddy.

During a science experiment, a rat in a cage refused to push a lever for food when he saw that another rat received an electric shock as a result. In a separate experiment, a male Diana monkey who learned to insert a token into a slot to obtain food helped a female who couldn't get the hang of the trick; the male inserted the token for her and allowed her to eat the food reward.

In other incidents, a female fruit-eating bat helped an unrelated female give birth by showing her how to hang in the proper way. A cat named Libby led her elderly deaf and blind dog friend, Cashew, away from obstacles and to food. In a group of chimpanzees at the Arnhem Zoo in the Netherlands, individuals punish other chimpanzees who are late for dinner because no one eats until they're all present.

Do these examples show that animals display moral behavior, that they can be compassionate, empathic, altruistic, and fair? Do animals display a kind of moral intelligence? Yes, they do.

Here's a story sent to me by Linda Alvarez. Linda wrote about her two dogs, a male named Volt and his sidekick, Lola.

Lola is four-and-a-half-months-old, and she was recently spayed. I brought her home with her e-collar on. She was obviously frustrated with this space-like sphere around her neck. The times when the e-collar seemed to bother her most were, I guess, when the stitches were causing an itching sensation. Periodically, she would start bucking around like a wild stallion and bark at me as if attempting to say, "Hey, my stomach itches. Can you help me out here?" I sympathized, but I left the e-collar on for fear that she might rip off the stitches.

Seeing that I didn't really do anything to alleviate her problem, she tried the next best thing: Volt. Whenever Lola started acting this way, Volt would watch her; he seemed to be observing and trying to figure out what her issue was. Then, on one occasion Lola came over to Volt, who was laying on the grass, stood right over him, so that her surgical incision was right over his face, and then started to make grunting sounds. Volt propped up his ears, sniffed her stomach, and then started licking her wound. I thought this was awesome!

I'm sure dogs and other animals do this all the time, but I just thought it was fascinating that Lola figured out a way to work around the e-collar problem.

I think it's also fascinating that Volt showed the simple caring we would expect of any family member. Is this not the right thing to do? Is this not moral intelligence?

## Binti Jua's Rescue: A Sign of Compassion or Just Good Training?

The popular and scientific media constantly remind us of the amazing things animals can do, know, and feel, and these often surprise us — we didn't know animals could do *that*! However, correctly understanding animal behavior is also tricky; sometimes, there are several plausible, alternate explanations, and it's important to examine them all. When it comes to animals displaying a sense of justice and compassion, the answer typically hinges on a basic question: is the animal displaying what appears to be self-aware intelligence and other-directed empathy, or is the animal's response unthinking, self-centered, and automatic? Is the animal blindly following instinct, or is the animal making a choice guided by a combination of an inborn predisposition and of learning, which shows that the animal is being flexible and adapting to a specific situation?

Consider the story of a female Western Lowland gorilla named Binti Jua — Swahili for "daughter of sunshine" — who lived in the Brookfield Zoo in Illinois. One summer day in 1996, a three-year-old boy climbed the wall of the gorilla enclosure at Brookfield and fell twenty feet onto the concrete floor below. As spectators gaped and the boy's mother screamed in terror, Binti Jua approached the unconscious boy. She reached down and gently lifted him, cradling him in her arms while her own infant, Koola, clung to her back. Growling warnings at the other gorillas who tried to get close, Binti Jua carried the boy safely to an access gate and the waiting zoo staff. Her face and posture showed deep concern.

This story made headlines worldwide, and Binti Jua was widely hailed as an animal hero. She was even awarded a medal from the American Legion. However, behind the splashy news, the gorilla's story added fuel to an already smoldering debate about what goes on inside the mind and heart of an animal like Binti Jua. That is, was Binti Jua's behavior really a deliberate act of kindness — did she know what she was doing — or did it simply reflect her previous training by zoo staff?

In the mid-1990s, there remained considerable skepticism among scientists that an animal, even an intelligent animal like a gorilla, could have the cognitive and emotional resources to respond to a novel situation with what appeared to be intelligence and compassion. Skeptics argued that the most likely explanation for Binti Jua's "heroism" was her particular experience as a captive animal. Because Binti Jua had been hand-raised by zoo staff, she had not learned, as she would have in the wild, the skills of gorilla mothering. She had to be taught these skills by humans, who used a stuffed toy as a pretend baby to show her how to care for her own daughter. She had even been trained to bring her "baby" to zoo staff. Thus, some scientists argued that she was probably simply replaying this training exercise, having mistaken the young boy for another stuffed toy.

At the time, several scientists disagreed with their skeptical colleagues and argued that at least some animals, particularly primates, probably do have the capacity for empathy, altruism, and compassion and were intelligent enough to assess the situation and understand that the boy needed help. Binti Jua's manner showed evident care and concern, and combined with her warnings to the other gorillas, displayed an awareness that she held an injured living being and not an inanimate doll. Her prior training perhaps helped her know what to do, but she applied that knowledge to an entirely new and different situation. To support this understanding, the scientists pointed to a small but growing body of research hinting that animals have cognitive and emotional lives rich beyond our understanding.

We'll never know exactly why Binti Jua did what she did. But now, years later, the staggering amount of information that we have about animal intelligence and animal emotions brings us much closer to answering the larger question raised by her behavior: Can animals really act with compassion, altruism, and empathy? Among scientists who study animal behavior, the answer has become an unequivocal "Yes." This doesn't mean that animals always act in these ways; humans certainly don't. But considering Binti Jua today, we have every reason to believe that she made a deliberate, empathetic choice to rescue the young boy — as well as unintentionally liberating some of my colleagues from the grip of timeworn and outdated views of our fellow animals and opening the door for much-needed discussion about their cognitive and emotional lives.

## All in the Family: The Love of Pets

Nearly anyone who has cared for a companion animal (or pet) knows that animals are capable of love and compassion. Domestic animals exhibit these qualities so naturally and powerfully that they are enlisted in numerous programs to help heal and care for humans, to bring happiness and joy to those who are sick, disabled, elderly, or otherwise alone. Dogs, for example, are taken to assisted-living homes and catalyze happiness in people who have little else in their lives. Dogs and other animals also bring joy to troubled children and adults. They truly are our companions, helping us through difficult times — failing health, the loss of friends and family members — just as we do for them. In his memoir *Dog Years*, poet Mark Doty describes his moving relationship with his two dogs, Arden and Beau, trying to understand and express the complexities of cross-species love, compassion, communication, and understanding. Doty eloquently describes how his dogs helped heal and care for him and his partner during their emotional and physical illnesses, and how Doty later did the same for his dogs as they grew old and died.

Consider a study conducted by psychologist Carolyn Zahn-Waxler: she wanted to observe the responses of young children to the distress of a family member, so she went into the homes of a number of families and observed how children reacted to parental distress. However, the behavior of the household pet turned out to be just as interesting as the behavior of the child. When a family member feigned sadness or distress — when he or she pretended to cry or choke — the household dogs would often show more concern than the children, hovering nearby or nudging their owners, or gently resting their head on the distressed person's lap. In a completely different study, one focused on alleviating stress, Karen Allen, a researcher at the School of Medicine at the State University of New York at Buffalo, also discovered that our pets might actually provide better support and reassurance than our loved ones.

When it comes to our pets and domestic companions, if the question is "Are animals capable of compassion and empathy?" then it seems we have already answered it.

## Measuring Compassion: It's in the Eyes

As we've seen, scientists have a hard time coming up with rigorous, replicable experiments to measure emotion, empathy, and love. Indeed, what's in an individual's heart is hard to quantify, and is often inexpressible, even among humans who share language, culture, and history. What do we find when we look into the eyes of our spouse, our children, anyone we love?

For this reason, evidence for compassion between animals often relies on anecdote and subjective impressions. Let me share two stories that exemplify this and that highlight the power of eyes. The first was sent to me by Alexandria Neonakis, who wrote in an email:

> My entire life has been touched by birds. I am fascinated by them. I'm one of those people who will scream "Oh my God!" and stop on a highway if I see an osprey or a hawk flying overhead. As a twenty-three year old, my friends find this kind of funny. They always get a bit of a shock when I yell and pull to the side of the road, and they always sort of give me a bored/exasperated look and roll their eyes at me with the obligatory, "It's just a bird, Alex." But to me, birds are something special.
>
> When I was in the tenth grade, I got my first real taste of heartbreak. I was staying with my grandmother while my mom was camping with my siblings.

Walking along a street, I saw a bird in the middle of the road. Assuming it was dead, I kept walking, but out of the corner of my eye, as I passed it, I noticed it move its head. I looked back, but at that moment a car was coming. It passed over it, narrowly missing him. He made a small squeaking noise, so I rushed over and put my hand down toward it, not really knowing what to expect. He immediately jumped into my hands. I was startled at first. He was a starling, and this was not normal behavior for a bird. I pulled him close to me and sat on the side of the road to inspect him. He had been hit by a car. His wings were badly mangled. As I held him in my hands, I could feel his heart thumping against my fingertips. I could tell he was scared. So I started to sing to him really softly and pet his back. He looked up at me and watched me as I sang to him. I could feel him calming down, and he became kind of inquisitive, looking at me, cocking his head to the side, kind of like a puppy does. I continued to rub his back. Then in an instant, a change came over him. His heart rate was slowing. I could feel it. He looked at me and his eyes said something that I couldn't explain in that moment. It was like nothing I'd ever seen. He closed them slowly, and died in my hands. I held him for a long time after he died, singing softly to him, and rubbing his back. Then I carried him home and buried him under a bush in my grandmother's garden.

I thought long and hard about what had happened in the instant before he died. There was something about the way he looked at me. It was gratitude. But it wasn't the gratitude a human feels toward another human, or even that which a bird feels toward another bird. It was the gratitude shared only between him and I. It was him thanking me for letting him finally calm down enough to just let go and die, as he was too afraid to calm down enough to just let it happen, as he sat on the road watching death pass over him every few seconds.

Shannon Griffith sent me the following, equally moving story:

Last winter I was walking my dog in the woods near my home. He ended up chasing this gull that was sitting down by the water into a thicket bush. This gull was all tangled up, and the briars were in knots around his wings. I could not have left him because he would have surely been dinner for some other hungry animal. I approached this bird — who was very scared and hissing and trying to peck me with his bill — and I tried to unwrap his wings. I then quietly said to him, "It's okay, I am here to help." And he immediately stopped moving, hissing, and pecking. I think he understood me; maybe not my words, but the tone of my voice probably soothed him. I finally got him all untangled from the bushes, lifted him up in my arms — which was an amazing experience — and then he took off like an eagle from my hands. He looked back at me and stared, and it almost looked like he nodded his head. I knew by the way he looked back at me that he was saying "Thank you," and I simply said, "You're welcome."

## Saying Good-bye to Jethro:
## Our Obligation of Compassion

When it comes to our companion animals, the individuals with whom we share our homes, we all recognize that we have accepted an obligation to care for them, to show them compassion, to the end of their lives. But isn't it equally true that the entire world is our home, and all beings share it, so that all beings have an obligation to care for one another? Isn't this what the stories of Binti Jua and Shannon Griffith demonstrate — that all beings feel this obligation, and that it springs forth naturally, innately, even across species? When my dog buddy Jethro died in July 2002, I wrote an epitaph about his life I'd like to share:

> Jethro never hesitated to tell me when it was time for a hike, dinner, or a belly rub. I was constantly on call for him, a large German shepherd/Rottweiler mix with whom I shared my home for twelve years. I rescued Jethro from the Humane Society in Boulder, but in many ways he rescued me.
>
> As he got older, it became clear that our lives together soon would be over. The uninhibited and exuberant wagging of his whip-like tail, which fanned me in the summer, occasionally knocked glasses off the table, and told me how happy he was, would soon stop.
>
> What should I do? Let him live in misery or help him die peacefully, with dignity? It was my call and a hard one at that. But just as I was there for him in life, I needed to be there for him as he approached death, to put his interests before mine, to help end his suffering,

to help him cross into his mysterious future with grace, dignity, and love. For sure, easier said than done.

Dogs trust us unconditionally. It's great to be trusted and loved, and no one does it better than dogs. Jethro was no exception. But along with trust and love come many serious responsibilities and difficult moral choices. I find it easiest to think about dog trust in terms of what they expect from us. They have great faith in us; they expect we'll always have their best interests in mind, that we'll care for them and make them as happy as we can. Indeed, we welcome them into our homes as family members who bring us much joy and deep friendship.

We're responsible for giving each and every individual the best life we can. Even in death we must let our friends go with compassion, empathy, and love, putting their interests ahead of our own. Because they're so dependent on us, we're also responsible for making difficult decisions about when to end their lives. I've been faced with this situation many times and have anguished trying to "do what's right" for my buddies. Should I let them live a bit longer or has the time really come to say good-bye? When Jethro got old and could hardly walk, eat, or hold his water, the time had come for me to put him out of his misery. He was dying right in front of my eyes, and in my heart, I knew it. Even when eating a bagel he was miserable. His eyes had lost much of their luster and glee.

Finally, I chose to let Jethro leave Earth in peace. After countless hugs and "I love you's," to this day I swear that Jethro knew what was happening. When he went for his last car ride, something he loved to do, he accepted his fate with valor, grace, and honor. And I feel he also told me that the moral dilemma with which I was faced was no predicament at all, that I had indeed done all I could and that his trust in me was not compromised one bit, but, perhaps, strengthened. I made the right choice and he openly thanked me for it. And he wished me well, that I could go on with no remorse or apologies.

Let's thank our animal companions for who they are, let's rejoice and embrace them as the amazing beings they are. If we open our hearts to them, we can learn much from their selfless lessons in compassion, humility, generosity, kindness, devotion, respect, spirituality, and love. By honoring our dogs' trust, we tap into our own spirituality, into our hearts and souls.

And sometimes that means not only killing them with love, but also mercifully taking their lives when their own spirit has died and life's flame has been irreversibly extinguished. Our companions are counting on us to be there for them in all situations, to let them go and not to let their lives deteriorate into base, undignified humiliation while we ponder our own needs in lieu of theirs. We are obliged to do so. We can do no less. Our commitment never ends.

Finally, here is a well-known passage by Harry Beston from his wonderful book *The Outermost House*, which summarizes poetically how our fellow animals might indeed ask humans to reconceive our life together:

We need another and a wiser and perhaps a more mystical concept of animals. Remote from universal nature, and living by complicated artifice, man in civilization surveys the creature through the glass of his knowledge and sees thereby a feather magnified and the whole image in distortion. We patronize them for their incompleteness, for their tragic fate of having taken form so far below ourselves. And therein we err, and greatly err. For the animal shall not be measured by man. In a world older and more complete than ours they move finished and complete, gifted with extensions of the senses we have lost or never attained, living by voices we shall never hear. They are not brethren, they are not underlings; they are other nations caught with ourselves in the net of life and time, fellow prisoners of the splendour and travail of the earth.

# REASON 4

## *Connection Breeds Caring, Alienation Breeds Disrespect*

"You have just dined, and however scrupulously the slaughterhouse is concealed in the graceful distance of miles, there is complicity."

— Ralph Waldo Emerson

IF ANIMALS WROTE A MANIFESTO, they would surely insist that they are not in competition with humans to dominate and control the world. Ecosystems thrive when they are in balance, and species that throw ecosystems out of balance usually suffer. No one is exempt from the wanton destruction that humans wreak on the planet and beyond. In fact, animals would, I believe, scoff at the still-prevalent idea among humans that "evolution" is essentially a "survival of the fittest" competitive game. The strongest and biggest species do not always prevail, nor could top-of-the-food-chain predators live long if every other link in that chain isn't nurtured and respected. The reverse is also true, incidentally; we have discovered that when ecosystems lose their top predators, other species are thrown just as firmly out of balance and into jeopardy.

Instead, survival requires both competition and cooperation, selfishness and reciprocity. Compassion and empathy are also essential. We are apparently hardwired to understand that caring for others spills over to caring for ourselves. In the big picture, when all nonhuman beings thrive, we thrive too. It's not really a dog-eat-dog world because dogs don't eat other dogs.

What this means is that if we nurture our connection with animals and care for them better, we humans will benefit directly. The "animal manifesto" this book represents would, if adopted, improve the lives of all animals, including humans. For instance, I feel very close to most animals, but this doesn't distance or alienate me from other humans. In fact, over the years I feel that I have become more aware of the human condition as a result of my devotion to the plight of animals. Compassion begets compassion. As we develop compassion, we expand our moral circle to include all animals and people; this is the ultimate goal of expanding our compassion footprint.

This concept of interdependence is not new. Thomas Berry stresses that no living being nourishes itself; each is dependent on every other member of the community for nourishment and the assistance it needs for its own survival. This is likely the evolutionary seed of compassion, which as Dacher Keltner notes in *Born to Be Good*, is the central ethic of all world religions and spiritual philosophies — compassion generates more compassion and brings diverse peoples together. Keltner also reports that empirical research shows that exercising compassion makes people feel more connected to vulnerable groups, such as the homeless, the ill, and the elderly. This surely extends to nonhuman animals. Whenever we expand our compassion footprint, we only gain more compassion, and we increase the likelihood that we ourselves will be met with kindness. We receive what we give.

Naturally, even tragically, the reverse is also true. When we foster alienation and disconnection, we increase these in all our relationships. This is vividly demonstrated in this and the next chapter, as we look more closely at the current state of our interrelationships with animals. To heal the environment and improve our lives, we need to break through the cycle of alienation that exists between humans and our fellow animals in our modern world. As we take steps to do this, expanding our compassion footprint along the way, our natural inclination to respect and care for all living beings will grow and flourish.

## Embrace Your Inner Animal

Humans are animals and we should embrace our membership in this kingdom. However, modern culture typically portrays "being an animal" as not just bad but exemplifying the worst aspects of humanity: it usually means we've been ruthlessly competitive, angry, and violent. The result? We tend to distance ourselves from other animals and emphasize our differences. We need to change this.

First of all, helping other animals recover from trauma or simply treating them with kindness, respect, dignity, and love, all based in deep empathy, is a two-way street. We feel better when we help other beings, no matter what their species. In *Made for Each Other*, Meg Daley Olmert reported on a study that found that when people feel that wild animals trust them, it enhances their self-esteem. Animals open the door to understanding, trust, cooperation, community, and hope.

It feels good to interact with animals because it's in our evolutionary heritage. Our old, reptilian brains get a bad rap, but having them means we are tightly tied to other animals and to nature. However, modern culture pulls us away from having close relationships with our animal kin. Our lifestyles and jobs and cities disconnect us from the natural world, forcing us to deny the innate pull we feel toward animals and nature. But we have to learn to live — to coexist — this way. Children experience a natural and immediate connection with animals. Their senses haven't been dulled, and they aren't made to feel guilty for their love and empathy for animals. However, our current lifestyles can easily alienate children from animals and the natural world.

We suffer when we are alienated from animals because it's fundamentally unnatural. We benefit from their presence. We know that when we pet a dog, for example, our heart rate and blood pressure decrease, as do the heart rate and blood pressure of the dog. As we saw in the last chapter, dogs and other animals are often used to calm patients in various healthcare facilities — their mere presence makes the patients feel good. If mimicking animals brings out the worst in us, how could this be?

In order to distance ourselves from animals, we've ill-defined our own "human nature" — but we're not the only rational, conscious, sentient, tool-using, moral beings. Animals, as we've seen, share these qualities to varying degrees. Our effort to define ourselves as separate merely isolates us. We foster our own alienation from nature by insisting, falsely, that we're unique and superior. As a result, we suffer from what author, and chairman of the Children and Nature Network, Richard Louv calls "nature-deficit disorder."

Australian environmental ethicist Rod Bennison has developed the notion of "ecological inclusion." He writes, "Implicit within an ecologically inclusive worldview is the recognition that, no matter what perceptions of nature may be held by any human individual, there is an overarching oneness or unity within nature and that all life forms have an inherent worth or intrinsic value." Bennison focuses on identifying those destructive practices that exclude animals from the moral arena and allow us to exploit them for our own selfish purposes.

This deliberate, self-created alienation from our fellow animals fosters disrespect and gives us permission to mistreat them. It allows us to think of animals as property, mere objects, or products with which we can do anything we choose. It allows us to legally keep chimpanzees in five-foot-square cages. It allows us to poach wild animals and to destroy their habitat to the point that they are imperiled. It allows us to torture animals for unneeded food and to trap animals for unneeded clothing.

Overcoming our objectification of animals often requires just simple proximity. Australian wildlife biologist Clive Marks writes about a poignant experience he had in which a student's seeming brutality was transformed by a few minutes with the wild animals he had previously regarded as objects:

Not long ago I lectured a group of keen university students and offered as a reward for their endurance an introduction to the menagerie of animals we kept for our research. We crossed the lawns and the acrid smell of foxes wafted towards us. As we ambled, one student enthusiastically told me of how foxes could be caught with shark fishing hooks baited with meat, with the bait suspended a metre from the ground. The fox would be found hanging, hook in mouth, the next day. Shortly afterwards, he spent a few minutes with some tame foxes who examined his shoes, looked him in the eyes and indulged in the usual cacophony of fox sounds. I recall the perplexed look on this earnest young man's face as we walked back to the lecture theatre. He uttered some simple, if not facile words, that seemed to belie his obvious intelligence: "I didn't realise that they were real animals."

## It's All in a Name

"That's the way hunting works. The *thing* you're hunting for is the *thing* you don't see."

— Idaho hunter on the first day of
wolf hunting season (emphasis added)

When I visited the Qiming Animal Rescue Centre outside of Chengdu, China, in October 2008 with people from the Moon Bear Rescue Centre, we brought five dogs back to the Moon Bear facility for medical treatment. I was given the honor of naming them: Henry (whose front right leg had been chopped off by a butcher after Henry stole some meat), Matilde (who was then emaciated but now is thriving), Lady Lobster (whose untreated broken front right leg healed like a lobster claw), Stevie (whose blinded eyes were seriously infected), and Butch (who was blind in one eye after a fight with another dog). Heather Bacon, the talented and tireless veterinarian at the Moon Bear Rescue Centre, amputated the rest of Henry's leg, and I was told that he's now morphed into a kangaroo, happily hopping about here and there.

Already living at the Moon Bear Centre were two dogs who had been rescued in the wake of a devastating earthquake that shook the region and killed tens of thousands of people in May 2008. The dogs were aptly named Tremor — whom I nicknamed Rambo because of his confident manner, which belied his pint-sized stature — and Richter. Naming these dogs was important. The names allowed people to immediately identify with the animals and their maladies, and some were adopted by workers at the Moon Bear Centre itself, even though they were already seriously overworked because of their dedication to rehabilitating rescued bears.

In parts of Africa they say when you give someone a name they become your responsibility. Naming animals immediately creates an identity and a connection; a name indicates that we are meeting an individual being with feelings and an autobiography. A name can open neurological floodgates of emotion. In the 1960s, Jane Goodall rocked the world of animal behavior when she named the chimpanzees she studied. She refused to give them numbers for the purpose of publishing her results in professional journals. In the process, she changed the way people, including researchers, viewed animals. No longer were animals merely interchangeable numbered things, but rather they were individuals with distinct personalities and unique capabilities.

There's a reason that researchers number animals rather than name them, especially laboratory animals. Referring to a dog as "subject 4886" helps the scientist deny the subjectivity of the animal; it alienates the researcher, creating an emotional disconnection. In this way, the scientist can justify experiments that in another context and with another animal would be considered cruel and abusive. I know many researchers who mistreat dogs and cats in the laboratory, and yet they name their companion dogs and cats and shower them with love and affection. During the past few years I've noted a trend that younger researchers are naming research animals, and some professional journals are allowing researchers to use the names in print. About thirty years ago I was initially told I could not use the names I'd given to the coyotes I studied in Grand Teton National Park, but soon after the editor relented. Biologist Anne Innis Dagg mentions in her book *The Social Behavior of Older Animals* that one biologist who was involved in the reintroduction of wolves to Yellowstone National Park noted that wolves were numbered and not named because "the survival of one is not as important as the survival of the group." So says the biologist, not the wolf.

Naming can dramatically change how we feel about eating animals. Recently, my friend Carolyn Hornung told me about her family's latest addition, a crayfish: at her child's school, the students had studied the behavior of these fascinating crustaceans (who, like lobsters, feel pain), and some students were allowed to bring one home. Once Carolyn's family decided to name the crayfish Bubbles, she found it impossible to think of doing the creature any harm, including eating her. In January 2009, a New York restaurant purchased a just-caught 140-year-old lobster, named him George, and used him as a mascot; George generated so much affectionate publicity, it led to calls to release him back to the ocean, which the restaurant agreed to do. Occasionally, I remind people that a bacon, lettuce, and tomato sandwich is really a Babe, lettuce, and tomato sandwich; this was enough for one friend to vow she wouldn't eat pigs again. Indeed, how might our diets change if we knew who we were eating by name?

A name immediately, and almost by definition, confers subjectivity and sentience. Names don't lead us to mistake animals for people, but they lead us to take their sentience seriously, whether or not it resembles ours. In his book *Animals as Persons*, activist and lawyer Gary Francione argues, in fact, that since many animals share the very traits we use to confer "personhood" on humans, we should grant animals "personhood" as well. Generally, the following criteria are used to designate a being as a "person": being conscious of one's surroundings, being able to reason, experiencing various emotions, having a sense of self, being able to communicate with others, adjusting to changing situations, and performing various cognitive and intellectual tasks. Of course, not every human fulfills all of these criteria all of the time — consider babies or infants, those suffering emotional disorders like Alzheimer's, and seriously mentally challenged adults. Nevertheless, we rightfully consider these humans to be "persons."

Now, what about other animals? For instance, my late companion dog Jethro was very active, could feed and groom himself, could communicate, was aware of his surroundings, and was very emotional. He was a fully autonomous dog. He might not have wanted to be called a "person," but he met the criteria — except, that is, for not being a member of the human species. The point, ultimately, isn't to debate the definition of the word "person," but to show that animals meet most if not all of the standards of the term "personhood." As such, why shouldn't they be granted the same attendant moral and legal standing that "personhood" confers on humans? Granting this doesn't lessen or take away from the moral and legal standing of humans, just as my love for Jethro and all animals doesn't lessen or take away from my love for my family or any other human. But names and titles matter; they make a difference in how we allow ourselves to treat another being. If we humans use the term "personhood" to indicate a being who deserves to be treated with respect, compassion, and love, and who should be protected from undue suffering, then animals qualify as "persons" and should be given equal consideration.

## In the Kitchen and on the Farm: The Morality of Eating

"Nothing will benefit human health and increase chances of survival for life on earth as much as the evolution to a vegetarian diet."

— Albert Einstein

Without a doubt the one area where our alienation from animals leads us to make morally questionable decisions is with the food we choose to eat. *Who* — not what — we eat presents us with major dilemmas. A number of excellent books have appeared recently that tackle these concerns, such as author Michael Pollan's *The Omnivore's Dilemma* and *In Defense of Food* and Gene Baur's *Farm Sanctuary*, a superb review of the horrors of factory farming. Today, when we eat animals and animal products, we're usually consuming misery.

Who we put in our mouths is a moral act. George Washington University professor David DeGrazia notes, "When it comes to the consumption of meat and other animal products, there is a remarkable disconnect between what people do and what makes moral sense." This disconnection touches every aspect of eating meat, from the animals we choose to eat and how we treat those animals to the negative impacts of industrial agriculture on human health and our environment. Too often, what should inspire gratitude — that animals literally feed us — is replaced with unthinking gluttony, as exemplified by events like the nationally televised Thanksgiving Day "Turkey Bowl," in which contestants race to eat a twenty-pound bird the fastest. George Shea, the organizer, was quoted in 2007 as saying, "Seeing those guys go at a 20lb turkey is like poetry." But what if, every Thanksgiving, the abuse and suffering that routinely define the existence of these sentient animals was also broadcast on national TV? Would that also be considered "poetry"?

In fact, before we begin, we have to honestly acknowledge what "eating meat" means in the first place. For instance, in our urban and suburban twenty-first-century world, children often don't know that a hamburger was once a living, sentient cow, or that eating bacon, pork, and sausage means they're eating Babe the pig. The animal him- or herself, much less their suffering and death, is absent from their worldview; indeed, many adults have no idea what happens to animals in order to turn them into the food on their plate. Children don't even know what the word "meat" refers to, and when they find out, they can get upset and sometimes want to become vegetarians. In a 2009 article, psychologist William Crain wrote: "In a study of urban, middle class children, Alina Pavlakos found that most five-year-olds didn't know where meat comes from. They knew they ate meat, but when asked, 'Do you eat animals?' most said, 'Nooo!' — as if the idea were outrageous."

Even children in 4-H programs, who are learning about humane animal husbandry, don't always appreciate that the "good life" their animals have with them still ends brutally at the slaughterhouse door. The former mayor of Ojai, California, Suza Francina, has written that 4-H programs should include a trip to the slaughterhouse, so that students understand that, from an animal's point of view, being sold at the annual county auction is not a happy ending.

Simply put, humans have developed a strong conceptual disconnect because of the distance — physical and emotional — from the slaughterhouse to their house. Sarah Bexell, a conservation and humane educator who has done wonderful work in China to help make children more empathetic, calls it "emotional dissonance." The individual animal's torturous journey of indignity is kept hidden and remains unacknowledged by everyone. While we can surely sanitize the animal's trip for young children, there is no reason they shouldn't be aware of what "meat" is. For adults, there is no reason they shouldn't be completely aware of the entire process.

Awareness begins with language, as Crain points out: "We eat pork, not pigs; veal, not calves; meat, not flesh." When humans rely on euphemisms to describe something, it often indicates moral discomfort, if not outright shame. If we can't use honest language to describe our food, then we should change who we eat and/or how we care for food animals until we can.

The moral dilemma concerning who we eat is about making humane choices based on what we know about animals, not denying what we know so that we humans can feel less shame about how we treat them: Lobsters feel pain, and don't like being dropped in boiling water. Fish feel pain, and don't like hooks in their mouths. Cows and pigs are sentient, emotional animals; they know what happens to them and their loved ones in the slaughterhouse. If we would ask certain animals to give their lives for us, we should treat them with the respect such a request deserves.

## *Old MacDonald Did Not Run a Factory Farm*

It's been estimated that about 95 percent of all animal use is in agriculture. Thus, the amount of cruelty, pain, suffering, and death that takes place in factory farms far surpasses the total amount of cruelty, pain, suffering, and death in all other venues combined. This is another reason why changing how we treat animals in agriculture is so urgent: it's the single fastest way to improve the lives of the most animals.

How many animals are we talking about? Every five minutes more than 250,000 animals are slaughtered for food in the United States alone; annually, that amounts to millions of mammals and billions of birds, for an estimated total of approximately 27 billion cows, pigs, chickens, turkeys, and other animals killed each year in the United States "in the name of food." According to the Food and Agriculture Organization, the total number of chickens reared for meat worldwide was nearly 47 billion in 2004, of which approximately 19 percent were produced in the United States, 15 percent in China, 13 percent in the European Union, and 11 percent in Brazil. In Australia 470 million chickens were slaughtered from 2006 to 2007 to feed a demand that has grown a staggering 600 percent in the past fifty years. Heather Moore, who works for People for the Ethical Treatment of Animals, has calculated that an average American eats about 2,500 chickens if they live to age seventy-seven.

It almost goes without saying that the way humans raise these animals is done solely for economic gain and our convenience. The animals are nonconsenting victims of reprehensible torture. Indeed, so much has been published recently about the horrific conditions at factory farms that I won't dwell on it here. Once in the slaughterhouse, it takes about thirty minutes to turn a cow into a steak, during which time these sentient beings suffer immensely; in addition, as they wait to be killed, they also see, hear, and smell other cows on their way to becoming a burger. One slaughterhouse worker notes of food animals, "They die piece by piece." Imagine what it would be like to be a cow hanging upside down in a slaughterhouse waiting to have your throat slashed or a bolt driven into your head. Or a turkey being stomped to death, as was documented in 2008 at the Aviagen Turkeys plant in Lewisburg, West Virginia.

The amount of cruelty that pervades slaughterhouses worldwide is incalculable, and it's made worse because animals have awareness and feelings. Cows display strong emotions; they feel pain, fear, and anxiety, and studies have shown they worry about the future. They and other agricultural animals make and miss their friends. Veterinarian John Webster and his colleagues have shown how cows within a herd form smaller friendship groups of between two and four animals with whom they spend most of their time, often grooming and licking each other. They also dislike other cows and can bear grudges for months or years. There's no doubt that cows and other farm animals are sentient beings who care very much about what happens to them. While some have suggested that one solution would be to genetically engineer "pain-free" animals — who wouldn't suffer physical pain as they went through the grueling process of becoming a meal — the fact that these are still living beings with emotions, and feelings for others, warrants against using them in ways that result in their death.

This is also true for the billions of birds, fish, and invertebrates humans eat. We know fish feel pain and recent research at Queen's University in Belfast, Ireland, shows that lobsters also feel pain; both show a response to painful stimuli that resembles that of humans. Intensively farmed fish suffer from a range of welfare problems, including physical injuries such as fin erosion, eye cataracts, skeletal deformities, soft tissue anomalies, increased susceptibility to disease, sea lice infestation, high mortality rates, and, in some countries, often inhumane slaughter methods.

Indeed, a natural result of the abusive living conditions on factory farms is that many agricultural animals suffer from disease and illness. Called "downers," cows sometimes become too sick or weak to stand on their own, and until recently, these animals were still processed as food. The shocking abuse of "downer" cows occurs not just at slaughter plants but may be an everyday happening at livestock auctions and stockyards in the United States, according to an undercover investigation by the U.S. Humane Society. However, there has been some good news recently — in July 2008, California Governor Arnold Schwarzenegger strengthened the legal protections for downer cows in California, and in March 2009 the United States government banned the use of downer cows for food.

These protections, though laudable, are still less concerned for the animals than for the humans eating them. Raising animals in conditions that foster disease has led, not surprisingly, to a high prevalence of infectious disease in factory-farmed meat. This includes streptococcus, nipah virus, multidrug-resistant bacteria, SARS, avian flu, and other diseases. There is also concern that the incredibly contagious H1N1 virus (or what used to be called "swine flu") came from factory farms. There's even evidence that workers who kill pigs suffer nerve damage. Physicians at the Austin Medical Center in Minnesota were mystified by three patients who had the same highly unusual symptoms, including fatigue, pain, weakness, numbness, and tingling in the legs and feet. But the patients had something else in common — all worked at a local meatpacking plant.

Yet another concern is the rampant use of antibiotics with farm animals, which are considered necessary to fight the diseases factory farms make rampant. In the *New York Times*, Nicholas Kristof notes: "We continue to allow agribusiness companies to add antibiotics to animal feed so that piglets stay healthy and don't get ear infections. Seventy percent of all antibiotics in the United States go to healthy livestock, according to a careful study by the Union of Concerned Scientists — and that's one reason we're seeing the rise of pathogens that defy antibiotics." In a recent study, five of ninety samples of retail pork tested positive for MRSA, an antibiotic-resistant staph infection, in a store in Louisiana, and a new strain called ST398 is on the rise and appears to be prevalent in hog farms.

It is a biological imperative that we must eat to live, but is there a healthy link in this chain? The connection between alienation and illness couldn't be clearer: our alienation from animals has led to an abusive agricultural industry that fosters disease, and humans are being made sick by what that industry produces.

### Unsustainable: How Agriculture Is Poisoning Our World

"We don't let hog or dairy farms spread their waste unregulated, and we wouldn't let a town of 25,000 people dump human manure untreated on open lands. So why should we allow a farm with 150,000 chickens do it?"

— Gerald Winegrad, former Maryland state senator, voicing concerns about chicken-farm pollution in Maryland

Industrial agriculture doesn't work well for animals, and we have many reasons to believe it's not very good for humans either. Raising animals for food involves a host of extremely important ethical questions, in addition to our health concerns about the way the industry currently works. Last but not least, there are serious environmental concerns. For the moment, let's put aside the welfare of our fellow animals. Instead, let's consider to what degree industrial meat production is harming the planet, helping spur climate change, and degrading life for all species.

For example, it's estimated that by 2025 about 64 percent of humanity will be living in areas of water shortage. The livestock sector is responsible for over 8 percent of global human water use, with 7 percent of global water being used for irrigating crops grown for animal feed. Animal agriculture is responsible for 18 percent of global anthropogenic greenhouse gases. In New Zealand, 34.2 million sheep, 9.7 million cattle, 1.4 million deer, and 155,000 goats emit almost 50 percent of that country's greenhouse gases in the form of methane and nitrous oxide. People are now talking about a "carbon hoofprint" and calling livestock "living smokestacks," as ways to characterize the large amount of greenhouse gases released into the atmosphere. For example, one Swedish study found that "producing a pound of beef creates 11 times as much greenhouse gas emission as a pound of chicken and 100 times more than a pound of carrots."

According to a 2008 essay in the *New York Times*, titled "Rethinking the Meat-Guzzler":

Global demand for meat has multiplied in recent years, encouraged by growing affluence and nourished by the proliferation of huge, confined animal feeding operations. These assembly-line meat factories consume enormous amounts of energy, pollute water supplies, generate significant greenhouse gases and require ever-increasing amounts of corn, soy and other grains, a dependency that has led to the destruction of vast swaths of the world's tropical rain forests.... The world's total meat supply was 71 million tons in 1961. In 2007, it was estimated to be 284 million tons. Per capita consumption has more than doubled over that period. (In the developing world, it rose twice as fast, doubling in the last 20 years.) World meat consumption is expected to double again by 2050.

These are daunting and haunting figures that spell doom for much fertile habitat. Indeed, the article noted that over a five-month span in 2007, 1,250 square miles of Brazilian rain forest were cut down for agriculture and ranching, leading Brazil's president to announce emergency measures to halt the destruction. In addition to all the resources factory farms consume, we have to cope with how their byproducts damage the environment: how to handle the enormous amounts of manure they generate is perhaps the most obvious concern. Another is that pharmaceutical medicines, pesticides, and chemicals used to treat and protect agricultural animals from sickness can run off directly into waterways and wetlands, harming water quality and other species.

If you're an environmentalist, it's impossible to justify eating factory-farmed meat. The facts don't lie about the incredible and irreversible environmental destruction wrought by factory farms. Indeed, this was made "official" in 2007 by the Intergovernmental Panel on Climate Change — the United Nation's Nobel Prize–winning scientific panel. As one article summarized the report, "Don't eat meat, ride a bike, and be a frugal shopper — that's how you can help brake global warming." The panel's head, Rajendra Pachauri, even pleaded directly, saying, "Please eat less meat — meat is a very carbon intensive commodity."

In fact, when comparing the relative environmental impact of being a vegetarian versus being a "locavore," a 2008 study at Carnegie Mellon University found that "foregoing red meat and dairy just one day a week achieves more greenhouse gas reductions than eating an entire week's worth of locally sourced foods. That's because the carbon footprint of food miles is dwarfed by that of food production. In fact, 83 percent of the average U.S. household's carbon footprint for food consumption comes from production; transportation represents only 11 percent; wholesaling and retailing account for 5 percent." It's been calculated that the carbon footprint of meat-eaters is almost twice that of vegetarians.

To help emphasize the urgency of this, it's been calculated that, on average, the world's 6.7 billion humans are now consuming all resources 30 percent faster than the sustainable rate of replenishment. In the United States, people are consuming resources nearly 90 percent faster than the Earth can replenish them.

By most definitions of "sustainable" — doing something in a way that meets the needs of the present without compromising the ability of future generations to meet their needs — today's commercial meat production clearly is not sustainable. If we expand our definition of *sustainable* to include animals — doing something that meets human needs without compromising the needs of other species — then there is no question: factory farms fail every moral and practical test.

## A Full Menu of Compassionate Choices

I travel a lot and meet wonderful people and wonderful animals. I've noticed two trends: One is that most people don't spend much time thinking about what they eat or wear or the many ways the lives of animals are intertwined with our everyday choices. The other is that, whenever people become aware of how certain choices lead to harm for animals, their compassion and concern naturally spring forth and can lead them to change.

In July 2008 I was sitting in a hotel restaurant in Budapest, Hungary, when four women on holiday from the United Kingdom sat down next to me. One asked another what she was going to eat, and her friend responded, "Oh, some bacon." Then they started a lively conversation about their previous late night out on the town. A few minutes later, a friend joined me at my table, and we began to talk with the British women. We told them we were attending an international meeting on the behavior of dogs, and they laughed that a meeting about dogs would be important enough to attract people from all over the world. They asked what sort of research my friend and I did, and when I mentioned that I was interested in animal emotions, they seemed to get more interested. Eventually, the conversation shifted to how we use animals, how factory farming works, and how factory-farmed animals are treated in the process of becoming a meal. Led by their questions, and without being preachy or prescriptive, I talked about sentience and suffering and pointed out that the pig who became the bacon on their plates had suffered greatly along the way. One woman, Diana, was openly moved and agreed to cut back on her consumption of meat, even though she wasn't ready to "go veggie."

Her friends agreed, and while I don't know what they did after we parted, I do believe that our brief conversation made a difference. They'd never really put it together, they said. But we all agreed that each of us is responsible for the decisions we make and that we could all do more to expand our compassion footprint.

It's really easy to make a positive and noble difference in the lives of animals, and we can all begin right now. We don't have to go out and protest or found a movement. We just have to eat compassionately. We can make an immediate difference with every meal. We don't necessarily need to go "cold turkey" and stop eating meat entirely this second, but it's extremely easy to cut back, and to do it slowly and steadily so it's a progressive and lasting change. Many people with whom I speak tell me that they know that the animals they eat suffer immensely, but then they dismissively say, "Oh, but I love my steak." I acknowledge their tastes, but then explain to them how easy it would be for them to expand their compassion footprint by making more humane choices; many say they'll try.

It's getting easier to avoid meat from factory farms, and to avoid wearing fur and leather. Eliminating meat entirely from our diet is one of the healthiest and most compassionate choices we can make — for animals, for the environment, and for ourselves — but even dedicated carnivores can make a huge positive difference simply by cutting back. We increase our compassion footprint and decrease our carbon footprint whenever we choose not to eat or wear animals. In a talk I attended by Thich Nhat Hanh in August 2007, this awe-inspiring man suggested that, as a start, humans should cut back on meat consumption by 50 percent. This obviously would add more compassion to the world.

A new term that links these issues is "environmental vegetarianism." Environmental vegetarians seek to reduce first-
world consumption of meat, especially in the United States.
According to the United Nations Population Fund, "Each U.S.
citizen consumes an average of 260 lbs. of meat per year, the
world's highest rate. That is about 1.5 times the industrial world
average, three times the East Asian average, and 40 times the
average in Bangladesh." Furthermore, "the ecological footprint
of an average person in a high-income country is about six
times bigger than that of someone in a low-income country, and
many more times bigger than in the least-developed countries."
A 2008 essay in *New Scientist* magazine noted, "Switching from
the average American diet to a vegetarian one could cut emissions by 1.5 tonnes of $CO_2$ per person."

Thus, when it comes to agricultural animals, we accrue
compassion credits as we accrue carbon credits, and vice versa.
Increased compassion for animals can readily lead to less carbon because there's an inverse relationship between these
markers, especially in our consumption of factory-farmed
meat from highly abused animals. Every individual can make
positive changes for all living beings and our planet by weaving more compassion, empathy, respect, dignity, peace, and
love into their lives. Simply take compassion into account when
deciding what to eat and wear, and what animal "entertainment" to patronize.

What does this look like in everyday terms? When in a
restaurant, ask about the source of the animals on the menu,
and if the restaurant doesn't know or the only choices are from
factory farms, choose a vegetarian alternative. Even asking has
an effect, as it shows the restaurant there is a public desire for
more humane food products; every individual decision ripples

out into larger community effects. When shopping, avoid buying factory-farmed meat and wean away from organically farmed animals as well. We can also teach children that our hamburger was a cow and our bacon and sausage were a pig; that these animals had families and friends and that factory farms create for them a horrific life. We can let them know *who*, not *what*, they're eating — that they're eating *a* chicken, not just chicken.

As a society, we might also consider difficult questions that most people avoid, such as, "Might it be more sustainable to eat what are called 'surplus' dogs rather than raise cows, pigs, and sheep for food?" We need to question our assumptions: why, for instance, does eating dogs make us uncomfortable, but eating pigs does not? What are some alternatives to the unsustainable, compassionless food industry that now exists? Suffice it to say, we can all make more ethical and humane choices right now that will make the world a more compassionate place without sacrificing our quality of life.

Our alienation from other beings ends when we approach every being with respect and dignity. Entire nations of animals are treated as second-class citizens, or worse, as beings whose sole purpose is to serve human ends. While we may not all agree on what constitutes dignity, we all know when we lose it, and so do our fellow animals. We must embrace animals with our senses and our heart. We must allow animals to bring joy into our lives. We increase dignity for all and for ourselves whenever we look out for one another.

# Our World Is Not Compassionate to Animals

"The zoo is not a window on nature but rather a prism that bends the light according to the culture it is set in. Both the design of zoo exhibits and the ways in which zoos use their money reveal much about our culture's view of animals — what we value them for and whether we regard them as objects to be used by us or as living beings who are valuable in their own right."

— Vicki Croke, *The Modern Zoo*

ANIMALS ASK US FOR COMPASSION. They ask to be treated with dignity as fellow living beings. It doesn't matter where we encounter them, whether by accident or choice: animals want humans to respect their well-being for their own sake as sentient, emotional, sometimes moral fellow animals. This requires a much-needed and long-overdue paradigm shift on our part that incorporates compassion and empathy for all other beings, a change in our ways that will benefit other animals and ourselves.

As we've seen, all species are interdependent on each other for their own survival and to maintain the health of our world's ecosystems. When humans abuse animals, we suffer along with them. This is true not only when abuse occurs "in the name of food." When humans justify animal cruelty "in the name of science" or "in the name of entertainment," we suffer as well. Humans have incorporated animals into our lives in a multitude of ways, and in each arena, if humans treated animals with respect and care, it wouldn't be a selfless act. If we did this, we would improve our own lives, our own health, our own compassion and dignity.

This chapter looks at the myriad ways in which humans use animals in our modern world. Throughout, I ask two central questions: Are we caring for the animal's well-being? And is using animals in this way or in this setting necessary? With few exceptions the answers are no and no. In nearly every area — whether it be science, education, industrial farming, clothing, zoos, circuses, rodeos, the wildlife trade, and so on — we are abusing animals, sometimes horrifically, and we are doing so by choice. Though we may justify the abuse as "necessary," upon closer inspection, this is almost never the case.

Animal advocate and author Nick Taussig points out in *Gorilla Guerrilla* that the brutality with which we treat other animals belies our intelligence. How can we big-brained, intelligent mammals routinely do what we do to other animals with little or no regard for how we are making them suffer? How did people come up with the idea of factory-farmed animals to begin with, and how can we continue supporting them, considering how little we do about the incredible suffering they create? How can scientists in research laboratories deprive animals of water and food, confine them to cages, bolt their heads, isolate them, force them to endure painful electric shocks, and expose them to diseases and harmful drugs until the animals die? How can zoos and circuses abuse animals the way they often do, and audiences enjoy these sad displays?

Self-justifying "necessity" is one reason. Another is that animal abuse, particularly the worst instances, is kept hidden from the public as much as possible. Circus audiences don't see and aren't told how lions were trained to perform. Drug companies don't explain how many unsafe products were tested on animals before a safe product was developed. Scientists don't detail the cruelty they design into their animal research. In all areas, we need constant inspection of what is happening behind closed doors by those who have no vested interest in the particular company or research project. These reports then must be made publicly available, so that people can see what is happening. Only then will the full ethics and morality of our choices be clear. It's no longer acceptable for scientists to dismiss the ethics of their animal research simply because it's "science." As with the food industry, all of human society is complicit in the choices we collectively make and in the abuse that's allowed, whether in the name of medicine, science, business, or entertainment.

Furthermore, animal abuse makes for bad science, and bad science doesn't work. Exposing animal abuse is important to expose faulty research, which does nothing to benefit human health. Indeed, the U.S. National Research Council recently concluded that the testing of toxic substances on animals is of little value, yet very few people know of this important report. A similar report by medical experts in England concluded that using animals to research chronic pain has "limited value" and should be ended. Plus, scientific studies on animals produce different results depending on who's doing the research. Scientists claim to be objective, but they have a subjectivity that can influence their methods and outcomes. Sometimes, results just seem to reflect funding. Noted science writer Sharon Begley discovered that "153 out of 167 government-funded studies of bisphenol-A, a chemical used to make plastic, find toxic effects in animals, such as low sperm counts." On the other hand, "No industry-funded studies find any problem."

I fully realize that there are difficult situations where there isn't a clear right or wrong solution. Certain situations may work well for some species but not others. Some animals love to perform and can be taught with kindness. When animals find themselves held in zoos, their interactions with caring people can be enriching. The same is true for animals who are kept in laboratories. But there are innumerable instances in which we simply ignore the interests of animals and do the wrong thing because it's easier. And in general, as Matthew Scully says in his book *Dominion*, "our society has turned its gaze away from animals, and countenanced a shameful climate of exploitation and cruelty toward them."

If you think I'm being overdramatic about the extent to which we violate the lives of animals, rent the 2005 documentary film *Earthlings*, which graphically demonstrates everything this and chapter 4 describes. Of course, humans do a lot of good things on behalf of animals, but the larger point is that it's not enough. This book is a critique of who we are and what we have done to animals for millennia. The reason animals ask for compassion is because it does not yet define their relationship with humans.

### HEADLINE NEWS:
### Trainer Stabs Elephant! Monkey Boiled Alive!

Just as it makes headlines whenever animals display their sentience and emotions, we notice when animal cruelty and tragedy is made public. Here is just a handful of recent incidents:

## Army Shoots Live Pigs for Medical Drill
MSNBC, July 18, 2008

"The Army says it's critical to saving the lives of wounded soldiers. Animal-rights activists call the training cruel and outdated.

"Despite opposition by the People for the Ethical Treatment of Animals, the Army proceeded to shoot live pigs and treat their gunshot wounds in a medical trauma exercise Friday at Schofield Barracks for soldiers headed to Iraq....

"'It's to teach Army personnel how to manage critically injured patients within the first few hours of their injury,' [an Army spokesperson] said. The soldiers are learning emergency lifesaving skills needed on the battlefield when there are no medics, doctors or facility nearby, he said.

"PETA, however, said there are more advanced and humane options available, including high-tech human simulators. In a letter, PETA urged the Army to end all use of animals, 'as the overwhelming majority of North American medical schools have already done.... Shooting and maiming pigs is as outdated as Civil War rifles.'"

## Videos Renew Debate on Military Use of Animals
CNN, June 5, 2009

"Newly released videos are raising questions about the military's continued use of live animals in simulated battlefield medical training... [and] are evidence that the military is violating its own animal-welfare regulations. Military officials counter that the training is legal and vital to saving the lives of service members in the field.

"In one of the training videos, a live vervet monkey is anesthetized and then injected with a dose of physostigmine, a simulated nerve agent.... The military says trainees observe the effects of the physostigmine and then take steps to relieve them, injecting the animal with an antidote....

" 'The animals recover completely and display no behavioral or physical ill effects from the exercise,' a military spokesman said in an email about the procedure. 'No animal has ever died as a result of the exercise.'

"In another video, a medical instructor uses a scalpel to slice open the leg of an anesthetized goat. The video goes on to show medical personnel applying a tourniquet and then dressing the wound. A third video shows a chest tube being inserted into an anesthetized goat."

### Dolphin Dies After Aerial Collision In US
*Sydney Morning Herald*, April 29, 2008

"A dolphin has died after colliding with another dolphin while performing aerial tricks at a US marine park. Sharkey, a 30-year-old dolphin, died after the accident on Saturday at the Discovery Cove park — a sister property to Sea World in Orlando, Florida.

"About 30 visitors were standing in a lagoon while the dolphins did tricks, but something went amiss when the two mammals leapt from the water and collided mid-air.

"The second dolphin did not appear to have been injured.... 'This is a very unfortunate and very rare incident,' [a spokesperson] said."

### Unbearable Zoo Mystery Turns Into Potboiler
*Sydney Morning Herald*, March 29, 2008

"The Berlin Zoo is under pressure to explain the fate of hundreds of animals which have vanished amid claims they were slaughtered and in some cases turned into potency-boosting drugs. Claudia Hammerling, a Green party politician, backed by several animal rights organisations, . . . claims to have evidence that four Asian black bears and a hippopotamus were transported to the Belgian town of Wortel, which has no zoo, but which does have an abattoir.

"According to Ms. Hammerling these animals were slaughtered. She said the systematic 'overproduction of animals' at zoos, designed to attract more visitors, was to blame. Ms. Hammerling said she also knew of several tigers and leopards from Berlin that ended up in a tiger breeding farm in China that promoted itself as a purveyor of traditional potency-boosting medicines made from big cats. She alleges the animals' remains were turned into drugs.

"[The zoo director] strongly denies the charges. . . . Rearing animals was central to his work and visitors should have the chance to observe the rearing process, he said.

"However, at Nuremberg zoo, the deputy director . . . has been reported as saying: 'If we cannot find good homes for the animals, we kill them and use them as feed.' At Nuremberg recently an antelope was fed to caged lions as visitors watched in outrage."

### Zoo Rocked by Abuse Allegations
*The Age*, January 19, 2008

"Senior zoo experts, staff and the RSPCA have accused the Melbourne Zoo of abuse and neglect of animals. . . . A confidential internal memo . . . reported the stabbing in May last year of a 13-year-old elephant, Dokkoon, with a marlin spike — a large, needle-like implement used to untie rope knots.

"The memo...says [the] animal trainer...was trying to control the elephant using a hooked implement known as an ankus or bullhook. 'After a time trying to control the elephant, [the trainer] appeared to become extremely angry and used his marlin spike to stab at the elephant's leg repeatedly in excess of a dozen times. The elephants seemed obviously distressed, standing back to back, vocalising and defecating.'

"In other incidents confirmed by the zoo:...Four seals have suffered partial blindness after being moved to a small swimming pool — out of public view and possibly for up to three years....The eye problems have been caused by chlorine in the pool.

"The eyelids of a Malayan tapir were sewn together, also because of eye trouble....Lack of tree cover and over-exposure to the sun is believed to have contributed to the animal's eye damage."

### Orangutan Drowns in German Zoo
*Der Spiegel*, July 31, 2008

"Staff at a Hamburg zoo say one of their orangutans died needlessly after a visitor broke park rules against feeding animals. The animal, they claim, drowned in pursuit of a bread roll that had been lobbed into her enclosure.

"The chief zookeeper...said a visitor was responsible for the drowning. 'Leila wanted to get the roll, but instead fell into the water and drowned.'"

### 32 Research Monkeys Die in Accident at Nevada Lab
Associated Press, August 7, 2008

"Thirty-two research monkeys at a Nevada laboratory died because human errors made the room too hot, officials for the drug company that runs the lab said Thursday.... Charles River Laboratories Inc. issued a statement saying the monkeys died in Sparks on May 28. The company, based in Wilmington, Mass., attributed the deaths to incorrect climate-control operation.

"[A PETA spokesperson said]: 'That monkeys were literally cooked to death by a heating system failure, as a whistleblower alleges, shows that the facility did not even have a simple alarm system in place to alert staff to the malfunction.'"

### Monkey Boiled Alive at Research Lab

KIRO TV, January 31, 2008

"A monkey, slotted to be used in a drug-product research experiment, was instead boiled alive inside an Everett laboratory, a KIRO Team 7 Investigation found. It's a deadly error, but not the first one...uncovered at SNBL USA....

"KIRO Team 7 Investigators confirmed someone placed a wire kennel, with a healthy female macaque monkey still inside, into a giant rack-washer. The 180-degree water, caustic foam and detergent killed the primate at some point during the 20-minute cycle....

"[A former Animal Care Supervisor for SNBL] says she was recently fired after telling federal inspectors that some SNBL employees were abusing primates and failing to follow other US Department of Agriculture guidelines. Her list of complaints include: employees carelessly spraying monkeys with acid and intentionally slamming primates on the floor."

## By the Numbers: Quantifying Death and Cruelty

The number of animals used by humans is staggering. Far and away the most animals are used in agriculture, but we encounter animals in numerous different venues in our complex and demanding world. Indeed, we typically don't even realize how extensive animal use is. Each of us is pulled in many different directions as we go through the day, and it's easy not to notice or to forget about the animals imprisoned in laboratories, slaughterhouses, rodeos, circuses, zoos, fur farms, and more. It's hard to coexist and be compassionate with beings we never see. Out of sight, scent, or hearing is out of mind and out of heart.

Yet when one looks at the number of animals who are routinely and cavalierly abused behind closed doors and shaded windows, it makes for a frightening portrait that is at once sobering, stunning, and sickening. It makes me embarrassed to be human.

Consider scientific research. U.S. Department of Agriculture statistics for the fiscal year 2005 listed a total of 1,177,566 primates, dogs, cats, rabbits, guinea pigs, hamsters, and other species as being subjected to experimental procedures; this was an increase of 7 percent from the previous year. This included 66,610 dogs, 57,531 primates, 58,598 pigs, 245,786 rabbits, 22,921 cats, 176,988 hamsters, 64,146 other farm animals, 32,260 sheep, 231,440 other animals, and 221,286 guinea pigs. However, animals such as mice and rats are not protected by the federal Animal Welfare Act and they are not even counted; if they were, the total would be over 20 million animals in the United States alone. Worldwide in 2005, it was estimated that in 179 countries about 58.3 million living nonhuman vertebrates were subjected to fundamental or medically-applied biomedical research, toxicity testing, or educational use.

Veterinarian Andrew Knight has estimated that 68,607,807 additional animals may have been killed for the provision of experimental tissues, used to maintain established genetically modified strains, or bred for laboratory use but then killed as surplus to requirements. Knight also cautions that the estimate of 17.3 million living vertebrates used within the United States is significantly less than a 2000 U.S. Animal Plant Health Inspection Service estimate of 31–156 million. In November 2008 it was reported that primate experimentation increased to a record of 69,990 animals, and at least 20 million animals are killed in biomedical research and in laboratories that test various products.

Despite a growing consensus among scientists that animal testing should be decreased for ethical and practical reasons, it nevertheless increases. In 2008, Britain reported that experiments on animals rose to 3.2 million in that country, an increase of 6 percent over the previous year. Further, animal experiments in England have increased steadily over the past eleven years by a total of 21 percent. In the United States, there has been a marked increase in primates imported from other countries: in 2006, the total number was 26,638, a 44 percent increase since 2004, and in 2008 the total number rose to over 28,000. Nearly all were destined for research labs.

While many people certainly show kindness to the animals they meet in their everyday lives, that doesn't mean everyone does. England reported that in 2007 the number of people convicted of cruelty to animals in that country rose by 24 percent. One newspaper story said: "In all, 1,149 people were convicted in 2007 for crimes against animals, up from 927 the previous year, the RSPCA said. Convictions for cruelty to dogs went up by 34% to 1,197, to cats by 15% to 277 and to horses by 13% to 119. The number of jail terms rose by 42% while suspended prison sentences rose by 39% to 71." Uncounted in these numbers are the approximately 40,000 retired racehorses that are slaughtered each year and the millions of cats and dogs killed in animal shelters.

Obviously, people love their pets, but the market for purebred or pedigree dogs has led to the rise of abusive "puppy mills," in which dogs are consciously and intentionally bred and inbred, leading to severe anatomical, physiological, and genetic defects that shorten their lives and cause them to suffer when they're alive. Renowned Australian veterinarian Paul McGreevy laments, "Pedigree dogs, as they are currently defined, are doomed. Inherited disorders will only become more and more common unless the breeding rules are changed." In March 2009 the BBC dropped its coverage of the prestigious Crufts dog show because of the way in which dogs suffer after they're bred for various physical traits to achieve "winning looks." Public outcry was concerned with such breeds as pugs and Pekingese, whose faces are so flat that they have difficulty breathing and regulating their body temperature. An editorial in the *Times of London* noted, "It is difficult to see dog as man's best friend when we castrate them, make them commit incest and parade them under bright lights in Birmingham."

Internationally, millions of wild animals are traded illegally as if they were mere commodities like televisions or couches. The commercial trade in wild animals is a multibillion dollar business that threatens the survival of many species, and it involves a vast range of people, desires, and businesses, from finding exotic pets and stocking zoos to providing unusual leathers, furs, food, traditional medicine, and more.

Clearly, many people still consider leather and fur stylish, but that doesn't make them necessary as clothing. And what is the cost in lives and suffering? It's been well documented that fur farms are purveyors of pure torture, in which the bones of a fox, chinchilla, or mink go snap, crackle, and pop in the process of turning them into a coat. Yet the number of animal skins needed to make a forty-inch fur coat may surprise you — 60 mink, 50 muskrats, 42 red foxes, 40 raccoons, 20 badgers, 18 lynx, 16 coyotes, and 15 beavers. According to animal activist Camilla Fox (in my *Encyclopedia of Animal Behavior*), over 50 million animals worldwide are killed for their fur annualy. Although the number of wild animals trapped in the United States has decreased from nearly 14 million in 1987 to less than 4 million in 2005, increasing overseas fur markets and the growing popularity of fur trim could reverse this trend. Moreover, many former fur trappers, unable to profit from their trade, have switched to "nuisance" or "damage control" trapping, a fast-growing, highly unregulated industry capitalizing on increased urban/suburban conflicts with wildlife and employing the same body-gripping traps used in fur trapping.

Fox also stresses the suffering that trapping causes. Ethical concerns abound. Many animals caught and killed for their fur suffer out of our view beneath the surface of lakes and rivers. Consider what Fox wrote about trapping aquatic animals: "Leghold and submarine traps act by restraining the animals underwater until they drown. Most semi-aquatic animals, including mink, muskrat, and beaver, are adapted to diving by means of special oxygen conservation mechanisms. The experience of drowning in a trap must be extremely terrifying. Biologists Frederick Gilbert and Norman Gofton discovered that animals display intense and violent struggling and were found to take up to four minutes for mink to die, nine minutes for muskrats to die, and ten to thirteen minutes for beavers to die. Mink have been shown to struggle frantically prior to loss of consciousness, an indication of extreme trauma." Most animals caught in aquatic traps struggle for more than three minutes before losing consciousness.

The time it takes an animal to die is one way to judge the cruelty of a method of killing. Whales are another prime example: once they are harpooned or shot, as cetacean expert Philippa Brakes documented in *Troubled Waters: A Review of the Welfare Implications of Modern Whaling Activities*, it can take from two to more than forty minutes for them to die, depending on how they are hunted and how wounded they are; during this time, Brakes wonders, "Do whales scream?" Worldwide, as many as 300,000 cetaceans slowly meet their death when they get entangled as accidental bycatch in fishing nets. When their bodies are recovered, it's obvious that they had desperately struggled to escape from their entrapment and that they sustained horrific injuries while doing so; there is nothing quick about this. Trapped individuals sustain deep cuts and skin abrasions from the rope and the netting, and fins and tail flukes can be partially or completely amputated. They also have broken teeth, beaks, or jaws, torn muscles, hemorrhaging, and serious internal injuries.

The suffering of these sentient beings goes unnoticed because it is shrouded by the water in which they live, but it's safe to say that it would not be tolerated if it happened on land in situations such as commercial meat production. What is simply unacceptable is that there isn't any legislation that is concerned with this hidden problem. Because most fur animals trapped in aquatic sets struggle for more than three minutes before losing consciousness, biologists have argued that they did not meet basic trap standards and therefore can't be considered humane. Camilla Fox concluded, "For an activity that affects millions of wild animals each year, it is astounding that so little is known about the full impact of trapping on individual animals, wildlife populations and ecosystem health."

In his book *The Great Compassion*, activist and Buddhist scholar Norm Phelps notes in a chapter titled "The Rosary of Death" that worldwide about 48 billion animals are killed annually for food and fabric, of whom 46 billion are chickens, ducks, turkeys, and geese. But what about the 115 million wild animals who are killed annually just for the pleasure of it? Sport hunting is the second leading form of animal killing in the United States, although it is decreasing. Still, there's now evidence that hunting is having an effect on the size of animals who survive the nonselective onslaught of humans, and hunting and commercial fishing may hurt the long-term survival of some species. Over the course of a thirty-year study on Ram Mountain in Alberta, Canada, biologist Marco Festa-Bianchet Sherbrooke discovered that both male and female sheep were getting smaller and that the size of the horns of bighorn sheep declined by about 25 percent. Biologists argue that hunting has led to a form of "evolution in reverse." Festa-Bianchet notes, "When you take them [larger and more fit individuals] systematically out of the population for several years, you end up leaving essentially a bunch of losers doing the breeding." This threatens the viability of the species and actually leaves fewer of the prized "trophy animals" hunters want in the first place.

Of course, death is easy to quantify. When we are keeping rather than killing animals, judging what treatment qualifies as "cruel" can be less clear. However, take circuses: elephants spend between 72 to 96 percent of the time chained, big cats are confined to small cages upwards of 95 percent of the time, and horses are tethered up to 98 percent of the time. Would a human performer put up with this? In February 2009, a suit was filed against Ringling Brothers and Barnum & Bailey Circus claiming that the circus abused their elephants and used fear to get them to cooperate and perform, which challenged the circus's claim that the elephants were happy, healthy, and well cared for. In addition, a recent British study found that about 54 percent of elephants in U.K. zoos suffer from daytime behavioral problems. As we'll explore more later, it's now well documented that zoos can't satisfy the social, emotional, or physical needs of elephants, and elephant exhibits are being phased out at some major U.S. zoos, despite the fact that they're moneymakers. Zoos, according to renowned New York University philosopher and ethicist Dale Jamieson, remain "more or less random collections of animals kept under largely bad conditions."

Indeed, what if zoos contained only those animals who could be well cared for in conditions reasonably close to their actual natural habitats? What animals would then be left, and what would zoo visitors really lose if this happened? Wouldn't zoos without elephants and lions — and perhaps many other species — become lessons in compassion? Children and all visitors would learn that animals are not commodities to be controlled and exploited for human ends, but individuals with whom humans seek to connect and treat with dignity. Wouldn't this turn zoos into places where everyone in them — animals and humans alike — was for the most part happier?

## Animal Rights and Human Laws

We're only fooling ourselves whenever we claim that animals are adequately protected from pain and suffering. In the

United States, the minimum standard of care for animals in most settings — such as research, commercial sale and transportation, exhibition, and others — is established by the Animal Welfare Act (AWA), which is governed by the U.S. Department of Agriculture. However, only about 1 percent of animals used in research in the United States are protected under the AWA. Or, put differently, around 99 percent of research animals have no legal protections. This is because the AWA has sometimes been amended in nonsensical ways to accommodate the "needs" of researchers. For example, in 2004, mice, rats, and birds bred for research were excluded from the AWA's definition of "animal," and farmed animals are not covered by federal legislation, yet these animals are the most frequently used and abused animals in research.

Despite the extremely limited number of animals the AWA covers, from 2002 to 2007, violations of the Animal Welfare Act in the United States increased more than 90 percent. In 2006 alone there were 2,107 known violations of the AWA, with the highest level of violations occurring in the areas of Institutional Animal Care and Use Committees (which oversee research; 58 percent) and veterinary care (25 percent). It's been estimated that about 75 percent of all laboratories violate the AWA at one time or another.

Karen Davis, president of United Poultry Concerns, notes:

> Millions of birds suffer miserably each year in government, university, and private corporation laboratories, especially considering the huge numbers of chickens, turkeys, ducks, quails, and pigeons being used in agricultural research throughout the world, in addition to the increasing experimental use of adult chickens and chicken embryos to replace

mammalian species in basic and biomedical research. For example, Colgate-Palmolive sponsored the development of the CAM (Chorioallantoic Membrane) Test, an eye irritation test in which vivisection of fertilized chicken eggs is necessary to expose the egg's interior membrane to the materials being tested....

Slaughter experiments are also routinely performed on live chickens, turkeys, ducks, ostriches, and emus, in which these birds are subjected to varying levels of electric shock in order to test the effect of various voltages on their muscle tissue for the meat industry. For example, the Spring 2002 issue of the *Journal of Applied Poultry Research* has an article in which USDA researchers describe shocking 250 hens in a laboratory simulation of commercial slaughter conditions to show that "subjecting mature chickens to electrical stimulation will allow breast muscle deboning after 2 hours in the chiller with little or no additional holding time."

Clearly, animal laws and their enforcement are both inadequate protections from arrogant, self-centered "research" like this. Even the prestigious journal *Nature*, which largely defends animal research, noted in 2009: "The federal government should conduct a thorough review of the regulations concerning animal research to eliminate gaps, ensure compliance and strengthen penalties. Ideally, the oversight powers would be consolidated within a single organization. But, in any case such measures might boost public confidence in animal research."

It is incumbent on all people who work with animals to take responsibility for their practices and always to use the most humane and noninvasive techniques possible. Not only will this produce more reliable data but it will also set an example for future researchers, including young children, who might want to pursue a career in science. Not only is it incumbent on us to conduct humane research, and treat animals well in every setting, but we must own our actions. Far too many people, including practicing scientists, ignore the fact that each of us is individually responsible for our own choices. If we harm animals, even if we are just doing our job in a research lab, we still are the ones causing intentional suffering, pain, or death. Most people who work with animals on a daily basis come to care about and even love the animals, and they feel bad when the animals suffer and die. In particular, a 2008 story in the *New Scientist* looked at researchers who weep for the animals they must kill, and sometimes seek counseling and hold memorial services to cope with their grief.

The article quotes Gill Langley of the Dr. Hadwen Trust for Humane Research, who said, "Omitting any mention of the suffering caused to animals during experimental procedures, the technicians seemed to care only about the moment of euthanasia. What a bizarre reversal of priorities that animal technicians, who freely apply for and continue with their jobs, should seek emotional support for the remorse and grief they cause themselves by harming and killing animals, albeit in the name of science. Rather than wasting resources on commemorative services, more would be achieved by replacing animal research and testing methods with humane alternatives. That way, animals, human patients and technicians would all benefit."

# The Unlucky Puppy:
# The Faulty Logic of Animal Testing

"Mice are lousy models for clinical studies."

— Mark Davis, PhD,
Director of the Stanford Institute for Immunity

"Since President Richard Nixon declared the war on cancer in his famous State of the Union address of 1971, cancer has become the second-biggest killer of Americans. Two in every five of us will be diagnosed with cancer, and one of us will die from it. Millions of dogs, cats, monkeys, guinea pigs, rabbits and mice have lost their lives, and billions of taxpayer dollars have been spent, in the quest for a cure. Yet, despite decades of intense effort, age-adjusted mortality rates have slowly increased, and experts such as Dr. J. C. Bailar III, former chief administrator of the war on cancer, tell us that all these efforts focused largely on improving treatment must be judged a 'qualified failure.' How could this be so, when researchers tell us that animals are so similar to human beings that drugging, irradiating and dissecting them provides a valid model for a human cancer victim? Perhaps it is because, as the researchers also tell us, animals are in fact so different from humans that these things may be done without consent, kindness, painkillers or adequate medical care, as undercover investigations of laboratories repeatedly reveal. Perhaps those differences have something to do with the fact that adverse reactions to drugs deemed safe after passing animal tests are the fourth-leading killer of Americans, killing more people each year than all illegal drugs combined."

— Veterinarian Andrew Knight

An increasing number of scientists are growing skeptical about the use of animal models in scientific research. But there are some hangers-on who ignore the warnings of their colleagues and use misleading moral arguments to justify their treatment of animals. The U.S. National Institutes of Health, in conjunction with an animal research trade group, promotes a children's coloring book called *The Lucky Puppy* that presents a false view of what animal experimentation entails, so much so that the Physicians Committee for Responsible Medicine has called attention to the misleading messages that this book presents. *The Lucky Puppy* implies that researchers are trying to cure animals who are already sick, rather than purposely infecting them with diseases, and it ignores the fact that animals suffer and die in the process. The only thing such propaganda reveals is the dishonesty of the people who created it.

In a recent discussion of the use of animals to study human pain, psychologists and animal experimenters Stuart Derbyshire and Andrew Bagshaw wrote, "We believe that animals are sufficiently different from us that pursuing experimentation with animals to advance human interests is morally justified." Clearly these researchers want it both ways — animals are different enough so that it's moral to cause them pain but similar enough that we can learn about human pain by torturing them. Further confirming their self-serving logic, Derbyshire and Bagshaw note that we don't do the same things to humans that we do to animals because it would be immoral on humans. Meanwhile, Roberto Caminiti, chair of the Programme of European Neuroscience Schools, argues that it will never be possible to replace animals in research, yet Caminiti conveniently avoids any discussion of the numerous nonanimal alternatives that are available, many of which are currently being used successfully.

Bill Crum of the Centre for Neuroimaging Sciences at the Institute of Psychiatry at King's College London counters Caminiti as follows: "To my mind, there is a moral inconsistency attached to studies of higher brain function in non-human primates: namely, the stronger the evidence that non-human primates provide excellent experimental models of human cognition, the stronger the moral case against using them for invasive medical experiments. From this perspective, 'replacement' should be embraced as a future goal."

## False Hopes and Few Results

Unfortunately, the use of animal models often creates false hopes for humans in need. While the human mortality rate has declined since 1900, it is estimated that only 1 to 3.5 percent of the decline stems from the results of animal research. If all of the current animal research going on today were equally "successful," we must ask ourselves, will it be worth the death and suffering it causes so that humans can, on average, live a year or so longer?

Innumerable animals are used in biomedical research, but compelling data show that studies on animals — particularly mice and great apes such as chimpanzees — make little contribution to progress in treating diseases. In a recent review of the ability of animal models to predict human outcomes, a team of a medical doctor, a veterinarian, and a philosopher concluded: "When one empirically analyzes animal models using scientific tools they fall far short of being able to predict human responses. This is not surprising considering what we have learned from fields such [as] evolutionary and developmental biology, gene regulation and expression, epigenetics, complexity theory, and comparative genomics." Concerning mice, another report summarized, "When it comes to adapting therapeutic interventions that seem to cure all kinds of infectious disease, cancers and autoimmune conditions in mice for use in human beings, the record is not so good. The vast majority of clinical trials designed to test these interventions in people end in failure."

In a paper titled "The Poor Contribution of Chimpanzee Experiments to Biomedical Progress," veterinarian Andrew Knight reported that few papers based on these experiments are ever cited in future research and that a detailed examination of these medical papers revealed that, rather than animal-related research, in vitro studies, human clinical and epidemiological studies, molecular assays and methods, and genomic studies contributed the most to their development. Knight also showed that in toxicology testing, animal models were frequently equivocal or inconsistent with human outcomes.

The bottom line is that animal models have very limited utility, they are very expensive, and they raise all sorts of ethical questions. Why pursue research methods that harm animals and provide results that are not particularly relevant for humans? Consistent with these concerns, in February 2008 top officials from the U.S. National Institutes of Health and the Environmental Protection Agency announced a five-year deal to share technology, information, and other resources that will improve the toxicity testing of chemical compounds used in food, medicine, and other products using robots rather than lab animals.

Often it's not clear why experimenters conduct animal studies when they already have compelling results from human studies. Consider one study that found that monkeys can control a mechanical arm with their thoughts. This research, as reported in 2008 in the *New York Times*, would hopefully help people suffering from paralysis to gain more control over their lives. What I found interesting was that the article went on to state: "In previous studies, researchers showed that humans who had been paralyzed for years could learn to control a cursor on a computer screen with their brain waves and that non-human primates could use their thoughts to move a mechanical arm, a robotic hand or a robot on a treadmill." If scientists already knew this, why use more monkeys? Wouldn't the most fruitful route for this sort of research, which has very important implications for humans with severe motor deficits, be to study humans?

In the behavioral sciences, two examples of the inadequacy of animal models are the use of maternal and social deprivation (depriving young animals of mothering and other social contact) to learn about human depression, and the use of animals to study human eating disorders, including obesity, anorexia, and bulimia. The deplorable maternal-deprivation studies of Harry Harlow at the University of Wisconsin proved the obvious, and ever since, socially deprived monkeys have been commonly used to study the psychological and physiological aspects of depression. Individuals typically are removed from their mothers and other family members soon after birth and raised alone, often in small, dark, barren cages called "depression pits." In their impoverished prisons, isolated monkeys scream in despair, become self-destructive, and eventually withdraw from the world. The only social contacts with these unsocialized, frightened, and distraught monkeys occur when blood is drawn or other physiological measures are taken, or when they are introduced to other monkeys, whom they avoid or who maim or occasionally kill them.

Besides the fact that these types of studies are ethically revolting, numerous flaws plague deprivation studies, including the lack of human clinical relevance. Researchers view human depression as a distinctly human condition. Simplistic animal models of human depression do not work for the diagnosis, treatment, or prevention of human depression. Nonetheless, federal agencies heavily fund (with taxpayers' money) these studies in which baby monkeys are torn from their mothers and made to suffer panic attacks, anxiety, and depression. Even people who accept other forms of animal research are offended by the horrors of deprivation research. Many in the public believe it should be stopped immediately. No ends justify these means.

Psychologist Kenneth Shapiro has written extensively about the use of animal models in psychological research, specifically in eating disorders. Despite research in which animals are starved, force-fed, or subjected to binge-purge cycles, Shapiro found that only 37 percent of clinicians who treat people for eating disorders even know about the results of such research. Of those who do know about the research, 87 percent said animal models were not used to design human treatment programs. Thus, the success rate of animal models for application in human clinical practice is extremely low. If you had the same chance of arriving at a theater to see a movie, you probably would not even try to go.

For scientific research, the minds and emotions of our fellow animals are simply too much like us to morally justify doing them harm, yet they remain too physically different to make them useful models for helping humans. In February 2006 the prestigious Diabetes Research Institute published a report stating that scientists "have shown that the composition of a human islet is so different than that of the rodent model, it is no longer relevant for human studies." This bad animal research leads to bad human medicine. An essay published in the *Journal of the American Medical Association* estimated that 106,000 people die each year in hospitals from adverse reactions to drugs that had previously been tested on animals and approved by the U.S. Food and Drug Administration (FDA). Adverse drug reactions are now the fifth leading cause of death in the United States, following heart disease, cancer, stroke, and lung disease. Vioxx, a popular drug for arthritis, caused about 27,500 heart attacks, of which about 7,000 were fatal. According to the FDA, 92 of every 100 drugs that pass animal trials fail during human clinical trials, meaning that about 90 percent of drugs tested as safe and effective on animals don't work on humans. Plus, more than 50 percent of those that are given to people are withdrawn because of toxic effects on humans not predicted in animal experiments. Drugs would actually be safer if animal testing was eliminated. John Pippin, a cardiologist, points out, "The monoclonal antibody TGN1412 was safe in monkeys at 500 times the dose tested in humans, yet all six British volunteers who received the drug in 2006 nearly died. Conversely, simple aspirin produces birth defects in at least seven animal species, yet is safe in human pregnancy."

Stress is also a problem in research on captive animals. Jonathan Balcombe and his colleagues analyzed eighty published studies to assess the potential stress associated with three routine laboratory procedures that are commonly performed on animals: handling, blood collection, and the use of stomach tubes (or force-feeding). They published their results in the professional journal *Contemporary Topics in Laboratory Animal Science* in 2004. What they found is that simply picking up a mouse and holding the animal briefly can affect the animal's heart rate and blood pressure significantly (along with other stress indicators), and the effects can last from half an hour to an hour. They found that, the particular experiment aside, life in the lab for animals is so stressful that it alone impairs their immune system, which of course affects the results for many types of research, such as tumor growth, cardiovascular disorders, immune function, and psychological studies, among others.

All in all, a paradigm change is needed. It's not just animal protectionists who argue against animal research. Scientists who care about solid, effective science are also becoming skeptical. Human health and compassion will both improve when research focuses more on humans, rather than on animal surrogates.

## No More Cutting:
## The End of Dissection and Vivisection

"I am not interested to know whether vivisection produces results that are profitable to the human race or doesn't. . . . The pain which it inflicts upon unconsenting animals is the basis of my enmity toward it, and it is to me sufficient justification of the enmity without looking further."

— Mark Twain

For centuries, medical schools and universities have cut up animals to teach students. Yet ever since the late nineteenth century, an antivivisection movement has argued that these practices are immoral and unnecessary for learning. Today, schools of all kinds and at all levels around the world are finally banning this practice, not only because of ethical issues, but because non-animal alternatives are as good or better for teaching. More than thirty published studies show that the use of alternatives such as computer software, models, and transparencies are at least as likely as dissection to achieve the intended educational goals.

Technological advances, in fact, provide overwhelming advantages to dissection — such as imaging that allows students to view the nervous system, to rotate the image, to make certain layers opaque and others transparent, to cut away certain layers, and to repeat these operations in reverse.

Educators around the world agree. At Bhavnager University in Gujyrat, India, the annual use of over three thousand animals has been replaced with alternatives; Israel banned vivisection in schools in 2003; and in March 2008 the Faculty of Zoology at Tomsk Agricultural Institute in Russia ended the use of animals for dissection, even though Russian president and *Time* magazine's person of the year, Vladimir Putin, harassed rats when he was young.

Medical schools in the United States are also "swapping pigs for plastic." In an essay in *Nature*, it was noted that while doctors used to try out their surgical skills on animals before being allowed to work on patients, now only a handful of medical schools in the United States still have animal labs. Live-animal experiments were on the curriculum in 77 of 125 medical schools in 1994, but now only about 11 of 126 schools still use them. In January 2008, the *New York Times* reported that all American medical schools have abandoned dog labs for teaching cardiology. The newspaper quoted Francis Belloni, a dean at New York Medical College, as saying that, though animal use "was not done lightly and had value," students would "become just as good doctors without it."

## Studying Wild Animals: Traps and Dung

Fieldwork — or studying and researching animals in the wild — is far better than studying animals in cages and labs. Yet fieldwork can also be invasive, and the current regulations used to protect animals are not good enough. In order to study wild animals and track their habits, scientists not only observe animals as unobtrusively as they can but also capture individuals, measure them, weigh them, evaluate their health, often tag them, and then release them; these practices extract a cost on the animal and can lead to misleading data.

For instance, wildlife researcher and veterinarian Marc Cattet and his colleagues recently conducted a study evaluating the long-term capture-and-handling effects on bears. Cattet discovered that these methods can seriously injure and impact the bears, causing scientists to gather spurious data. One bear died ten days after a capture because it suffered from "such a severe case of capture myopathy — a kind of muscle meltdown some captured animals suffer when they overexert themselves trying to escape — that its chest, bicep and pectoral muscles were pure white and as brittle as chalk."

Further, "blood analyses of 127 grizzlies caught in Alberta between 1999 and 2005 revealed a significant number of those animals were showing signs of serious stress for alarmingly long periods of time after they were processed and released back in the wild," and about two-thirds of the animals caught in leghold traps suffered muscle injuries.

While Marc Cattet and other researchers aren't ready to give up wildlife research, it is heartening that he concludes that we can do much more: "I think that a number of things can be done to perhaps minimize restraint times and capture-related injuries," Cattet said. "We could use motion activated video cameras at trap sites that would allow researchers to assess animals' reactions to capture. I think that what this study underscores is that the status quo is not the answer. It also underscores the reality that it is not only bears that suffer. There's every reason to believe that other animals are suffering too when they are captured and released."

There are alternatives to trapping and immobilizing animals that work very well. Collecting dung is one. When I visited Iain Douglas-Hamilton and his coworkers as they studied elephants in Samburu National Reserve in Northern Kenya, I had the pleasure of collecting elephant dung with George Wittemyer. Samples of dung are collected, then sent off for genetic analyses that help George and his colleagues further understand the elephants. By analyzing fecal hormones, scientists can get information on stress levels; for instance, it's known that stress hormones increase when a matriarch is killed and are higher in areas with high levels of poaching. What are called "fecal-centric approaches" to wildlife behavior and ecology are becoming more popular because these scatological techniques are noninvasive.

Research ecologist Robert Long and his colleagues recently published a book titled *Noninvasive Survey Methods for Carnivores* that surely will help wild animals and be a win-win for all involved in field research. John Brusher and Jennifer Schull have developed nonlethal methods for determining the age of fish using the characteristics of dorsal spines. Many researchers realize that they don't have to kill animals to study them, and we can look forward to the development of more and more noninvasive techniques for studying a wide variety of animals. Even a 2009 essay in the *New York Times* noted the effectiveness of noninvasive research on wildlife, such as the wealth of information that can be gleaned from an animal's hair.

Admittedly, it's a difficult situation because we need to do the research to learn more about the animals we want to understand and protect. But we can always do it more ethically and humanely — to make sure we don't harm animals in our pursuit of knowledge about them, and to be sure that the information we collect reflects their actual needs and behavior in the wild.

## Performing Animals: Circuses and Rodeos

Given the choice, would animals find circuses and rodeos as entertaining as people do? Unlike zoos (which I address next), circuses, rodeos, and other types of animal "performance" don't promise any higher redeeming value, such as education, conservation, and so on. They are for amusement and entertainment, pure and simple. But, are the animals amused and entertained?

In fact, so much has been written about the serious ethical concerns surrounding these venues that the short answer is simple: No. There simply are no data that show that there is much, if anything, good for the animals who are kept for human amusement and entertainment. Like humans, some animals show evidence that they are natural "performers," but the business of animal entertainment is synonymous with abuse. Circuses deprive animals of any chance to have their emotional needs met; they're an insult to both animals and humans and rob us all of our dignity. It will be a great day when all circus animals are allowed to live out their lives with respect and dignity in appropriate animal sanctuaries. Circuses also set a bad example for children, as the underlying lesson they teach is that it's okay for animals to be treated as objects for entertainment and amusement.

Concerning circuses, Boulder, Colorado, animal activist Donna Marino sums up the dire situation by asking, "Would you knowingly pay to watch an elephant jabbed with an electric prod until his body collapsed in pain? How about watching a lion prodded by a trainer with a steel hook until blood spurts from one of his legs?" Marino notes that if you pay to see the circus, that's exactly where your money goes. She goes on to write:

> For years, circuses have abused animals to get them to perform tricks for the 'entertainment' of humans. Since animals do not naturally or voluntarily ride bicycles or jump through rings of fire, their trainers must force them to perform these tricks. The methods are generally barbaric and involve the use of whips, tight collars, muzzles, electric prods, bull hooks, and other brutal tools of the trade. Some animals are kept muzzled to subdue them and discourage them from defending themselves if they feel threatened. Others are drugged to make them manageable and some even have their teeth removed to prevent biting. Because circus animals travel long distances on a grueling schedule in order to earn the most profit for their owners, these creatures are often confined for 20 hours or more a day in small cages. During that time, they cannot satisfy their natural needs and may not even see the light of day until they're unloaded for a performance.

As I noted above, one study revealed that large circus animals like elephants, big cats, and horses spend virtually all their time chained and confined in cages. Furthermore, captive bears engage in stereotyped back-and-forth pacing about 30 percent of the time. Many animals display repetitive stereotyped movements in captivity that are not seen in the wild, and Israeli scientists are using the behavior of disturbed animals in zoos to help them understand obsessive-compulsive disorder in humans. Let's hope the animals also benefit from these studies.

Rodeos and bull riding are also insults to the animals who are abused and objectified solely for our own entertainment. Despite the assurances of rodeo advocates that great care is taken to provide for the animals' welfare, injuries in rodeos are very common, including paralysis from spinal cord injuries, severed tracheas, as well as broken backs and legs. A common activity, calf roping, is incredibly inhumane. Even Bud Kerby, owner and operator of Bar T Rodeos, agrees; he was quoted as saying he "wouldn't mind seeing calf roping phased out." Stock shows around the country allow young kids to engage in "mutton busting," in which children are placed on scared, bucking sheep. This endangers the sheep and the children, and it most assuredly doesn't promote kindness and respect for animals. Indeed, despite claims by advocates otherwise, rodeos are dangerous for people; for instance, in June 2009 in Longmont, Colorado, a twelve-year-old boy was killed when a bull he was trying to ride stomped on his stomach.

## It's Not Happening at the Zoo

Zoos and aquariums are meant to be entertaining, but many also operate with a "higher calling." They are first and foremost supposed to be educational institutions that aim to teach people about our fellow animals, and they also hope to aid the conservation of species. While education and conservation are admirable goals, the evidence is so far lacking that zoos achieve either one very well; nor is there evidence that zoos are the *best* way to accomplish them. Despite being founded explicitly to care for animals, zoos have a disturbing record of failing the very animals they hold.

Let me begin by saying that most people who work in zoos care about the animals with whom they work, and they do the very best they can for them. Many zoo and aquarium employees are deeply committed to education, conservation, and animal protection, and it's imperative to keep them in the discussion about the best means for achieving these goals.

Nonetheless, I've been told from time to time that zoos are good for animals because they get free meals, a safe place to live and to sleep, and health insurance (veterinary care). These luxuries keep them content and happy. But are animals really happy in zoos? Do zoos adequately provide for them? The answer can vary depending on the zoo and the animal, but the record is extremely mixed, and it gets worse with the larger, most complex species — typically, the zoo's moneymaking "star attractions." Yet all by itself, providing comfortable quarters is not reason enough to justify keeping animals in captivity, at which point it becomes a lame excuse.

For instance, in January 2007, Ralph, an adolescent, twenty-two-foot-long whale shark, died mysteriously at the Georgia Aquarium, despite being as well cared for as perhaps any whale shark in captivity. This raised questions about whether whale sharks, a species about which little is known, should ever be taken from the wild. Despite a zoo's or aquarium's best efforts, captivity can never replicate a healthy natural environment; for some species, it's so inadequate as to be fatal. Only a month earlier, a beluga whale at the Georgia Aquarium became seriously ill and died.

In December 2007, in another high-profile example, Tatiana, a female Siberian tiger at the San Francisco Zoo, got out of her aging, inadequate enclosure and attacked three men, killing one of them. Tatiana's story illustrates a number of problems with zoo care, and it attracted worldwide press because not only was it a terribly sad event but it also could have been avoided. First of all, in this case, the zoo wasn't properly protecting either the animal or the public; the enclosure's walls were very old and four feet lower than the current recommended standard. If tigers can't get out, they can't hurt anyone.

But also, a year before, Tatiana had attacked a keeper and chewed his arm. Large carnivores simply do not belong in zoos, but Tatiana may have been particularly agitated. Tatiana had lived at the Denver Zoo and was shipped to San Francisco because Denver wanted to redecorate their facility. Animals are sentient and emotional beings, and it affects them when they are shipped here and there as if they were couches. During her two years in the San Francisco Zoo, between the time she was transferred and when she was shot by San Francisco police, she'd lost 50 pounds. Her weight dropped from 292 pounds to 242 pounds. At the Denver Zoo, she was fed 42 pounds of food a week. At the San Francisco Zoo, she was fed between 32 and 36 pounds of food a week. Her keeper's notes show a pattern: "Tatiana frantic for food." Given her history, an essay in *Time* magazine even speculated whether Tatiana held a grudge against people.

In addition, the men Tatiana attacked had been taunting her, an activity that is rather common at zoos. In the mid-1990s my students and I discovered that 20 to 25 percent of visitors at the Denver Zoo taunted animals by mimicking, yelling, and throwing things at them and that carnivorous predators were the most likely targets. It's quite possible Tatiana had been taunted many times, and in this case, it made her so mad she found a way to fight back. However, at the time, Stephen Zawistowski, science adviser for the American Society for the Prevention of Cruelty to Animals, said that taunting probably was not the sole reason for Tatiana's attack, though it likely played a role. Indeed, the likelihood that lions, tigers, bears, gorillas, and so on will be taunted should be taken into account when building enclosures. The Association of Zoos and Aquariums (AZA) must build taunt-proof cages, and zoos should be vigilant about removing people who taunt animals.

Robert Jenkins, director of animal care at the San Francisco Zoo, claimed that, "We don't know how [the tiger] was able to get out." Then the zoo and the AZA traded blame, with the AZA saying they had told the zoo the enclosure wasn't high enough for Siberian tigers, and the zoo saying they didn't know this. Lost in the debate was Tatiana herself, an animal with a point of view who did not like being treated as if she were an inanimate object. She was a highly evolved predator who didn't like being imprisoned. When will zoos learn this lesson? How many more people and animals will have to be injured or killed? Isn't it about time that the AZA start investigating how to remove certain animals from zoos and send them off to sanctuaries so they can live out their lives with dignity?

In many ways the Association of Zoos and Aquariums and some zoo advocates are their own worst enemies. The AZA has a history of lax enforcement of their stated standards and of reaccrediting zoos with extremely poor records. Take, for instance, the prestigious National Zoo in Washington, DC, which some consider the flagship institution in the United States. Major problems were documented at the National Zoo in the late 1990s through the early 2000s that seriously compromised the well-being of its residents, but which didn't compromise its AZA accreditation.

When you look into the eyes of animals in zoos, you immediately know when something isn't right. I confirmed this when I was a reader for the "Review of the Smithsonian Institution's National Zoological Park," a zoo report resulting from a study conducted by the National Academy of Sciences' National Research Board on Agriculture and Natural Resources. The purpose of the study was to "identify strengths, weaknesses, needs and gaps in the current infrastructure" at the National Zoo because of suspicions of mismanagement and inadequate animal treatment. The report documented a long history of problems, with numerous infractions of federal statutes, laws, and other guidelines (as well as common sense) that were serious and inexcusable.

One of the most egregious violations was the alteration of veterinary records. It was disquieting that infractions and abuses occurred even though the zoo's veterinarians are board-certified by the American Veterinary Medical Association. Questions from the public finally surfaced when two red pandas died after being exposed to rat poison. Safety managers, who could have prevented these unnecessary deaths, were nowhere to be found. Overall, there was a shameful lack of concern for animal welfare by some of the administrators responsible for overseeing the zoo's operation.

Other concerns included the lack of documentation for the preventative medicine program, the lack of compliance with standard veterinary medicine, and the shortcomings of the animal nutrition program (despite supposed world-class research) that led to animal fatalities. Further worries included the disregard for requirements for research given by the Public Health Service, the Animal Welfare Act, the American Zoo and Aquarium Association, and the Institutional Animal Care and Use Committees, in addition to the zoo's own policies and procedures for animal health and welfare. Poor record-keeping — such as the failure to keep adequate animal husbandry and management records — and poor compliance with the zoo's own policies were commonplace.

Unfortunately, the AZA didn't hesitate to reaccredit the zoo in the spring of 2004, apparently turning a blind eye to the zoo's appalling state and no doubt yielding to political pressure. Even though a previous AZA accreditation report had asked the National Zoo to develop a strategic plan, they still hadn't done so, and this in and of itself justified withholding accreditation until the zoo made major adjustments. While the report was meant to foster significant changes, many problems were blatantly ignored.

I found myself wondering how things could have gotten so bad at such a high-profile zoo. How and why did conditions deteriorate despite close scrutiny by organizations and individuals who are supposed to be responsible for overseeing zoos and despite repeated and deep expressions of concern by the public that appeared in regional and national media? If these things weren't enough to keep the National Zoo from providing substandard care, then what could possibly ensure adequate care for animals at all the other smaller, lower-profile zoos around the country and the world? In how many other places is the same story unfolding, and how easy will it be for it to keep happening?

## Letting Elephants Go

Currently five major zoos in the United States — the Bronx Zoo and those in Detroit, Chicago, San Francisco, and Philadelphia — are phasing out their elephant exhibits, despite the fact that they're moneymakers. They are doing this because zoos cannot meet the social, emotional, and physical needs of these awesome mammoths, and also because of the high cost of keeping captive elephants. Elephants are highly intelligent, extremely emotional, very social, and like to roam. By definition, zoos are antithetical to these needs.

In contrast, in Colorado, a debate has arisen over the Denver Zoo's plan to spend $52 million to increase the size of its Asian elephant habitat and to boost the number of captive elephants from two to as many as eight. But the Denver Zoo's proposed ten-acre elephant park — which would include a "hot tub" — would merely be a bigger but still thoroughly inadequate cage.

The Denver Zoo justifies its intentions by claiming that its park will help to conserve this endangered species. In an interview I did on Colorado Public Radio with Craig Piper, vicepresident of the Denver Zoo, Piper called the Denver Zoo elephants an "insurance population." But, insurance for what? For the day all wild Asian elephants are gone? The AZA has developed what it calls the Species Survival Plan (SSP), which attempts to ensure the survival of certain wildlife species using managed breeding programs and reintroducing captive-bred wildlife into proper habitat. Yet the Denver Zoo puts less than 10 percent of its annual budget into conservation efforts (and about the same into education); by comparison, that's one-quarter of what the Bronx Zoo devotes to conservation. Piper admitted that it's extremely unlikely — really impossible — that any of these "insurance" elephants would ever be reintroduced to the wild. Every conservation biologist knows that retaining suitable habitat for animals is enormously difficult, and there's no hope that habitat into which elephants could be released would be saved for them in their absence. If wild Asian elephants don't have habitat and protections enough to maintain themselves in the wild, then neither will reintroduced captive elephants. Captive elephants merely insure a zoo's income.

Or, as Terry Maple, renowned director of Zoo Atlanta, has noted, "Any zoo that sits around and tells you that the strength of zoos is the SSP is blowing smoke."

Keeping elephants in captivity, then, fails two of a zoo's stated goals: humane care and conservation. For example, Piper said that the zoo might be able to house perhaps six bull elephants and use them for breeding and also for sending around to other zoos. Redecorating zoos with any animal raises serious ethical questions. Yet elephant groups are particularly important; if, in order to maintain Denver's elephant park, individuals will be shipped in and out, then the strong and enduring social bonds elephants create will be broken repeatedly. Elephants are highly emotional, sentient beings, and they suffer from post-traumatic stress disorder and psychological flashbacks. They grieve, often irreversibly, when life-long friendships are broken. Elephants have thick skins, but tender hearts.

Officials at the Denver Zoo already know this, since they've had experience with what can go wrong. In spring 2001, Dolly, a thirty-two-year-old female Asian elephant at the Denver Zoo, was removed from her friends, Mimi and Candy, and sent to Missouri on her "honeymoon," as the zoo called it, to breed. A few months later, Hope, a mature female, and Amigo, a two-year-old male (who had been taken from his mother), were sent to the Denver Zoo, where they lived next door to Mimi and Candy.

In the following months, Mimi got increasingly agitated. In June 2001, Mimi pushed Candy over; when Candy couldn't get up, she had to be euthanized (the zoo didn't have a proper elephant hoist). Two days after Candy died, Hope got angry, escaped from her keepers, and rampaged through the zoo. Miraculously, no one was seriously injured. Hope was then transferred out of the zoo, and a new elephant, Rosie, was brought in. When the social order of elephants is severely disrupted, individuals get very upset. I've seen this firsthand among wild elephants in Kenya, and not surprisingly, this is what happened at the Denver Zoo. Playing "musical chairs" with animals is a serious business that can have dire consequences.

All of which raises a larger question: if the Denver Zoo, or any zoo, wants to spend tens of millions of dollars helping to conserve Asian elephants, why don't they spend it helping wild elephants? If captive Asian elephants aren't likely to help conserve the species, then why not put our efforts into preserving habitat that's useful to wild elephants? There's no reason the zoos can't publicize their efforts and educate the public (and make money doing so), but why not act in ways that actually help the animals, rather than just help the zoo?

Georgia Mason, a professor in the Animal Science Department at the University of Guelph in Canada, and an acknowledged expert on the behavior of animals in captivity, has made exactly this case: "In the past 10 years Western zoos have spent or committed something like $500 million improving the enclosures of something like just over 200 elephants — all of it evidence-free. These sums are worrying because they are staggering compared with what it would take to conserve these animals better in Africa and Asia.... The Oklahoma City zoo has announced plans to create a $23 million enclosure that would keep a handful of elephants.... That sum is about the same as the annual budget of the Kenya Wildlife Service or the South African National Parks Authority."

Zoos are no place for elephants. The purposes zoos serve, and the animals we keep in them, are up to us to decide, so let's make the correct choice — phase out the elephant exhibit and send these amazing animals to sanctuaries where they can live out their lives with social and emotional stability, respect, and dignity. The Denver Zoo should use its money to improve the lives of the residents it already has, or to help preserve the habitats of wild animals so they will never know a cage.

### What Do Zoos Teach Us?

Most people come to zoos to be entertained, to be amazed by exotic creatures, and to experience a rare interaction and connection with our fellow animals. These same desires often inspire our adventures into the wilderness. But as we saw with Tatiana, the Siberian tiger, for a minority of visitors (but perhaps as many as a quarter), the interaction they most enjoy is the power zoos give them to mock and antagonize otherwise fearsome predators.

However, I'm told that zoos do indeed also educate, and I find this to be a reasonable claim. Yet there is only scant evidence that this results in any attitude and behavior changes concerning conservation, or that it leads to improved animal welfare. If zoos want to claim that they are conducting *conservation* education, they need to find a way to prove that their efforts are resulting in behavior changes that preserve biodiversity. However, until we have proof, it is more fair to say that zoos are conducting what Sarah Bexell calls "wildlife natural history education" that has yet to be shown to engender humane attitudes and biodiversity preservation.

A recent study conducted by the Association of Zoos and Aquariums attempted to quantify the educational impact of zoos and aquariums. The assessment was titled "Groundbreaking Study Identifies Impact of Zoo and Aquarium Visits," and it surveyed 5,500 out of about 157,000 visitors to twelve zoos. The results showed that about 60 percent of visitors said they had their values and attitudes toward conservation reinforced, 42 percent believed that zoos and aquariums played an important role in conservation education and animal care, and 57 percent said that their visit strengthened their connection to nature.

From this, the AZA concluded, "zoos and aquariums all over this country are making a difference for wildlife and wild places." In fact, this survey only confirms what visitors say about how a zoo influences their attitudes, not whether zoos improve the lives of animals. Actually, only about 11 percent of animals confined in zoos are threatened or endangered, animals are rarely if ever reintroduced to the wild, and animals in zoos do not have healthier lives. When a report was published that captive Asian elephants show higher mortality rates than their wild relatives, Paul Boyle, a conservation official with the AZA, became very upset and extolled the virtues of zoos by claiming: "When you get a seventh-grader next to an elephant, there's that hay smell. It's huge. They look up and see these eyelashes that are 4 inches long....And they begin to ask questions."

But do they? Or do they just look in amazement and move on to the next animal? There is no empirical evidence that the experiences zoos provide, as warm as they can be, actually inspire lasting action or changes in attitudes. Sarah Bexell, an expert on the educational role of zoos, has noted that even seeing animals such as pandas playing doesn't motivate people to ask questions about the conservation of these charismatic animals. In one study conducted at the Edinburgh Zoo in Scotland, only 4 percent of zoo visitors said they went to the zoo to be educated. Even if people become interested, this does not lead to monetary contributions or any long-lasting education effect that actually benefits the animals. Animals in zoos surely aren't ambassadors for their wild relatives. How can an individual who is caged and has lost his or her freedom be an ambassador for their species? As former zoo director David Hancocks says, zoos are "a different nature" and, indeed, a paradox, for they represent animals in misleading ways.

Of course, I realize research on attitude and behavioral changes toward animals is difficult to conduct and evaluate. Still, there are effective ways of teaching conservation and compassion for animals. For instance, take the conservation camps in Chengdu, China, which Sarah Bexell and her Chinese colleagues have organized. The camps were developed for children ages eight to twelve, and they were designed to encourage the acquisition of knowledge about animals, care for animals, compassion toward animals, and environmental stewardship. The program guided children along what they called a "continuum of care." To facilitate this process, students first met small animals (rabbits, guinea pigs, hamsters, parakeets, and tortoises) as *individuals* (not merely members of a species), and they were encouraged to recognize them as individuals with personalities and feelings similar to ours. They also met exotic captive animals (including giant pandas, red pandas, zebras, golden monkeys, giraffes, and lemurs) as individuals. Bexell and her colleagues found statistically significant self-reported increases of knowledge, level of care, and propensity for animal and environmental stewardship. Anecdotally from observation as well as from parental responses, they also learned that some students became kinder toward their peers, especially younger campers. This program and its evaluation allowed the researchers to document one way that young people can develop positive and humane attitudes and behavior toward animals and nature, and it can serve as a model for other much-needed studies elsewhere.

To conclude, let's consider what the Association of Zoos and Aquariums itself has to say in their own executive statement, which notes: "Little to no systematic research has been conducted on the impact of visits to zoos and aquariums on visitor conservation knowledge, awareness, affect, or behavior." Enough said. There's little groundbreaking information contained in the AZA's reports, and the burden of proof still falls on those who want to keep animals in captivity. Thus far, they have been unable to provide any convincing evidence that zoos do much of anything for "the good of a species." All zoos must show that they are living up to their stated educational and conservation goals, and the public must hold them accountable. The animals, of course, can't do this for themselves.

## "Good Welfare" Isn't "Good Enough"

Clearly, the way we treat animals today doesn't work. It doesn't work for our fellow animals, and quite often it doesn't work for us. Just about everyone I know says they care about animals. Many people work hard to protect animals. Some people say they love animals and yet harm them nonetheless; I'm glad those people don't love me. While most of us have good intentions, judging by the state of animal welfare today, good intentions aren't enough. Despite global attempts to protect animals from wanton use and abuse, the institutions and industries we've created kill and torture billions of animals every year — what currently passes for "good welfare" just isn't "good enough." Humans still tend to deny that the wanton abuse of animals occurs in numerous venues, and when they acknowledge it, they still sometimes justify it by saying that animals don't have emotions and don't understand what's going on. But at this point, given the constant reminders in the popular media about animal sentience and suffering, only a hermit could really say, "Oh, I didn't know animals could feel."

Our relationships with our fellow animals are complicated, frustrating, exhilarating, ambiguous, and paradoxical; they range all over the place. Our fellow animals challenge us to take a hard look at who we are and who (not what) they are. Our relationships with animals are scattered across the love-hate spectrum, and this causes problems for animals and for us.

According to existing laws and regulations, "good welfare" in research allows mice to be shocked and otherwise tortured, rats to be starved or force-fed, pigs to be castrated without anesthetic, cats to be blinded, dogs to be shot with bullets, and primates to have their brains invaded with electrodes. We need to ask ourselves what "good welfare" really means. Is it just synonymous with "convenient for humans," or is this really the best that humans can do on behalf of animals? Consider the real-life scenarios we've already read about, which occur in laboratories, zoos, slaughterhouses, and in the wild nearly every day:

Is injuring coyotes and bears in leghold traps so we can study them "good welfare"?

Is shooting pigs to teach medical procedures for treating bullet wounds "good welfare"?

Is drowning minks in aquatic traps "good welfare"?

Is slaughtering hens so we can learn how to debone them faster "good welfare"?

Is injecting a disease into a chimpanzee "good welfare"?

Is blinding seals in chlorinated pools "good welfare"?

Is placing tigers in cages where they can be taunted "good welfare"?

Is moving elephants from zoo to zoo "good welfare"?

Are factory farms that create "downer" cows "good welfare"?

Is chaining circus horses and elephants over 90 percent of the time "good welfare"?

Clearly, "good" isn't good enough. Treatment that humans regard as acceptable is unacceptable to animals. It is also disquieting that the results of a national survey of 157 veterinary faculty in the United States show that only 71 percent of respondents self-characterized their attitude toward farm animal welfare as "we can use animals for the greater human good but have an obligation to provide for the majority of the animals' physiologic and behavioral needs."

When it comes to deciding what constitutes "good welfare," I often ask people: Would you do this to your dog? Would you trade places with the animal? If not, then why would any animal want to be treated in ways that, though legal, are abusive enough that you would not tolerate them, either for yourself or an animal you love? I ask these questions because we need to be very clear about what we do to animals and why we do it. It is possible for a dog to live in a closet or a cage as long as she or he is fed and given medical care when needed. They might not like it — indeed, they wouldn't — but they could survive. We need to ask ourselves if we're being consistent in deciding who to treat with compassion, and if not, why. We need to unravel what we mean by "good welfare" from the point of view of our fellow animals.

Françoise Wemelsfelder stresses in her excellent work, which focuses on how we assess the quality of life of animals, that good welfare is more than just an absence of suffering. It concerns the quality of the individual's entire relationship with his or her environment, how she or he copes with their environment, and our willingness to treat animals as sentient beings with feelings, as individuals who care about what happens to them. In other words, animals don't want us to merely stop acting cruelly toward them; they need us to also provide a compassionate world in which they can thrive.

## What Animals Want: All We Have to Do Is Ask

If we ask, is it possible for animals to tell us what they want? Apparently so. Renowned ape-language researcher Sue Savage-Rumbaugh did just this with the bonobos she has studied for years, Kanzi, Panbanisha, and Nyota. Then she coauthored a peer-reviewed paper of her discoveries in the *Journal of*

*Applied Animal Welfare Science*. Sue and her colleagues developed a method for conducting two-way conversations with these amazing beings using a keyboard with symbols (or lexigrams), and using this, she could actually ask them questions and record their responses. Sue notes, "Although it is true that I chose the items listed as critical to the welfare of these bonobos and facilitated the discussion of these particular items, I did not create this list arbitrarily. These items represent a distillation of the things that these bonobos have requested repeatedly during my decades of research with them."

Sue discovered that these were the items the bonobos agreed were important for their welfare:

1. Having food that is fresh and of their choice.
2. Traveling from place to place.
3. Going to places they have never been before.
4. Planning ways of maximizing travel and resource procurement.
5. Being able to leave and rejoin the group, to explore, and to share information regarding distant locations.
6. Being able to be apart from others for periods of time.
7. Maintaining lifelong contact with individuals whom they love.
8. Transmitting their cultural knowledge to their offspring.
9. Developing and fulfilling a unique role in the social group.
10. Experiencing the judgment of their peers regarding their capacity to fulfill their roles, for the good of the group.

11. Living free from the fear of human beings attacking them.
12. Receiving recognition, from the humans who keep them in captivity, of their level of linguistic competency and their ability to self-determine and self-express through language.

The bonobos live in captivity, yet they articulated a range of seemingly universal needs and desires: to eat well, to have the freedom to move about, to have time alone as well as to be an active, admired member of a social group, to be stimulated by novelty, to be appreciated for the beings they are, and to live free from fear. Enriched and challenging social and physical environments are clearly important to them, as they would be to most animals, but perhaps particularly to those living in confined situations with limited options. If we could apply these same communication techniques with other species, how revolutionary would that be? Our fellow animals could tell us what they want and need, and by doing this, we could make "good welfare" reflect true compassion.

I realize that no one is perfect. Without meaning to, good people can do bad things to animals. Yet we all can do more to make the world a more compassionate and less cruel place for all beings. What is important is that we lead by example and that we engage in compassionate activism, hopefully proactively. Although we live in an imperfect world and although we're all fallible, this does not mean that anything goes. Rather, it means that we all must work that much harder to make more sustainable, ethical, and humane choices. We can make a positive difference, each and every one of us, by working together to create a more compassionate world. Isn't that why we are here?

# Acting Compassionately
# Helps All Beings and Our World

"To see animals who have been tortured all their lives be able to live on this ranch and be loved, to have someone fall in love with one of the animals and want to care for it, is one of the most wonderful feelings in the world."

— David Groobman, founder of Kindness Ranch

ANY MANIFESTO IS A CALL TO ACTION. This animal manifesto is a plea to regard animals as fellow sentient, emotional beings, to recognize the cruelty that too often defines our relationship with them, and to change that by acting compassionately on their behalf. To a very large extent, we control the lives of our fellow animals. We're their lifeguards. It's essential that we move rapidly to make kindness and compassion the basis of our interactions with animals. We shouldn't be afraid to make changes that improve animals' lives. Indeed, we should embrace them. Such changes will only help heal ourselves and our world.

At a meeting in Palermo, Italy, a veterinarian who was in charge of the well-being of cows going to slaughter told me that he saw a cow cry. While he wasn't absolutely certain the water dripping from the cow's eye was a tear, the cow had reason to grieve, for she had just seen, heard, and smelled her friends being killed. The experience was enough for the veterinarian to request a transfer to another job.

As difficult as it can be, we must remain open to the emotions, and too often the pain, of our fellow creatures, and we must let this spur us to action. Our alienation from animals and nature kills our hearts, and we don't even realize how numb we've become until we witness the beauty of nature and the wonder of life: something as simple as a squirrel performing acrobatics as she runs across a telephone wire, a bird alighting on a tree limb and singing a beautiful melody, a bee circling a flower, or a child reveling at a line of ants crossing a hiking trail. In these small moments, we feel our inherent connection to all creatures and all of nature. What will future generations say when they look back and see how, despite what we knew, we still tortured animals and decimated pristine habitats for our own gain? How could we miss the obvious connection? That when we destroy them we destroy ourselves? As the philosopher and master magician David Abram constantly reminds us, we live in a more-than-human-world, and we must never forget this.

## Building an Animal Protection Movement

Those who care about animals and Earth are involved in an ever-growing social and political movement, and the time has indeed come to move forward proactively to educate, to raise consciousness, and to effect change in the lives of animals.

There is already a lot happening to make animal protection a meaningful part of the political agenda, and it's encouraging news. In 2002, the Party for the Animals was founded in the

Netherlands, and in 2006 it gained two seats in the Dutch parliament, becoming the world's first party to gain parliamentary seats with an agenda focused primarily on animal rights. Though it was founded to fight for animal rights and welfare, it also seeks to be more than a single-issue political party. As of January 1, 2007, the Party for the Animals had 6,370 members.

In August 2008, the International Primatological Congress held in Edinburgh, Scotland, held a symposium on invasive research on great apes, one of the first of its kind ever at this prestigious meeting. This important gathering occurred at the same time that the European Union was considering revising and updating its regulations over the use of animals in research (Directive 86/609), potentially to include a total ban on the use of great apes and wild-caught primates in invasive research. Then, in November 2008, the European Parliament adopted a written declaration urging the European Union to enact this change, along with establishing a timetable for replacing the use of all primates in scientific experiments with alternatives. In June 2009, animal activist Jasmijn de Boo, cofounder of the organization Animals Count, put animals on the agenda of the European Parliament elections. It turns out that EU politicians receive more mail on issues of animal protection than on any other topic.

In July 2009, China drafted the country's first law on animal protection, which would cover all wild and domestic animals. This is the first Chinese legislation to propose criminal punishment for animal cruelty. Even in Spain, an anti-bullfighting movement is succeeding. In 2007, official government statistics tallied 2,622 bullfighting events that used 12,167 innocent animals, and the Spanish government subsidized bullfighting to the tune of 560 million euros. But as physician and animal activist Núria Querol i Viñas tells me, attitudes are changing.

According to a recent survey, 72 percent of Spaniards have no interest in bullfighting, and only 8 percent of Spaniards consider themselves supporters. In 1989, Tossa de Mar became the first city to declare itself as anti-bullfighting, and so far forty-seven cities have joined, including Barcelona in 2004. In the small Portuguese town of Viana do Castelo, which has a bullfighting tradition dating back to 1871, the mayor banned bullfighting in early 2009.

In the United States, California has passed some major legislation. In July 2008 Governor Arnold Schwarzenegger signed a law that strengthened the protection of downed cows (prohibiting their sale or slaughter), and in November 2008, California voters passed Proposition 2, which helps protect farm animals from inhumane confinement and cages. In New Jersey, Farm Sanctuary achieved a precedent-setting victory after a ten-year battle with the state's Department of Agriculture. To quote Farm Sanctuary's press release: "In a monumental legal decision, the New Jersey Supreme Court unanimously declared that factory farming practices cannot be considered 'humane' simply because they are 'routine husbandry practices.'"

A few years ago I discovered the wonderful book titled *1968* by Mark Kurlansky, and I was reminded how great it was to be a child of the 1960s — how important it is to look into your heart and to get out and do something to change the world for the better. Kurlansky notes that in the 1960s there were many people who were fed up with what was happening and that "this gave the world a sense of hope...and a sense that where there is wrong, there are always people who will expose it and try to change it." What was happening then was simply not acceptable. This surely holds for animal use and abuse by humans today. As the late Gretchen Wyler, founder of the Ark Trust, used to say, "Cruelty can't stand the spot-light." And it can't.

·Every individual action shines a light, whether it's motivated by a desire to change society or simply to fix one injustice in the life of one animal. Also, we need to remain as light as we can despite the challenges and the abuse that breaks our hearts, to prevent our-selves from burnout. We need to speak to those who don't agree with us. I know that it's often exasperating, but there is hope, and every accomplishment, no matter how minor it seems, fuels our collective work on behalf of animals. Keep in mind what Henry Spira, founder of Animal Rights International, did in the 1970s working from his small apartment in New York City. Spira and his grassroots organization were responsible for having federal funding pulled on a project in which researchers at the American Museum of Natural History performed surgery on cat genitals and pumped them with various hormones to see how the mutilated cats would behave sexually. Spira also formed the Coalition to Abol-ish the Draize Test, a test that involves using rabbits to test eye makeup. The Draize test is torture, and rabbits, who have very sensitive eyes, suffer immensely. By 1981 the cosmetics industry itself awarded $1 million to Johns Hopkins University's School of Hygiene and Public Health to establish the Center for Alternatives to Animal Testing. Most cruelty-free products trace their history back to Spira's tireless and unflagging efforts to stop animal abuse.

A little bit of success here and there is all it takes to keep up our motivation to make the lives of animals better. Simply by speaking out, we can have an influence and change minds, and I'm happy to talk to those who need some convincing. In March 2006 I jumped at the opportunity to give a lecture at the annual meetings of the Institutional Animal Care and Use Com-mittees in Boston. I was received warmly and the discussion that followed my lecture on animal sentience and emotions was friendly, even if it was met with some skepticism. After my talk, a man who's responsible for enforcing the Animal Welfare Act at a major university admitted to me that I had confirmed his ambivalence about some of the research that's permitted under the act. From now on, he said, he would enforce the current legal standards more strictly and also work to establish more stringent regulations. As with this man, many people have mixed feelings about how animals in their care are treated, and they just need someone to confirm their intuition that the animals they work with are suffering. Though I don't know all that the man did afterward, I did learn that in 2008 he recommended that I be invited to a conference about enriching the lives of laboratory animals, and I was invited to such a meeting in November 2009 as a voice from the other side. Though I would like to see animal research phased out entirely, improving laboratory conditions is a first step, and clearly, this man had become one more person working with me to try to improve the lives of these animals.

HEADLINE NEWS:
### Veal Crates Banned! Wild Horses Saved!

Around the world, individual citizens, politicians, and governments are working to save animal lives and to establish new laws that give them increased rights and protections. Here are some recent headlines:

### Colorado Bans the Veal Crate and the Gestation Crate

"Compassion in World Farming" Press Release, May 19, 2008

"Colorado is now the first state in the country to ban the use of gestation crates and veal crates by action of a state legislature. Florida, Arizona and Oregon have prohibited gestation crates.

Arizona has prohibited veal crates. And a California measure to prohibit veal crates, gestation crates and battery cages recently qualified for November's ballot."

## Appealing to Dallas' Wallet,
## Lily Tomlin Keeps Trying to Move Jenny the Elephant
*Dallas Observer*, January 28, 2009

"[Lily] Tomlin last year took up the cause of Jenny the psychologically scarred elephant at the Dallas Zoo, joining in a communitywide effort to have her . . . relocated to a sanctuary in Tennessee. The zoo did eventually drop its plan to ship Jenny to a wildlife park in Mexico, but Jenny fans still haven't given up on landing Jenny a home in Tennessee.

" 'In today's hard times, one must question the economic sense of keeping Jenny at the Dallas Zoo, when she could retire at no cost to the city to the peace and safety of the sanctuary,' Tomlin wrote. . . . 'It costs hundreds of thousands of dollars annually to just maintain a single elephant in a zoo. The City of Dallas plans to spend $30 million alone to build a controversial elephant exhibit to house up to five elephants. . . . And, all the while, thousands of people in Dallas are losing their jobs and homes.' "

## A Dramatic Rescue for Doomed Wild Horses of the West
*Washington Post*, November 18, 2008

"The unwanted horses seemed destined for death. The wheels had been set in motion to put down about 2,000 healthy mustangs, those in a federally maintained herd of wild horses and burros that no one wanted to adopt.

"The Bureau of Land Management knew that euthanasia was a legal alternative, but officials were proceeding slowly, afraid of an intense public outcry.... Then... Madeleine Pickens, wife of billionaire T. Boone Pickens, made known her intentions to adopt not just the doomed wild horses but most or all of the 30,000 horses and burros kept in federal holding pens. Lifelong animal lovers, the Pickenses just a few years ago led the fight to close the last horse slaughterhouse in the United States."

## Spanish Parliament to Extend Rights to Apes
Reuters, June 25, 2008

"Spain's parliament voiced its support on Wednesday for the rights of great apes to life and freedom in what will apparently be the first time any national legislature has called for such rights for non-humans. Parliament's environmental committee approved resolutions urging Spain to comply with the Great Apes Project, devised by scientists and philosophers who say our closest genetic relatives deserve rights hitherto limited to humans.

" 'This is a historic day in the struggle for animal rights and in defense of our evolutionary comrades, which will doubtless go down in the history of humanity,' said the Spanish director of the Great Apes Project.

"Keeping apes for circuses, television commercials or filming will also be forbidden and breaking the new laws will become an offence under Spain's penal code."

## US Congress Moves Swiftly on Legislation
## to Stop "Pet" Primate Trade
Reuters, February 24, 2009

"Born Free USA...today congratulated the US House of Representatives for its swift passage of the Captive Primate Safety

Act (H.R.80) by an overwhelming vote of 323-95. The bill, sponsored by Representatives Earl Blumenauer (D-OR) and Mark Kirk (R-IL)..., prohibits interstate and international movement of nonhuman primates if they are to be kept as 'pets.'

" 'The primate trade involves enormous animal suffering and threats to human safety,' says...Born Free USA. 'These innocent animals may be confined in small cages or have their teeth or fingernails removed. We can't allow animals to be mutilated in the name of companionship. There is simply no excuse for keeping primates as pets and the trade must stop. Wildlife belongs in the wild.'

"Each year, there are numerous incidents of privately-held primates harming people. Just this month, in an incident that has garnered international attention, a woman was critically mauled by a 'pet' chimpanzee in Stamford, Connecticut....

" 'Primates are highly social and intelligent creatures who shouldn't be shipped around the country just to languish in people's bedrooms, basements, or backyards,' added the Executive Vice President of HSUS."

### Protection Boost for Rare Gorilla
*BBC News*, November 28, 2008

"The government of Cameroon has created a new national park aimed at protecting the critically endangered Cross River gorilla, the world's rarest. The total population of the subspecies is thought to be less than 300.

"The news comes as governments of 10 gorilla range states gather in Rome for the first meeting of a new partnership aimed at protecting the primates. The Gorilla Agreement was finalised in June, and brings together all the countries where the various species and subspecies are found.

"The Wildlife Conservation Society (WCS) helped establish the Takamanda park, and believes it will help curb the hunting and forest destruction that have brought Cross River numbers to such a minuscule level.

" 'By forming this national park, Cameroon sends a powerful message about the importance of conservation,' [said the WCS president].

"Gorillas should be able to move freely between the Takamanda reserve and Nigeria's Cross River National Park just across the border, helping to repair the fragmentation of habitat which can isolate tiny wildlife populations."

### Brussels Proposes Ban on Seal Cruelty
*EU Observer*, July 23, 2008

"The European Commission on Wednesday proposed a ban on seal products obtained by inhumane methods from entering or being produced within the European Union. 'Seal products coming from countries that practice cruel hunting methods must not be allowed to enter the EU,' said environment commissioner Stavros Dimas unveiling the proposal, which also covers sealing within the EU. 'The EU is committed to upholding high standards of animal welfare.'

"The regulation aims to ensure that the killing and skinning of seals during a hunt does not cause 'pain, distress or suffering.' Trade in seal products would in future be allowed only where a certification scheme, coupled possibly with a product label, could guarantee the product as coming from a country meeting strict animal welfare conditions."

## The Compassionate Activist

To improve the lives of the animals in our care, we must appeal to the people who care for them. We must convince the people who run our zoos, research centers, and farms that animals think and feel, and that they suffer from many of today's common practices. I know from experience that it's possible to change people's minds and attitudes, but this is always most successful when we appeal to a person's natural compassion, to their innate sense of kindness.

In October 2008 I visited the Chengdu Zoo in China with Jill Robinson and other people from the Moon Bear Rescue Centre. I'm always saddened when visiting these sorts of places, and I was warned that conditions at the zoo were terrible, but I knew I had to see what the zoo was like before I could complain. The visit truly was a mixed blessing — bored and lonely elephants, bears, and monkeys, simply horrible conditions for the chimpanzees sitting alone in totally barren cages, and lone tigers in empty concrete cells. I asked my colleagues whether I should write to the director of the zoo, and while they thought it was a good idea, they thought it unlikely that I would receive a letter back.

As an unwavering optimist and dreamer, I wrote a very strong letter criticizing zoo conditions in as gentle a manner as I could. I know not to fight fire with fire; a lesson that I've learned from Jethro and other animals is that getting in someone's face doesn't get you what you want. Compassion begets compassion, and you often do receive what you give. In the letter, I said that I knew the director and his coworkers really cared for the animals, but that the conditions themselves were horrible and I knew they could do better. I was not expecting a reply, but about ten days later I received a lovely letter from the director himself agreeing that they could and would do more. He thanked me for writing and wanted me, as a field biologist, to know that he would do more. And they are. Since then, they've been working with Jill and others to enrich the lives of the animals at the zoo, in part because they realize that they simply have to treat the animals with more respect and dignity and in part because they know people all over the world are scrutinizing them. For example, I've recently learned that the zoo is completing a new and more naturalistic primate facility where the chimpanzees and orangutans will live more enriched and better lives. Once again, we see that it really is true that "cruelty can't stand the spotlight." Time and again, calling attention to cruelty has resulted in people changing their ways, even though it often takes a good deal of time for them to do so.

In my travels to countries around the world, I've learned that there is a deeply shared commitment to work for animals who need our help. I've also learned that there are many diverse cultural attitudes and beliefs, and if we want to convince people in cultures different from our own to work for the betterment of animals, we need to be sensitive to these differences. For example, when I was in Taipei a few years ago, I met a woman who wanted to study biology and ultimately to help enrich the lives of captive animals. The woman's professor said she was required to dissect animals to complete his course, but she didn't want to do this. The student was in a deep dilemma and experiencing a lot of conflict; the situation seemed irresolvable. After we spoke, the woman asked if I would talk to her professor. I did, emphasizing all the nonanimal alternatives that would satisfy the professor's goals. The professor hadn't realized these alternatives existed, and he agreed that if she could learn the material using them, it would be all right if she didn't perform the dissections. Since then, the woman passed the course, and I like to believe that this professor will now grant similar requests not to dissect animals in his course. The key in this situation was that the professor didn't lose face; he was allowed to change his mind without it being seen as giving in to pressure. I've known other students who didn't want to dissect animals and directly confronted some of my colleagues, demanding not to do so. Because the professors felt pressured and cornered, they rarely yielded to the request.

We should, in other words, treat other people with the same dignity and respect we are asking them to extend to animals. Another story that exemplifies this was told to me by Leanne Deschenes, an intern with Green Mountain Animal Defenders in Burlington, Vermont. One day, Leanne became incredulous that some of her friends thought that it was just fine to kill a small bug who had walked across their picnic table. By talking to her friends gently, Leanne explained that the bug was here before they were and that being outdoors meant there would be bugs around. But equally important, as Leanne wrote: "Arguments and dialogues are sometimes necessary, oftentimes stimulating, and here and there discouraging, but we must demonstrate compassion to every person in every moment for them to see and feel the benefits. It is this way in which compassion is taught; our actions flow into the actions of others and become their own. If we practice compassion toward people repeatedly, we will open their eyes, ultimately saving the life of a quirky little bug on a beautiful-day picnic table somewhere."

How right she is. We must remember that this is their turf, too, be it land, water, air, or picnic table.

## Protests, Threats, and the Canadian Lynx

Of course, personal conversations and letters are not always effective or appropriate. Different circumstances require different actions. In the late 1990s, I was concerned with the way a state program run by the Colorado Division of Wildlife (CDOW) to reintroduce the Canadian lynx into Southwestern Colorado was being handled, so I did something very simple: I organized protests and wrote letters to the local papers to call public attention to the project. I had serious ethical questions about this program. And it wasn't just me. Opposition was broad-based and involved people who rarely talked with one another, field and conservation biologists, animal rights activists, ranchers and woolgrowers; we all had shared concerns about the political, social, economic, and biological aspects of the project.

The reasoning behind the translocation seemed to indicate an effort that was either ill-conceived or not what it seemed. For instance, we were told a death rate of 50 percent was expected and acceptable because "they'll die up there anyway"; in Canada, the lynx were being trapped for their pelts. However, the area where they were to be moved in Colorado wasn't likely to have enough food to support them, as shown by a survey of the area by a CDOW employee, who was later removed from the project. At one point, Mr. S, who oversaw the project, referred to the lynx release as "an experiment of sorts" and admitted the project was rushed. I was offended at the cavalier attitude of the CDOW and felt their "dump and pray" strategy was a perfect example of irresponsible biology and was ethically indefensible, especially for people who supposedly love animals.

No public opinion survey concerning the lynx project was done. In addition, we learned that a ski resort company, Vail Associates, had given $200,000 to the project, which would allow its ski resort to expand into suitable lynx habitat, and that no lynx surveys had been conducted around Vail after their expansion was approved in 1994. Sometimes, reintroductions of species have been done simply to avoid having a species declared endangered, at which point the federal government steps in with its own restrictions. Was that going on here? I subsequently wrote an essay titled "Jinxed Lynx" and organized three protests.

As planned, however, the Canadian lynx were translocated to Colorado on February 3, 1999. As each lynx starved to death because of the predictable lack of food, others and I voiced our concerns. Our worries were ignored or categorically dismissed, but apparently raising public awareness had an effect. The response just became more personal than I expected.

I was teaching at the University of Colorado, and I learned that in March 1999, Mr. S wrote a letter to the president of the university that was an attempt to intimidate and coerce him into censuring me. Mr. S wrote that "my current will leaves 14% of my estate to the school of Environmental Studies at CU. Dr. Bekoff has seriously made me consider changing my will." He also indicated that, because of my efforts, he was considering diverting a $30,000 study grant from the University of Colorado to Colorado State University.

Rather than give in to this pressure, the president forwarded the letter to me, the Chancellor of the Boulder Campus, and other campus officials, and the university unequivocally supported me. Money, in this case, didn't talk. Yet in his letter, Mr. S made an interesting comment: "Animal rights is a difficult

subject to teach since it involves core values and would probably be better dealt with in one's quest for answers to spiritual
questions. Is Dr. Bekoff paid to teach animal rights? There is
considerable difference between animal behavior and animal
rights."

First, what I was being paid to teach wasn't the issue; the
lynx were the issue. And understanding the lynx was essential to evaluating whether their translocation made practical
and ethical sense. Is it right to move animals if the only result
will be they die of starvation in one place rather than by
human hands in another? Many people, including policy makers, make decisions about animal use and animal well-being
based on their behavior, based on what we know of their capacities to experience pain and suffering. In fact, there are
tight links between animal behavior and animal protection (or
rights).

What began as an inquiry as to why the Colorado Division of Wildlife was conducting this project went full circle to
a personal attack. But in the end activism paid off, at least partially: in response to our efforts, changes were made in the
ways in which lynx were transported and released that reduced
the mortality rate. We couldn't stop the project, but we made
it better for the lynx.

## Animals, Cultural Sensitivity, and Our Compassion Footprint

As I mention above, we need to respect cultural differences as
we work for animal rights; this is an integral part of expanding
our compassion footprint. I'd surely like to see the entire world
become vegan and drive less and pedal their bicycles more, but

I'm enough of a realist to know that this will not happen, even among people who would like to do so if they were able. We must resist judging others, and remember that improving the lives of animals frequently goes hand in hand with improving the lives of people.

A friend of mine told me that when she first went to South Africa she was incredibly naive about what life was like for many people there. She gave a well-received paper on ecofeminism and food, and she admonished people for eating animals. After her talk a mild-mannered woman approached her and said she really liked what she said, but that she needed to be more sensitive to cultural variations and poverty. The South African woman said she would love to be more of a vegetarian, but she simply didn't have access to the food she needed to keep healthy; her ability to help animals was hampered by her circumstances. In 2009, I read a very disturbing story about how soldiers in Zimbabwe are being fed elephant meat for their rations. This is terrible for the elephants, but it does no good to blame the soldiers, who are unable to even withdraw their salaries from banks as the country's economy collapses. We who are privileged need to work with fine-tuned humility with people of all sectors of society. Sometimes, we need to help other people before those people can help the animals with whom we share the Earth. Compassion begets compassion.

Sometimes poverty is a barrier. Sometimes it is cultural attitudes about animals. Only some people are intentionally cruel; many times, people just do not know or believe that when they harm animals they are slaughtering sentience. Even their understandings about what sentience is can be different. We need to educate people and raise consciousness, but be respectful of their point of view and circumstances. Some might ask who am I to make proclamations from the mountains of Colorado about how the people in other lands should treat the animals with whom they compete for space and resources. Indeed, in poorer countries, sometimes people do compete for resources, such as land, with wild animals; if animals are given preference, human welfare suffers. I'm very sensitive to these concerns and the fact that, as an American, I enjoy a very privileged lifestyle. I don't compete directly with the animals who share the land around my home. When people have their own essential needs met, it is far easier for them to extend kindness to others, whether human or animal. We must work to understand why people do what they do, and not fall into the trap of simply telling people what to do. To expand our compassion footprint on behalf of animals, we must respect the cultural pluralism of the diverse world in which we live.

Here is another excellent story that appeared in *Time* magazine that illustrates how, by helping people, we can help wildlife:

> If you want to protect wildlife in developing countries, the conventional wisdom has long been that you put the animals in a well-run reserve and safeguard it like it were a prison, keeping the wildlife separate from the people who actually live there. The locals, in this case, are the threat because they're the ones who poach endangered wildlife, whether for the ivory or skin trade, or just for meat. But, so far, this conventional wisdom hasn't led to much progress. According to the International Union for Conservation of Nature's annual report, nearly 40% of surveyed species are currently threatened, and their numbers are growing.

Dale Lewis has a different theory of conservation: Instead of helping the animals that are being hunted, help the people who are doing the hunting. In the West African country of Zambia, where he has lived and worked for nearly 30 years, Lewis has helped launch an innovative new program that seeks to save wildlife by improving the livelihoods of local people, giving them an economic incentive to give up poaching. The program is called Community Markets for Conservation (COMACO), and it may help change the way wildlife is protected. "I realized I could have told you all the vital statistics of an elephant, but not the vital statistics of the people who lived with an elephant," says Lewis, whose work is sponsored by the Wildlife Conservation Society. "Once you really begin to know what they're up against, you can really begin to understand [their behavior]." And once you understand that behavior, Lewis continues, you can change it.

## Born to Be Good: The Significance of *Jen*

In *Born to Be Good*, psychologist Dacher Keltner notes that Charles Darwin believed that sympathy was our strongest passion and that our positive emotions such as joy, compassion, sympathy, and gratitude "were the basis for our moral instinct and capacity for good." Darwin also believed that communities of sympathetic individuals were more successful in raising offspring. I found this to be true in studies I conducted with my students, in which we discovered that, among wild coyotes at least, there is a premium to playing fairly: individual coyotes who didn't were more likely to leave their group of their own accord because they were avoided or their invitations to play were ignored, and thus they suffered higher mortality rates than those who played fairly and remained with their group.

Recall that Keltner uses the Confucian concept of *jen*, which refers to "kindness, humanity, and reverence" to discuss our "good nature" and offers the concept of the *jen* ratio to "look at the relative balance of good and uplifting versus bad and cynical in life." I liken the *jen* ratio to the way we can consider the balance between our own compassion and cruelty. If we try to bring forth our innate compassion with every being we meet, whether they are human, animal, or plant, we will always be making progress and expanding our compassion footprint.

Author and filmmaker Michael Tobias often wonders how my Jain attitude toward animals can play out in the real world. As an eternal optimist, I don't worry about it all that much, for there are so many good people around the world working hard to make the lives of animals better, to restore respect, appreciation, and dignity to beings who we have abused for far too long. Everybody works in their own ways, within the confines of their own circumstances, but we can all accumulate compassion credits; compassion comes naturally if we let it. We can all wear smaller shoes and share Earth with all other beings. Socially responsible science, compassion, heart, and love can be blended into a productive recipe to learn more about the lives of other animals and the world where each one of us lives. Thomas Berry stresses we should strive for a "benign presence" in nature. Native Americans are proud to claim that "animals are all our relations." Animals and inanimate landscapes also speak for themselves, and it is up to us to listen to their messages very carefully. Trees and rocks need respect and love, too.

Every individual can make positive changes for all living beings by weaving compassion, empathy, respect, dignity, peace, and love into their lives. For instance, did you know that animal compassion has a gender gap? In a review of attitudes toward animals written for the *Encyclopedia of Animal Rights and Animal Welfare*, Jennifer Jackman notes that the renowned Yale University researcher and social ecologist Stephen Kellert and his colleague Joyce Berry concluded that gender is "among the most important demographic factors in determining attitudes about animals in our society." Jackman goes on to note that women are more likely than men to support animal welfare positions and to express concerns about the moral treatment of animals, and women are less likely to support animal use. While women and men share similar levels of concern about conservation, women are more supportive of strengthening the Endangered Species Act. Women also are more likely to oppose lethal wildlife management.

First and foremost, being more compassionate with animals is about our everyday choices: it's about what we eat and wear, how we educate students and conduct research, how we entertain ourselves. Political activism is also important, but if we only focused on changing our own lives, we would still influence the world.

For instance, as we discussed in chapter 4, factory-farmed meat is a significant factor in global warming. Factory farming is a global industry that's intricately tied into many national economies. How can individuals influence that? Simply by changing what we choose to put into our mouth. As Mike Tidwell points out in his essay "The Low-Carbon Diet," although he loves to eat meat, he's now a dedicated vegetarian because "I have an 11-year-old son whose future — like yours and mine — is rapidly unraveling due to global warming. And what we put on our plates can directly accelerate or decelerate the heating trend." Furthermore, Tidwell notes, "Simply put, raising beef, pigs, sheep, chicken, and eggs is very, very energy intensive. More than half of all the grains grown in America actually go to feed animals, not people, says the World Resources Institute. That means a huge fraction of the petroleum-based herbicides, pesticides, and fertilizers applied to grains, plus staggering percentages of all agricultural land and water use, are put in the service of livestock. Stop eating animals and you use dramatically less fossil fuels, as much as 250 gallons less oil per year for vegans, says Cornell University's David Pimentel, and 160 gallons less for egg-and-cheese-eating vegetarians."

Clearly, we can expand our compassion footprint simply by what we eat and the effects those choices have on everyone else. If we make ethical choices, we can change the way business is done. After all, money talks.

## Be Proactive:
## Inaction and Indifference Are Not Options

"In the relations of humans with the animals, with the flowers, with the objects of creation, there is a whole great ethic scarcely seen as yet, but which will eventually break through into the light and be the corollary and the complement to human ethics.... Doubtless it was first of all necessary to civilize man in relation to his fellow men. With this one must begin and the various lawmakers of the human spirit have been right to neglect every other care for this one. But it is also necessary to civilize humans in relation to nature. There, everything remains to be done."

— Victor Hugo

While there are many small, easy actions we can take to help animals, two things that are no longer acceptable are inaction and indifference. We've reached the point where enough is enough, or really, enough is simply too much — we cause far too much unnecessary suffering and pain in the world. There are canaries in coal mines around the world telling us that something is profoundly wrong.

Nobel laureate and peace activist Elie Wiesel encourages us: "Take sides. Neutrality helps the oppressor, never the victim. Silence encourages the tormentor, never the tormented." Silence is deadly for animals. There is a sense of urgency — time is not on our side. Indifference is far too costly. We need to act now with compassion and love for this magnificent world.

Naturally, we shouldn't let anger guide us. We need to remain compassionate activists at all times. This is what gives us real clout to influence others, but it also helps ourselves. Being kind makes us feel good; it is a profound and even spiritual experience to spread compassion, kindness, and love. It's also contagious. We need to be kind and empathic and cooperate with one another, so that we can define and work toward common goals, even when we disagree on the exact path. We can never be too kind, nor is anyone perfect. Humility and the way forward is recognizing our own imperfections even as we seek change in the actions of others. We should question a person's position and not attack people themselves.

Every day, we should look for opportunities to do something for animals, and create opportunities for others to do so. As we do, we need to be patient, for as long as we are moving in the right direction, things will get better for animals and Earth. As we've seen, there are costs to activism — such as harassment, intimidation, and frustration — but these are the price of putting one's beliefs on the line to prevent cruelty and save lives. Activism also takes a lot of time, but it's well worth it. Protest gently but forcefully; change actions as well as minds and hearts. Changes that are imposed on others are usually short-lived and make little difference.

Often it takes numerous efforts to accumulate the momentum needed to produce the deep changes in attitude and heart that truly make a difference. It's important to listen to all views. This is important to help find and solve the root causes of problems, but it is also smart tactics. We must master our opponents' arguments. Only by knowing your opponents' tactics and arguments can you mount a successful offense.

Sometimes activists get depressed and discouraged from working on so many heart-breaking problems, so it's also important to remember to have fun. Stay connected to joy. In his wonderful and bold book, *A World of Wounds*, renowned biologist Paul Ehrlich wrote: "Many of the students who have crossed my path in the last decade or so have wanted to do much, much more. They were drawn to ecology because they were brought up in a 'world of wounds,' and want to help heal it. But the current structure of ecology tends to dissuade them." When we become dissuaded, we are not as effective, and we become inclined to give up. But having fun, being sentimental, and doing solid science are not mutually exclusive activities. Once again, to quote Ehrlich, "In my view, no area of science can be successful (or much fun!) without a mutually supportive interaction between theory and empiricism.... So let's stop arguing about theory versus empiricism and worrying about the end of our science. Instead, let's cooperate more, change some of our priorities, and have fun while we're trying to save the world."

Indeed, the problems facing animals are so broad that they require creative proactive solutions drenched in deep humility, compassion, caring, respect, and love. We cannot allow our worries and fears to make us inactive and pessimistic, and we must not give in to cynicism. As we consider what to do, we need to be pro-something, not anti-something — we need to advocate for whales and mice as sentient beings, not think of our position as being anti-whaling or anti-animal research, though we don't favor either. Of course, advocating for mice means working to end invasive research on them, but in theory that research serves a purpose; we'll only achieve our goals when scientists find ways to satisfy their goals without such research. We need to be pro-elephants, not anti-zoos, to make a difference in the lives of elephants who suffer in zoos. We need to concentrate on being positive in difficult and challenging times and not let our frustration get the best of us. We need to act locally and think globally.

Finally, it's essential to remember that every individual counts and that every individual makes a difference. As Margaret Mead noted: "Never doubt that a small group of thoughtful, committed citizens can change the world. Indeed, it's the only thing that ever has." It's also important to remember that Gandhi was right — no matter how hard people fight against you, believing in what you're doing will eventually result in victory.

## Open Eyes and Open Hearts: Let Animals Move You

"Our stewardship of wild animals should continue to seek a balance of nature — but only ever upon a fulcrum of empathy."

— Clive Marks

It's impossible to develop a relationship with an animal and remain unmoved. We should encourage relationships with animals, particularly in our scientists, for we are always affected and changed by them. Surely, animals don't communicate like we do. They don't express themselves in the same ways. When they suffer, animals don't cry in the way that we do. But if our eyes are open, we recognize their pain anyway, and if our hearts are open, we feel it and are affected by it. When it comes to animals, we can be certain that their eyes and hearts are always open.

My friend and esteemed colleague Benjamin Beck, Director of Conservation at the Great Ape Trust, wrote the following notes:

> On the day of my retirement from the Smithsonian National Zoological Park in 2003, I walked around to say farewell and express thanks to the many people and animals with whom I had worked for 20 years. I saved two of my favorite animals, orangutans Azy and Indah, for last. I had known them since they were youngsters and worked with them collaboratively in cognitive research projects. We had close and trusting relationships, although Azy sometimes treated me as a competitor and performed impressive displays of his dominance. Indah was always sweet and curious, and was probably the brightest ape I have ever met. When I said goodbye to her, my emotions caught up and tears streamed down my cheeks. Indah had probably seen people cry before, but she had never seen me cry. She watched my tears closely, and then fixed my eyes. She reached out, and gently patted me on the shoulder and neck. She had

never before done this, usually preferring to examine my pockets or nudge me toward hidden treats whose location she, but not I, knew. I have no doubt that Indah was able to recognize my state of sadness, and that she responded appropriately, as a friend, with consolation. Later I realized that I had never seen Indah, or any other ape, cry. Our jobs would be easier if apes did cry, because we would have an observable measure of pain and sadness. Instead of tears we must rely on, in Jane Goodall's words, 'eyes filled with pain and hopelessness' in an ill-treated, newly motherless chimpanzee orphan.

Ben is a renowned hardcore scientist with a heart. His sentimentalism makes him more human and also shows clearly that he appreciates that the animals with whom he has worked are sentient beings worthy of respect and admiration. We must stop averting our gaze and closing our hearts to our fellow animals. If we remain aware and attentive, who knows how our lives might be transformed?

Take, for instance, the experience of Dan Southerland, executive editor of Radio Free Asia, who found his life briefly upended and his worldview changed by an errant butterfly. In 2008 in the *Washington Post*, he wrote about his encounter, beginning: "In July last year, a butterfly landed on my shoulder while I was taking a break from my office for a few minutes one afternoon to talk business with a colleague. I was sure the butterfly would soon fly off. We were walking through an L Street canyon near 19th Street NW that was surrounded by granite, concrete and glass. I had never seen a butterfly in this part of the city before. Now I had one clinging to me. It migrated to my shirt collar and stayed there." For over two hours, through a trip to a photo shop and lunch in a restaurant, the butterfly clung to Dan, who eventually decided to take him home in a taxicab. Dan named him Poppy, and the butterfly stayed in his family's backyard for over five weeks, fluttering out to "greet" Dan almost every evening when he returned home from work. Along the way, Dan discovered that he wasn't the first person to develop a relationship with a butterfly, and by his own admission, "my feelings at this point were approaching love for this small creature." Observing the butterfly's behavior so intimately, Dan came to believe Poppy "had a tremendous sense of joy," and "I began paying a lot more respect to all insects." One day, Poppy didn't return; presumably, his short life had ended. But, Dan wrote: "I can certify that at least one D.C. butterfly managed to escape [living in the city], take a taxi ride out of town and survive to have the time of his life in the suburbs."

This is the true "butterfly effect" that all animals can have: if we open our eyes and hearts to them once, we don't ever forget it. We are, in ways large and small, transformed. Sarah Bexell, in her work with her Chinese colleagues Luo Lan and Hu Yan, has noted a similar "light bulb effect" in the attitudes of children toward animals in China, in her studies of animal conservation camps. Bexell told me that, after their experience, many teachers and children said they would never think about animals with indifference again. The program participants spent time getting to know animals as individuals with emotions and personalities, and this alone transformed attitudes. Bexell summed up her findings aptly: "Once you see them, you can't unsee them."

Why should we expand our compassion footprint and respect an animal manifesto? Why should we care about animals and treat them better? There are numerous reasons I could list, and yet sometimes getting to know one animal is all we need.

Still, here is the list of reasons, a work in progress, I originally wrote as I developed this book:

- because they're smart
- because they feel
- because they are
- because they care
- because we don't have to use or abuse them
- because we can do better science without them
- because we'd be healthier if we didn't eat them
- because they're our buddies/consummate companions
- because we're so powerful
- because we all need to look out for each other
- because they're good for our souls and we are for theirs
- because we're a compassionate species
- because they're innocent
- because animals make us human
- because they bring us joy
- because we're all animals
- because silent springs are unacceptable
- because we're their voice
- because compassion begets compassion
- because by taking care of animals, we take care of ourselves
- because if we lose animals, we're screwed...we lose ourselves
- because we need more peace among all beings
- because animals do not harm Earth, humans do

This list is only a start. As we've seen, there are many more reasons to care for animals and to increase our compassion footprint, and these reasons generate even more reasons. I hope you will add to this list and do more for animals because there's always more that can be done. All of us animals will surely benefit.

## Deep Ethology and Cosmic Justice: Creating a Sense of Unity

"In reality there is a single integral community of the Earth. . . . In this community every being has its own role to fulfill, its own dignity, its inner spontaneity. Every being has its own voice. . . . We have no rights to disturb the basic functioning of the biosystems of the planet. We cannot own the Earth or any part of the Earth in any absolute manner."

— Thomas Berry, *The Great Work*

Most research nowadays supports what Dacher Keltner has said: "Human beings are wired to care . . . and it's probably our best route to happiness." It feels good to help others, and this is no accident. Egalitarianism as well as competition help shape animal societies, including human ones. It is natural to want to build a world based on compassion and unity, one that respects and cherishes the beautiful and magical webs of nature.

In order to transform our world, however, we have to transform ourselves. We owe it to future generations to transcend the present state of our relations to our fellow creatures, to dream of a better world, to step lightly, to move cautiously and with restraint. We all need to be both dreamers and doers. We owe it to ourselves and to our fellow animals. As big-brained, omnipresent mammals, we are the most powerful beings on Earth. We can influence every species and every ecosystem, and inextricably tied with that might are innumerable staggering responsibilities to be ethical. We can strive for no less, and we can always do more. "Good welfare" is never "good enough."

My notion of "deep ethology" applies here. Deep ethology is similar to the term "deep ecology," which asks people to recognize that not only are we an important part of nature but we have unique responsibilities to nature as moral agents. Deep ethological research pursues a detailed and compassionate understanding of the unique worlds of nonhuman animals in order to learn more about their own points of view — how they live, what they want, and how they experience emotions, pain, and suffering. Deep ethology recognizes that many animals have a broad set of feelings that function as social glue; these emotions are important for forming and maintaining social bonds among themselves and with human beings, they motivate specific actions and influence choices, and they insure behavioral flexibility, so that animals do what is appropriate in a given situation, whether with friends or competitors. By embracing deep ethology, we recognize animals as sentient beings, and as beings with intrinsic or inherent value with ways of life that deserve respect; living this belief, and working to improve the quality of life of our fellow animals when it's threatened or destroyed, naturally expands our compassion footprint.

We must also adopt what philosopher Gary Steiner, in his book *Animals and the Moral Community*, calls cosmic justice, the principle that demands nonviolence toward animals just as social justice demands nonviolence toward humans. Cosmic justice "will let animals be in such a way that we no longer project upon them a diminished reflection of our own image but instead value their mortality as we value our own." Animals aren't third-class citizens; they're nations of beings who deserve dignity and respect. So let's get hopping toward elevating their moral status right now, not later when it's more convenient for us and too late.

When we allow compassion, empathy, justice, and love to guide our actions, we surely will go a long way to healing wounds and dysfunctional relationships. If love is poured out in abundance, then it will be returned in abundance. There is no need to fear depleting the potent and self-reinforcing feeling of love, which only and continuously generates more compassion, respect, and love for life. Each and every individual plays an essential role, in part because each individual's spirit and love are intertwined with the spirit and love of others. These emergent interrelationships, which transcend an individual's embodied self, foster a sense of oneness. These interrelationships can work in harmony to make ours a better and more compassionate world for all beings. We must stroll with our kin and not leave them in the tumultuous wake of our rampant, self-serving destruction.

We need to replace "mindlessness" with "mindfulness" in our interactions with animals and Earth. If we do, nothing will be lost and much will be gained. We can never be too generous or too kind. Surely, we will come to feel better about ourselves if we know deep in our hearts that we did the best we could and took into account the well-being of the magnificent animals with whom we share Earth, the awesome and magical beings whose presence makes our lives richer, more challenging, and more enjoyable. Wouldn't it feel good to know that we have helped animals "out there," even if we cannot see, hear, or smell them? Wouldn't it feel good to know that we did something to help Earth and other humans, even if we do not see the fruits of our labor?

It's essential that we do better than our ancestors, and we

surely have the resources to do so. Foresight is becoming the new survival skill — we have the facts and heart, and now we must put them to proper use. Perhaps the biggest question of all is whether enough of us will choose to make the heartfelt commitment to making this a better world, a more compassionate world, before it is too late. I believe we have already embarked on this pilgrimage. My optimism leads me in no other direction.

My colleague Jessica Pierce says that we need more "ruth," a feeling of tender compassion for the suffering of others. Ruth is the opposite of ruthless, being cruel and lacking mercy. I agree. Kindness, living kindness, empathy, and compassion must always be first and foremost in our interactions with animals and every other being in this world. We need to remember that giving is a wonderful way of receiving. We need humility in head and resolve in heart. We must go from heartless to heart-full.

We owe it to all individual animals to make every attempt to come to a greater understanding and appreciation for who they are in their world and in ours. We must make kind and humane choices. We must all work together, for in the end we all want the same thing — a better life. Our better life must not come at the expense of other beings, and it is made truly better when it includes all beings. There's nothing to fear and much to gain by developing deep and reciprocal interactions with our fellow animals. Animals can teach us a great deal about responsibility, compassion, caring, forgiveness, and the value of deep friendship and love. Animals generously share their hearts with us, and we should do the same. Animals naturally respond to each other because we are all feeling and passionate beings. Let us embrace our fellow animals as the kindred spirits they are.

## Animal Stories:
## The Best of Times and the Worst of Times

Animals have no say in how humans change their lives. Animals simply live, doing the best they can in a human-dominated world. Taking the long view, it's hard to imagine that their lives have ever been harder or more compromised, and that's almost entirely due to us. To what degree do animals realize this? Birds can certainly witness the sweep of human civilization across continents, as can wolves, and even whales, who travel the globe and must have noticed long ago that humans are almost everywhere. Polar bears, too, who are losing precious ice floes due to climate change, along with urban wildlife, must alter their daily rhythms as they adapt to the way we've redecorated their homes. Domestic animals, certainly, understand on some level the human impact on their lives, for they live and die by our hands and are in constant contact with us.

In many ways and for most species, these are the worst of times. They may not recognize us as the cause, but animals certainly feel the pressure on their lives of the increasing global population of humans and our overconsumptive ways. As our society grows, there is less and less space for other animals without humans intruding into their lives and living rooms. People, meanwhile, deliberately manipulate the lives of animals almost relentlessly: killing them for sport and simply to lessen their numbers; catching and raising them for food and clothing; caging and dissecting them for research; and using them for entertainment. If our fellow animals don't understand it as such, they are certainly impacted by our society's alienation from nature in the way we treat animals in all these settings.

However, it's also true that more and more people around

the world are truly concerned about how we affect the lives of animals. More than ever, we understand that coexistence with other animals is essential, that our fate is tightly bound with them. Many people recognize that our species has been routinely overconsumptive for far too long, that we make messes wherever we go, and they are working to create a sustainable balance. Partly through our egregious errors, humans have learned how powerful a force in nature we are, and how essential it is to step lightly — to leave a smaller carbon footprint and a larger compassion footprint. More than ever, people are trying to change, so that our reliance on animals and our curiosity about them does not harm them. Though there is far too much work to be done, animals can no doubt look with hope that there are better times, and perhaps the best of times, to come. I'm an optimist and a dreamer and I do think that with hard work the future can be a much better one for animals, nonhuman and human.

It's important to note that I'm not a blind optimist. I know well that bad things happen to animals and the Earth. Thinking positively about what we can do for animals and the Earth, and concentrating on what works and moving ahead with hope, will enable us to put our finite amounts of time, energy, and passion into making life better for animals and for us. Anything that drains our energy from what needs to be done will have a negative effect. Thinking positively is a significant part of the much-needed paradigm shift about which this book is concerned.

There is much to gain and little to lose if we move forward with grace, humility, respect, compassion, empathy, and love. We are wired to be good, we are wired to be kind, and we are wired to be compassionate, but we also have a responsibility to be ethical. No more lame excuses for allowing the mistreatment of animals to continue. We will ultimately be judged by how we treat the least fortunate among us, so we need to treat animals better or leave them alone. Now is the time to tap into our innate goodness and kindness to make the world a better place for all beings. This revolutionary paradigm shift brings hope and life to our dreams for a more compassionate and peaceful planet.

# ACKNOWLEDGMENTS

First and foremost I thank Jason Gardner at New World Library for his patience, flexibility, and commitment to this book and for working with me on *The Emotional Lives of Animals*. There can be no better "ear" than Jason. Jason's got "ear" like border collies have "eye" — focused and sharp. Thanks also to Jeff Campbell for his masterful editing once again. Jeff has eye and ear. All of the other folks at New World also are a pleasure to work with, so many thanks to Monique Muhlenkamp, Ami Parkerson, Kristen Cashman, and Danielle Gotchet. Sarah Bexell offered numerous excellent suggestions for revisions and for ways to make a positive difference in the lives of animals. I'm grateful that she took the time to do so and for sharing her unbounded and unrelenting passion and for being in my life. Sarah also brought a much-needed global perspective. Emails and conversations with Dacher Keltner have reinforced my feelings about the innate goodness of human beings, and working on *Wild Justice* with Jessica Pierce has been a pleasure and an inspiration for seeing abundant kindness among nonhuman beings. Jessica also read the entire manuscript and is still sane and sighted.

I also thank Jill Robinson, founder and CEO of Animals Asia (animals asia.org), for bringing me to the Moon Bear Rescue Centre outside of Chengdu, China, and I thank Jasper and his Moon Bear buddies for allowing me to hang out with them and learn valuable lessons in compassion, trust, and hope. Philippa Brakes (also known as the "Green Tea Girl" and she knows why) of the Whale and Dolphin Conservation Society (wdcs.org) also has been a wonderful inspiration and source for my coming to a better understanding of what life under water is like for cetaceans. An outing in March 2008 on the beautiful waters outside of Adelaide, Australia, with Philippa and Mike Bossley, who discovered tail-walking in dolphins, opened my eyes to how much more there is to learn about these amazing beings and how their suffering is shrouded by the sea. Bruce Gottlieb, Christine Caldwell, and Carly Parry also offered helpful hints and laughter along the way, and Valerie Belt was a constant source of encouragement and "new findings" that I missed. I also thank Carron Meaney for becoming "more veggie" and for making the 2008 Thanksgiving dinner a vegetarian feast. And to my cycling buddies Brad, Andy, Randy, Scott, Chip, Daphne, Karen, Julia, Susie Mae, Christy, Anita, Annette, and April, who patiently listen to my nonstop chatter about animal behavior and animal protection and the virtues of eating more veggies (along with french fries, dark chocolate, good merlot, and peaty single malt): many thanks indeed for being tolerant and for having a great sense of humor about my ranting! My sisters Marjorie and Roberta also have been very supportive of my work, and very patient listening to me talk about animal behavior and animal protection.

I was fortunate to be able to complete this book at the beautiful home of Fabrizio Collova and Valeria Augello in Palermo, Italy. Fabrizio, Valeria, their four rescued dogs — Noor, Aston, Doxy, and Asia, along with Kiwi the love-bird, who liked to sit on my head — were most gracious in allowing me to eat their fine food, drink delicious wine, and relax as I edited the text.

I only wish my parents, Beatrice and Oscar, were alive to see this book. I know they'd say "bravo" and feel that they'd been successful. My folks knew from the start that I loved animals and reminded me that I always wanted to know what they were thinking and feeling — that I minded animals — and they allowed me to pursue my dreams, while on occasion — well, maybe more frequently than that — wondering what in the world I was doing. But they had faith that in the end something good would emerge. I miss them dearly. So thanks to two wonderful people who put up with me and trusted that I knew what I was doing most of the time. I've never met a more positive thinker than my father, and my mother was full of compassion and love. I know I've been most fortunate to be able to pursue my dreams of studying and working with animals and using what others and I have learned to better their lives, and my parents' role was surely instrumental. I can't thank Beatrice and Oscar enough for encouraging me to play a lot and also for providing the support, lightness, and love that reminded me that all would be okay and for allowing me to travel here and there, mentally and physically — and to dream about a more compassionate world. It's been a wonderful journey, and perhaps the best is yet to come.

# ENDNOTES

As much as possible, I have included websites for popular media and scholarly articles used during the research for this book. Quotes and references to books listed in the Resources section usually do not have a separate source note here.

## Introduction

Page 3, *polls show that just as green awareness is blossoming across the planet*: For 2006 Lake Research Partners poll, see Best Friends News Release, June 21, 2006, "In first annual Kindness Index," http://www.bestfriends.org/aboutus/pdfs/061906%20Kindness%20Index.pdf. The 2008 Gallup Environmental Poll is from the 2008 Deloitte publication, "Crossing the Green Divide," http://www.deloitte.com/dtt/cda/doc/content/us_es_CrossingtheGreenDivide.pdf.

Page 5, *Eight Belles broke her front ankles while running during the 134th Kentucky Derby*: Joe Drape, "At Kentucky Derby, Joy and Agony of Display," *New York Times*, May 4, 2008, http://www.iht.com/articles/2008/05/04/sports/HORSE.php. For more, see Lynn Reardon, *Beyond the Homestretch*.

Page 8, *when President Barack Obama nominated Harvard University law professor Cass Sunstein*: Jonathan Stein, "Is Obama's Regulatory Czar a 'Radical Animal Rights Activist'?" *Mother Jones*, January 28, 2009, http://www.motherjones.com/politics/2009/02/obamas-regulatory-czar-radical-animal-rights-activist.

Page 13, *I learned that the number of mountain gorillas*: For more on these stories, see Mark Kinver, "DR Congo Gorilla Numbers Up 12.5%," *BBC News*, January 27, 2009, http://news.bbc.co.uk/2/hi/science/nature/7852953.stm; "Emperor Penguins Face Extinction," *BBC News*, January 26, 2009, http://news.bbc.co.uk/2/hi/science/nature/7851276.stm; "Global Warming Is 'Irreversible,'" *BBC News*, January 27, 2009, http://news.bbc.co.uk/2/hi/science/nature/7852628.stm.

Page 13, *the first wildlife migration corridor through the Greater Yellowstone ecosystem*: "Ancient Pronghorn Path Becomes First US Wildlife Migration

Corridor," *Environment News Service*, June 17, 2008, http://www.ens
-newswire.com/ens/jun2008/2008-06-17-091.asp.

Page 13, *a study of primates that found that 303 species*: Lewis Smith, "Review of
Primates Finds 303 Species Threatened," *The Australian*, August 5, 2008,
http://www.theaustralian.news.com.au/story/0,25197,24131596
-2703,00.html.

Page 13, *imperiled right whales seem to be recovering*: For more on these stories,
see Cornelia Dean, "The Fall and Rise of the Right Whale," *New York Times*,
March 16, 2009, http://www.nytimes.com/2009/03/17/science/
17whal.html?_r=1&sq=fall%20rise%20right%20whale&st=cse&scp=1&page
wanted=all; VITA Animal Rights Center Press Release, "Russian
Authorities Have Fully Banned the Hunt for Baby Harp Seals," March 18,
2009, http://www.vita.org.ru/english/news.htm; Cornelia Dean,
"One-third of US Bird Species Endangered, Study Finds," *New York Times*,
March 19, 2009, http://www.nytimes.com/2009/03/20/science/earth/
20bird.html?scp=1&sq=one%20third%20bird&st=cse; Nora Schultz,
"Africa's First Bird Extinction Likely Within Four Years," *New Scientist*,
March 20, 2009, http://www.newscientist.com/article/dn16817-africas-first
-bird-extinction-likely-within-four-years.html.

Page 14, *sheep living on the remote island of Hirta off the coast of Scotland*: Michael
Marshall, "Incredible Shrinking Sheep Blamed on Climate Change," *New
Scientist*, July 2, 2009, http://www.newscientist.com/article/dn17407
-incredible-shrinking-sheep-blamed-on-climate-change.html.

Page 14, *three times as many polar bears are in a fasting state*: For these polar bear
stories, see Kate Ravilious, "More Polar Bears Going Hungry,"
*New Scientist*, January 1, 2009, http://www.newscientist.com/article/
mg20126882.700-more-polar-bears-going-hungry.html; Felicity Barringer,
"10 Polar Bears Are Seen Swimming in Open Water," *New York Times*,
August 22, 2008, http://www.nytimes.com/2008/08/23/science/
23bears.html?_r=1&scp=1&sq=10%20polar%20bears&st=cse&oref=
slogin; Allegra Stratton, "Polar Bear Shot Dead After 200-Mile Swim," *The
Guardian*, June 5, 2008, http://www.guardian.co.uk/uk/2008/jun/05/
animalwelfare.animalbehaviour.

Page 14, *As author Richard Nelson writes about polar bears: "I looked toward her"*:
excerpt from Steven Kazlowski, *The Last Polar Bear* (Seattle: Mountaineers
Books, 2008), appeared in Sierra Club newsletter, January/February 2008,
http://www.sierraclub.org/sierra/200801/chilling.asp.

Page 15, a *May 2007 issue of* Newsweek *contained an essay about the emotional
lives of elephants*: Hennie Lötter, "Deserving of Respect," *Newsweek*, May 7,
2007, http://www.newsweek.com/id/35114.

Page 15, *Wildlife biologists...described unique changes in the behavior of Tenino*:
Jay Mallonée, *Timber: A Perfect Life* (Whitehall, MT: New Perceptions Press,
2007).

Page 15, *the* New York Times *even published obituaries for two famous animals*: Benedict Carey, "Washoe, A Chimp of Many Words, Dies at 42," *New York Times*, November 1, 2007, http://www.nytimes.com/2007/11/01/ science/01chimp.html?_r=1&scp=1&sq=washoe&st=cse&oref=slogin; Benedict Carey, "Brainy Parrot Dies, Emotive to the End," *New York Times*, September 11, 2007, http://www.nytimes.com/2007/09/11/science/ 11parrot.html?scp=2&sq=ALEX+PARROT&st=nyt.

Page 16, *in October 2008, the* New York Times Magazine *published a major piece of investigative journalism about the plight of farm animals*: Maggie Jones, "Barnyard Strategist," *New York Times*, October 24, 2008, http://www.ny times.com/2008/10/26/magazine/26animal-t.html?_r=1&scp=1&sq= pacelle&st=cse&oref=slogin; "Standing, Stretching, Turning Around," editorial, *New York Times*, October 8, 2008, http://www.nytimes.com/ 2008/10/09/opinion/09thu3.html?_r=2&th&emc=th&oref= slogin&oref=slogin.

Page 19, *As teacher and writer Todd Nelson has pointed out*: Todd Nelson, "Our Civility Footprint or — Walk This Way," *Teachers.net Gazette*, March 1, 2008, http://teachers.net/gazette/MAR08/nelson. For the Animal Welfare Institute's "Compassion Index," see http://www.compassionindex.org.

Page 20, *Amirtharaj Christy Williams, a biologist with the World Wildlife Fund's Asian elephant and rhino program*: Amirtharaj Christy Williams, "Where Should the Elephants Go?" *BBC News*, January 14, 2009, http://news.bbc.co.uk/2/hi/science/nature/7828251.stm.

REASON 1: *All Animals Share the Earth and We Must Coexist*

Page 27: *Truth be told, the obliteration of animal dignity happens more than daily*: *UPI*, "USDA Report Allegedly Shows Abuse," December 4, 2008, http://www.upi.com/Science_News/2008/12/04/USDA_report_ allegedly_shows_abuse/UPI-63021228429229.

Page 29, *Noah Williams, a second-grade activist in Connecticut, wrote*: Jampa Williams and Noah Williams, "Is An Animal A Thing? Or a Being?" *Hartford Courant*, November 11, 2007, http://connecticutfor animals.blogspot.com/2007/11/hartford-courant-op-ed-7-yo-ct-ar_12.html.

Page 30, *Dominick LaCapra claims this is now the "century of the animal"*: Dominick LaCapra's claim was related to me by Walter Putnam after a lecture I gave at the University of New Mexico, February 6, 2008. In an email on February 9, 2008, Professor LaCapra gave me permission to quote him directly.

Page 31, *City University of New York psychologist William Crain reports*: William Crain, "Animal Feelings: Learning Not to Care and Not to Know," *Green Money Journal*, Fall 2009, http://www.greenmoneyjournal.com/ article.mpl?newsletterid=46&articleid=640.

Page 31, *as has happened with similar bequests, Ms. Helmsley's wishes were overturned*: Stephanie Strom, "Not All of Helmsley's Trust Has to Go to Dogs," *New York Times*, February 25, 2009, http://www.nytimes.com/2009/02/26/nyregion/26helmsley.html?scp=1&sq=unti&st=cse.

Page 32, *27 percent of pet owners buy birthday gifts*: "Pampered Pets," *Daily Camera*, June 16, 2008, http://www.dailycamera.com/news/2008/jun/16/pampered-pets; Paul Sheehan, "It's a Dog's Life — Without One," *Sydney Morning Herald*, September 3, 2007, http://www.smh.com.au /news opinion/its-a-dogs-life—without-one/2007/09/02 /1188671796072.html.

Page 32, *While racehorses often suffer abuse, they can also be extremely well cared for*: For the story of Barbaro, see http://en.wikipedia.org/wiki/Barbaro; for the story of Molly, see http://www.snopes.com/photos/animals/molly.asp, and http://www.greatpetnet.com/443/molly-the-fantastic-pony.

Page 36, *the Minnesota Department of Natural Resources (DNR) killed a male bear*: "Sad End for Bear with Jar on Head," *BBC News*, July 31, 2008, http://news.bbc.co.uk/2/hi/americas/7534325.stm.

Page 38, *In February 2009 a chimpanzee named Travis, who had lived in a human home*: Andy Newman and Anahad O'Connor, "Woman Mauled by Chimp Is Still in Critical Condition," *New York Times*, February 17, 2009, http://www.nytimes.com/2009/02/18/nyregion/18chimp.html.

Page 40, *Wisconsin lawmakers moved to lower the legal hunting age from twelve years of age to ten*: Ryan J. Foley, "Wisconsin Moves to Lower Hunting Age to 10," *Associated Press*, June 18, 2009, http://www.startribune.com/sports/outdoors/48543522.html.

Page 41, *As one employee of Wildlife Services was quoted as saying, "No one wants you"*: *Men's Journal*, January 2008, page 49.

Page 41, *In the fiscal year 2007, people working for Wildlife Services killed 2.4 million animals*: Jeff Barnard, "Agency Makes It Tough to Keep Tabs on Animal Kills," *AG Weekly*, July 31, 2008, http://www.agweekly.com/articles/2008/07/31/news/ag_news/news31.txt.

Page 42, *In 2008, Wildlife Services killed nearly five million wild animals and pets*: "Wildlife Services Exterminates 125% More Animals in 2008," WildEarth Guardians Press Release, June 17, 2009, http://www.wildearthguardians.org/library/paper.asp?nMode=1&nLibraryID=765.

Page 42, *In Wyoming alone during the fiscal year 2007, Wildlife Services gunned down*: "Coyote Killing Jumps in State," *Casper Star-Tribune*, August 1, 2008, http://casperstartribune.net/articles/2008/08/01/news/wyoming/90bcecfdeb42c30f8725749800030485.txt; for the Alaska wolves, see Rodger Schlickeisen, "14 Wolf Pups Executed in Alaska," *News Blaze*, August 1, 2008, http://newsblaze.com/story/20080801080734tsop.nb/topstory.html.

Page 42, *Wildlife Services had twenty-four accidents with seven fatalities between 1989 and 2006*: For the crash report, see the Sinapu blog, http://sinapu.word press.com/programs/protect-wildlife/the-air-war/aircraft-crashes/.

Page 45, *birds in different locations are known to mimic ambulance sirens*: For the
    details here, see Dawn Stover, "Not So Silent Spring," *Conservation Magazine*
    10 (Jan-Mar 2009), http://www.conservationmagazine.org/articles/
    v10n1/not-so-silent-spring; Mark Kinver, "City Birds Sing for Silent
    Nights," *BBC News*, April 25, 2007, http://news.bbc.co.uk/2/hi/science/
    nature/6591649.stm; Mark Kinver, "Light Pollution Forms 'Eco-Traps,'"
    *BBC News*, January 16, 2009, http://news.bbc.co.uk/2/hi/
    science/nature/7821298.stm.

Page 45, *As noted in the* New York Times, *"Most disturbing was the majority's"*:
    "Sonar Over Whales," *New York Times*, October 19, 2008, http://www.
    nytimes.com/2008/11/19/opinion/19iht-edwhales.1.17959146.html.

Page 46, *In February 2006, the Food and Agriculture Organization and in 1990,
    about 42 million marine mammals and sea birds were caught in drift nets*: Marc
    Bekoff, "Ethics and Marine Mammals." In *Encyclopedia of Marine Mammals*,
    2nd ed., edited by W. Perrin, B. Würsig, and H. Thewissen, 396–402
    (San Diego: Academic Press, 2008).

Page 47, *local changes in climate are responsible for an increase in tiger attacks*:
    "Climate Change Is Driving Increase in Tiger Attacks," *New Scientist*,
    October 21, 2008, http://www.newscientist.com/article/dn15000.

Page 47, *The migration patterns of Pacific brants, a sea goose, are changing*: Mark
    Kinver, "Warming Arctic 'Halts Migration,'" *BBC News*, September 17,
    2009, http://news.bbc.co.uk/2/hi/science/nature/8257299.stm.

Page 47, *recent studies have found that polar bears are getting smaller*: Victoria Gill,
    "'Stress' Is Shrinking Polar Bears," *BBC News*, August 25, 2009,
    http://news.bbc.co.uk/2/hi/science/nature/8214673.stm.

Page 47, *biologist William Laurance argues that other less charismatic species*:
    William Laurance, "Move Over, Polar Bear," *New Scientist*, January 7, 2009,
    http://www.newscientist.com/article/mg20126904.300-move-over
    -polar-bear.html.

Page 49, *John Hadidian, author of* Wild Neighbors: The Humane Approach to
    Living with Wildlife: Joyce Wadler, "There Are Other Ways," *New York
    Times*, June 5, 2008, http://query.nytimes.com/gst /fullpage.html?res=
    9805EFD81E3FF936A35755C0A96E9C8B63&scp=1&sq=hadidian&st=cse.

Page 49, *Indeed, recent studies of mountain lions living around Thousand Oaks,
    California*: Rachel McGrath, "Mountain Lions Are Learning to
    Live with Developments," *Ventura County Star*, January 20, 2009,
    http://www.venturacountystar.com/news/2009/jan/20/mountain
    -lions-are-learning-to-live-with.

REASON 2: *Animals Think and Feel*

Page 55, *In a 2008 essay in the* New York Times, *James Vlahos wrote about "pill-
    popping pets"*: James Vlahos, "Pill-Popping Pets," *New York Times Magazine*,
    July 13, 2008, http://www.nytimes.com /2008/07/13/magazine/13pets-t.html.

Page 56, *Birds are quickly being recognized as equal to mammals*: For these details, see Virginia Morell, "Minds of Their Own," *National Geographic*, March 2008, http://ngm.nationalgeographic.com/2008/03/animal-minds/virginia-morell-text; Brandon Keim, "Clever Critters: 8 Best Non-Human Tool Users," *Wired Science*, January 16, 2009, http://www.wired.com/wiredscience/2009/01/animaltools; Ed Yong, "The Evolutionary Story of the 'Language Gene,'" *New Scientist*, August 13, 2008, http://www.new scientist.com/channel/being-human/mg19926691.800-the-evolutionary-story-of-the-language-gene.html.

Page 57, *Consider, for instance, the ability of cormorants to count*: Erling Hoh, "Flying Fishes of Wucheng," *Natural History*, October 1998, http://find-articles.com/p/articles/mi_m1134/is_n8_v107/ai_21191222/pg_4?tag=artBody;col1.

Page 58, *"Queen's University says new research it conducted shows crabs"*: "Crabs 'Sense and Remember Pain,'" *BBC News*, March 27, 2009, http://news.bbc.co.uk/2/hi/uk_news/northern_ireland/7966807.stm.

Page 58, *"A South American river dolphin uses branches, weeds and lumps of clay"*: Richard Black, "Dolphin Woos with Wood and Grass," *BBC News*, March 26, 2008, http://news.bbc.co.uk/2/hi/science/nature/7313385.stm.

Page 59, *"Degus are highly social, intelligent rodents"*: Sandra Blakeslee, "What a Rodent Can Do With a Rake in Its Paw," *New York Times*, March 26, 2008, http://www.nytimes.com/2008/03/26/science/26rodentw.html.

Page 59, *"Recent research shows that cuttlefish can do things"*: Michael Brooks, "The Secret Language of Cuttlefish," *New Scientist*, April 26, 2008, http://www.newscientist.com/channel/life/mg19826531.000-the-secret-language-of-cuttlefish.html.

Page 59, *"A wild dolphin is apparently teaching other members"*: Richard Black, "Wild Dolphins Tail-walk on Water," *BBC News*, August 19, 2008, http://news.bbc.co.uk/2/hi/science/nature/7570097.stm.

Page 60, *"A 15-year-old South Australian school student has busted the myth"*: "Schoolboy Explodes Goldfish Memory Myth," *The Age*, February 18, 2008, http://www.theage.com.au/articles/2008/02/18/1203190696599.html; "Three-Second Memory Myth," *The Daily Mail*, January 7, 2009, http://www.dailymail.co.uk/sciencetech/article-1106884/Three-second-memory-myth-Fish-remember-months.html.

Page 60, *"Bees display a remarkable range of talents"*: Christof Koch, "Exploring Consciousness through the Study of Bees," *Scientific American*, December 2008, http://www.scientificamerican.com/article.cfm?id=exploring-consciousness.

Page 61, *"Worker ants in colonies with a queen are physically attacked"*: "Ants 'Get Aggressive with Cheats,'" *BBC News*, January 10, 2009, http://news.bbc.co.uk/2/hi/science/nature/7818692.stm.

Page 61, *"Female monkeys in Thailand have been observed showing their young"*: "Monkeys 'Teach Infants to Floss,'" *BBC News*, March 12, 2009, http://news.bbc.co.uk/2/hi/asia-pacific/7940052.stm.

Page 62, *"Scientists believe they have solved the mystery of why"*: Rebecca Morelle, "Chimps Craft Ultimate Fishing Rod," *BBC News*, March 4, 2009, http://news.bbc.co.uk/2/hi/science/nature/7922120.stm.

Page 62, *"Humpback whales have come up with a novel way"*: Rebecca Morelle, "Hungry Whales Steal Birds' Dinner," *BBC News*, March 17, 2009, http://news.bbc.co.uk/2/hi/science/nature/7940396.stm.

Page 63, *"Researchers have found that bearded capuchin monkeys"*: Henry Fountain, "For the Tough Nuts, Capuchin Monkeys Select the Right Stones," *New York Times*, January 16, 2009, http://www.nytimes.com/2009/01/20/science/20obtool.html?_r=1&scp=1&sq=monkeys%20pick%20right&st=cse.

Page 63, *"Monkeys can feel regret too — at least when playing"*: Fiona MacRae, "Monkeys Have Regrets Just Like Humans — At Least When They're Playing Deal or No Deal," *Daily Mail*, May 15, 2009, http://www.dailymail.co.uk/sciencetech/article-1181650/Monkeys-regrets-just-like-humans—theyre-playing-Deal-No-Deal.html#ixzz0M6DwoV3Q.

Page 64, *"The legendary 'bad temper' of mules is because"*: "Grumpy Mules 'Highly intelligent,'" *BBC News*, September 3, 2008, http://news.bbc.co.uk/2/hi/uk_news/england/devon/7596494.stm.

Page 64, *"Magpies can recognise themselves in a mirror, scientists have found"*: "Magpie 'Can Recognise Reflection,'" *BBC News*, August 19, 2008, http://news.bbc.co.uk/2/hi/science/nature/7570291.stm.

Page 65, *"A wild dolphin has been observed following a specific recipe"*: Christine Dell'Amore, "Dolphin 'Chef' Follows Cuttlefish Recipe," *National Geographic News*, January 28, 2009, http://news.nationalgeographic.com/news/2009/01/090128-dolphin-cuttlefish-meal.html.

Page 65, *"Sperm whales are one of the deepest diving whales"*: Richard Gray, "Sperm Whales Use Babysitters for Young," *The Telegraph*, June 13, 2009, http://www.telegraph.co.uk/earth/wildlife/5521920/Sperm-whales-use-babysitters-for-young.html.

Page 66, *"Dozens of people flocked the shoreline at Laniakea Beach"*: "Turtle Love Goes Beyond the Grave," *CNN*, July 24, 2008: for a clip of the CNN report, go to http://www.youtube.com/watch?v=YzfkeVtddIM; for a transcript, go to http://edition.cnn.com/TRANSCRIPTS/0807/24/cnr.02.html.

Page 66, *"Eleven-year-old gorilla Gana was holding her three-month-old baby"*: Marcus Dunk, "A Mother's Grief: Heartbroken Gorilla Cradles Her Dead Baby," *Daily News*, August 18, 2008, http://www.dailymail.co.uk/sciencetech/article-1046549/A-mothers-grief-Heartbroken-gorilla-cradles-dead-baby.html.

Page 68, *Christine Huffard, a graduate student at the University of California at Berkeley*: Rachel Tompa, "The Secret Love Lives of Octopi," *Monterey Herald*, April 12, 2008, http://www.racheltompa.com/documents/Herald/Octopi041208.pdf; "Sea of Love: Octopi Have Sophisticated Sex Lives," Bubblejam.net, April 2, 2008, http://www.bubblejam.net/brain/science.

Page 68, *Consider the reflections of George Schaller*: Michael Bond, "Interview: Feral and Free," *New Scientist*, April 5, 2007, http://www.newscientist.com/article/mg19425981.600-interview-feral-and-free.html.

Page 69, *Researcher James Burns and his colleagues reported in the prestigious journal* Ethology: J. G. Burns, A. Saravanan, and F. H. Rodd. "Rearing Environment Affects the Brain Size of Guppies: Lab-Reared Guppies Have Smaller Brains than Wild-Caught Guppies." *Ethology* 115 (2009): 122–33.

Page 70, *Masking emotions can be a very important social skill*: In general, see T. Dalgleish and M. Power, *Handbook of Cognition and Emotion* (New York: John Wiley & Sons, 1999), http://www.vhml.org/theses/wijayat/sources/writings/papers/facial_expression.pdf. For evidence in apes, see Joanne Tanner and Richard Byrne, "Concealing Facial Evidence of Mood: Perspective-taking in a Captive Gorilla?" *Primates* 34, no. 4 (October 1993), http://www.springerlink.com/content/p12153u435uvtu37.

Page 70, *"The life of bees is like a magic well"*: Quoted in Bert Hölldobler and E. O. Wilson, *The Superorganism: The Beauty, Elegance, and Strangeness of Insect Societies* (New York: W. W. Norton and Company, 2009), 73.

Page 70, *In China in December 2008, a trio of monkeys attacked their trainer*: "Performing Monkeys Attack Trainer in China," *The Telegraph*, December 17, 2008, http://www.telegraph.co.uk/news/newstopics/howaboutthat/3816785/Performing-monkeys-attack-trainer-in-China.html.

Page 70, *In another incident, a male chimpanzee at the Kolkata Zoo*: "Chimp Takes Revenge at Indian Zoo," *Mail & Guardian*, December 15, 2008, http://www.mg.co.za/article/2008-12-15-chimp-takes-revenge-at-indian-zoo.

Page 71, *Elephant expert Iain Douglas-Hamilton wrote to me in a recent email*: Quote from personal email to author, January 9, 2008. For more on elephant news, visit Save the Elephants (STE; http://www.savetheelephants.org/elephant-news-service.html), a news serve run by Melissa Groo.

Page 71, *researchers in Namibia's Etosha National Park are luring bull males*: James Morgan, "Vibrations 'Could Save Elephants,'" *BBC News*, February 14, 2009, http://news.bbc.co.uk/2/hi/science/nature/7890919.stm.

Page 71, *this moving account of a funeral service for a baby who was mauled to death*: Peter Jackson, "The Elephants' Farewell in Botswana," *Sunday Times*, January 28, 2007, http://travel.timesonline.co.uk/tol/life_and_style/travel/destinations/africa/article1271944.ece.

Page 72, *Elephants have also been observed mourning a black rhinoceros*: Schalk van Schalkwyk, "Elephant's Sad Farewell to Friend," *News24.com*, February 10, 2009, http://www.news24.com/News24 /South_Africa/News/0,2-7-1442_2467026,00.html.

Page 73, *I met some of these traumatized elephants at the David Sheldrick Wildlife Trust*: For more on this organization, see http://www.sheldrickwildlifetrust.org/index.asp.

Page 73, *A review of survivorship in Asian and African zoo elephants*: R. M. Clubb,

M. Rowcliffe, P. Lee, K. U. Mar, C. Moss, and G. Mason, "Compromised Survivorship in Zoo Elephants," *Science* 322 (2008): 1649.

Page 75, *in June 2006, researchers reported in the journal* Science: Dale J. Langford et al. "Social Modulation of Pain as Evidence for Empathy in Mice," *Science* 312 (2006): 1967.

Page 75, *In a study of "muskrat love," researchers separated nine male voles*: Denise Gellene, "Bonding with a Mate Changes Brain Chemistry, Researchers Find," *Los Angeles Times*, October 16, 2008, http://articles.latimes.com/2008/oct/16/science/sci-vole16.

Page 78, *I like what Australian Bradley Trevor Greive, writes*: Bradley Trevor Greive, *Priceless: The Vanishing Beauty of a Fragile Planet* (Kansas City, MO: Andrews McMeel Publishing, 2003), 93.

REASON 3: *Animals Have and Deserve Compassion*

Page 82, *"Scientists are gathering evidence that [walruses are]"*: Natalie Angier, "Who Is the Walrus?" *New York Times*, May 28, 2008, http://www.nytimes.com/2008/05/20/science/20walrus.html?_r=1&sq=walruses&st=cse&scp=2&pagewanted=all.

Page 82, *"By all accounts the baby kangaroo should have not survived"*: "Best Mates, the Baby Kangaroo and the Wonder Dog that Saved It," *Daily Mail*, March 31, 2008, http://www.dailymail.co.uk/news/article-551330/Best-mates-baby-kangaroo-wonder-dog-saved-it.html.

Page 83, *"A pygmy killer whale that beached itself on Maui"*: Dan Nakaso, "Podmates Aided Dying Whale in Its Last Days" *Honolulu Advertiser*, May 27, 2009, http://www.network54.com/Forum/235380/thread/1245336554/last-1245336554/Podmates+aided+dying+whale+in+its+last+days.

Page 83, *"It looks like a moment of terror — a diver"*: "The Amazing Moment Mila the Beluga Whale Saved a Stricken Diver's Life by Pushing Her to the Surface," *Daily Mail*, July 29, 2009, http://www.dailymail.co.uk/news/worldnews/article-1202941/Pictured-The-moment-Mila-brave-Beluga-whale-saved-stricken-divers-life-pushing-surface.html.

Page 84, *"In a case which gives the lie to the saying about 'fighting like cats and dogs'"*: "Hero Dog Risks Life to Save Kittens from Fire," *Reuters*, October 26, 2008, http://www.reuters.com/article/oddlyEnoughNews/idUSTRE49P1VZ20081026.

Page 84, *"The wandering 65-pound Pit Bull mix"*: Amy Lieberman, "Stray Pit Bull Saves Woman, Child from Attacker," *Zootoo Pet News*, November 5, 2008, http://www.zootoo.com/petnews/straydogsaveswomanchildheldatk.

Page 85, *"A dog is recovering after a Florida Keys carpenter dove in"*: "Man Dives In to Save Dog from Florida Shark Attack," *MSNBC*, September 30, 2008, http://www.msnbc.msn.com/id/26956958/?gt1=43001.

Page 85, *"A local security guard recently discovered a peculiar scene"*: "An Unusual Relationship Between Birds and Fishes," *Spluch Blogspot*, August 30, 2007,

http://spluch.blogspot.com/2007/08/unusual-relationship-between-birds
-and.html.

Page 86, *"A dolphin has come to the rescue of two whales"*: "New Zealand dolphin
Rescues Beached Whales," *BBC News*, March 12, 2008, http://news.bbc.co
.uk/2/hi/asia-pacific/7291501.stm.

Page 87, *"An eight-year-old dog has touched the hearts of Argentines"*: Daniel
Schweimler, "Argentine Dog Saves Abandoned Baby," *BBC News*, August
23, 2008, http://news.bbc.co.uk/2/hi/americas/7577275.stm.

Page 87, *"Trapped in a dark sewer, the six little mallard ducklings"*: Paul Sims,
"Amazing Rescue by a Mother Duck Who Went the Extra Mile," *Daily Mail*,
June 17, 2008, http://www.dailymail.co.uk/news/article-1026801/
Amazing-rescue-mother-duck-went-extra-mile.html.

Page 88, *"A 250-pound bear stranded under a bridge near Lake Tahoe"*: "Bear
Rescued from Bridge after Nearly Falling Off," *MSNBC*, October 1, 2007,
http://www.msnbc.msn.com/id/21078089.

Page 89, *Consider these scenarios. A teenage female elephant was once nursing*:
For more on the examples in this section, see Marc Bekoff, *Wild Justice*.

Page 93, *Domestic animals do this so naturally and powerfully*: One example of this
is the essay "The Healing Power of Dogs" by Tara Parker-Pope, *New York
Times*, January 8, 2008, http://well.blogs.nytimes.com/2008/
01/08/the-healing-power-of-dogs.

Page 94, *Consider a study conducted by psychologist Carolyn Zahn-Waxler*: C.
Zahn-Waxler, M. Radke-Yarrow, E. Wagner, and M. Chapman, "Development
of Concern for Others," *Developmental Psychology* 28 (1992): 126–36.

Page 94, *In a completely different study, one focused on alleviating stress, Karen
Allen*: Karen Allen et al., "Presence of Human Friends and Pet Dogs as
Moderators of Autonomic Responses to Stress in Women." *Journal of
Personality and Social Psychology* 61 (1991): 582–89.

Page 95, *"My entire life has been touched by birds"*: This story was sent by
Alexandria Neonakis to the author by email on August 14, 2008.

REASON 4: *Connection Breeds Caring, Alienation Breeds Disrespect*

Page 106, *we suffer from what . . . Richard Louv calls nature-deficit disorder*: See
Richard Louv, *Last Child in the Woods*, and the author's website,
http://richardlouv.com. For more on the Children and Nature Network, visit
http://www.childrenandnature.org.

Page 107, *Australian environmental ethicist Rod Bennison has developed the notion*:
Rod Bennison, "Ecological Inclusion: An History of the Ideas That Have
Shaped the Interaction Between Human and NonHuman Animals with a
View to a New Interrelationship," PhD diss., University of Newcastle,
Australia, 2007.

Page 107, *"Not long ago I lectured a group of keen university students"*: Clive
Marks, "When Extinction Becomes a Heresy," *Sydney Morning Herald*,
September 27, 2008, http://www.smh.com.au/news/environment/

conservation/when-extinction-becomes-a-heresy/2008/09/26/
1222217517619.html?page=fullpage#contentSwap2.

Page 108, *"That's the way hunting works. The* thing *you're hunting for"*: William
Yardley, "Wolves Aren't Making It Easy for Idaho Hunters," *New York
Times*, September 10, 2009, http://www.nytimes.com/2009/09/11/us/
11wolves.html?_r=1&hp. Emphasis added by author.

Page 109, *Already living at the Moon Bear Centre were two dogs*: For more about
the Moon Bear Centre, visit www.animalsasia.org. For more about Tremor
and Richter, visit http://www.animalsasia.org/blog/index.php?
entry=entry080804-204808 and http://www.animalsasia.org/
blog/index.php?entry=entry080723-001948.

Page 110, *a New York restaurant purchased a just-caught 140-year-old lobster*: "NY
Eatery Frees Ancient Lobster," *BBC News*, January 10, 2009,
http://news.bbc.co.uk/2/hi/americas/7821645.stm.

Page 113, *"Seeing those guys go at a 20lb turkey is like poetry"*: *Time*, December 3,
2007, page 29.

Page 113, *"In a study of urban, middle class children, Alina Pavlakos"*: William
Crain, "Animal Feelings: Learning Not to Care and Not to Know," *Green
Money Journal*, summer 2009, http://www.greenmoneyjournal.com/
article.mpl?newsletterid=46&articleid=640.

Page 114, *The former mayor of Ojai, California, Suza Francina, has written that
4-H programs*: Suza Francina, "4-H Responsibility Should Include Visit to
Slaughterhouse," *Ventura County Star*, August 16, 2009, http://www.ventura
countystar.com/news/2009/aug/16/4-h-responsibility-should-include
-visit-to.

Page 115, *In Australia 470 million chickens were slaughtered from 2006 to 2007*: For
more information, see *Voiceless*, the website of the Animal Protection
Institute in Australia; the numbers here are cited from the "Nest to
Nugget" report, http://www.voiceless.org.au/images/stories/reports/
from_nest_to_nugget_cas_online_final.pdf.

Page 116, *documented in 2008 at the Aviagen Turkeys plant in Lewisburg, West
Virginia*: Donald B. McNeil Jr., "Group Documents Cruelty to Turkeys,"
*New York Times*, November 18, 2008, http://www.nytimes.com/2008/
11/19/dining/19peta.html?scp=1&sq=cruelty%20turkeys&st=cse.

Page 116, *Cows display strong emotions; they feel pain, fear, and anxiety*: Jonathan
Leake, "The Secret Life of Moody Cows," *The Times*, February 27, 2005,
http://www.timesonline.co.uk/tol/news/uk/article416070.ece.

Page 116, *While some have suggested that one solution would be to genetically
engineer "pain-free" animals*: Ewen Callaway, "Pain-free Animals Could Take
Suffering Out of Farming," *New Scientist*, September 2, 2009,
http://www.newscientist.com/article/mg20327243.400-painfree
-animals-could-take-suffering-out-of-farming.html?full=true.

Page 117, *Intensively farmed fish suffer from a range of welfare problems*: Peter
Stevenson, "Closed Waters," the World Society for the Protection of

Animals, 2007 report, http://www.ciwf.org.uk/includes/documents/cm_docs/2008/c/closed_waters_welfare_of_farmed_atlantic_salmon.pdf.

Page 117, *The shocking abuse of "downer" cows . . . an undercover investigation by the U.S. Humane Society*: "Expanded Undercover Investigation Shows Mistreatment of Downer Cows Is Commonplace at Livestock Auctions," *HSUS*, May 7, 2008, http://www.hsus.org/farm/news/ournews/downer_investigation_050708.html.

Page 117, *in July 2008, California Governor Arnold Schwarzenegger strengthened the legal protections*: "Farm Sanctuary Applauds Governor Schwarzenegger for Strengthening Legal Protections," *Reuters*, July 23, 2008, http://www.reuters.com/article/pressRelease/idUS258696+23-Jul-2008+BW20080723; "Government Bans 'Downer' Cows from Food Supply," *Associated Press*, March 14, 2009, http://www.newsvine.com/_news/2009/03/14/2546655-government-bans-downer-cows-from-food-supply.

Page 117, *Raising animals in conditions that foster disease*: For more information on factory farms, see the Humane Farming Association (https://hfa.org) and the Humane Society of the United States Factory Farming Campaign (www.hsus.org/farm).

Page 117, *Physicians at the Austin Medical Center in Minnesota were mystified*: Denise Grady, "A Medical Mystery Unfolds at Minnesota Meatpacking Plant," *New York Times*, February 5, 2008, http://www.nytimes.com/2008/02/05/health/05iht-05pork.9742270.html.

Page 118, *"We continue to allow agribusiness companies to add antibiotics"*: Nicholas Kristof, "Pathogens in Our Pork," *New York Times*, March 14, 2009, http://www.nytimes.com/2009/03/15/opinion/15kristof.html?_r=1&scp=1&sq=pathogens%20pork&st=cse.

Page 118, *"We don't let hog or dairy farms spread their waste unregulated"*: Ian Urbina, "In Maryland, Focus on Poultry Industry Pollution," *New York Times*, November 28, 2008, http://www.nytimes.com/2008/11/29/us/29poultry.html?_r=1&scp=1&sq=maryland%20poultry&st=cse.

Page 119, *industrial meat production is harming the planet, helping spur climate change, and degrading life for all species*: For more information about industrial agriculture and the environment, see the *Compassion in World Farming* publications, http://www.ciwf.org.uk/resources/publications/environment_sustainability/default.aspx.

Page 119, *In New Zealand, 34.2 million sheep, 9.7 million cattle, 1.4 million deer*: Bijal Trivedi, "How Kangaroo Burgers Could Save the Planet," *New Scientist*, December 25, 2008, http://www.newscientist.com/article/mg20026873.100-how-kangaroo-burgers-could-save-the-planet.html.

Page 119, *"producing a pound of beef creates 11 times as much greenhouse gas emission"*: Elisabeth Rosenthal, "As More Eat Meat, a Bid to Cut Emissions," *New York Times*, December 3, 2008, http://www.nytimes.com/2008/12/04/science/earth/04meat.html?pagewanted=2&_r=1&ref=science.

Page 119, *"Global demand for meat has multiplied in recent years"*: Mark Bittman,

"Rethinking the Meat-Guzzler," *New York Times*, January 27, 2008, http://www.nytimes.com/2008/01/27/weekinreview/27bittman.html.

Page 120, *pharmaceutical medicines, pesticides, and chemicals used to treat and protect agricultural animals*: Peter M. J. Fisher and Ross Scott, "Evaluating and Controlling Pharmaceutical Emissions from Dairy Farms: A Critical First Step in Developing a Preventative Management Approach," *Journal of Cleaner Production* 16, no. 14 (September 2008), http://www.sciencedirect.com/science?_ob=ArticleURL&_udi=B6VFX4SSGCH02&_user=10&_rdoc=1&_fmt=&_orig=search&_sort=d&view=c&_version=1&_urlVersion=0&_userid=10&md5=dcf6dc9401f4ab66fc65757e55adef91.

Page 120, *one article summarized the report, "Don't eat meat, ride a bike, and be a frugal shopper"*: "Lifestyle Changes Can Curb Climate Change: IPCC Chief," *Agence France-Presse*, January 15, 2008, http://afp.google.com/article/ALeqM5iIVBkZpOUA9Hz3Xc2u-61mDlrwoQ.

Page 121, *a 2008 study at Carnegie Mellon University found that "foregoing red meat and dairy just one day a week"*: Natasha Loder, Elizabeth Finkel, Craig Meisner, and Pamela Ronald, "The Problem of What to Eat," *Conservation Magazine* 9, no. 3 (July/September 2008), http://www.conservationmagazine.org/articles/v9n3/the-problem-of-what-to-eat.

Page 121, *the carbon footprint of meat-eaters is almost twice that of vegetarians*: A. C. Bert, "Love Mother Earth? Slash Carbon Footprint by Going Veggie," *Now Public* blog, August 26, 2008, http://www.nowpublic.com/environment/love-mother-earth-slash-carbon-footprint-going-veggie

Page 121, *humans are now consuming all resources 30 percent faster than the sustainable rate of replenishment*: "6.7 Billion People Overconsume by 30%," *World Population Balance Newsletter*, August 2009, http://www.worldpopulationbalance.org/wpb_newsletters/wpb_newsletter_2009aug.pdf.

Page 124, *"Switching from the average American diet to a vegetarian one"*: Bijal Trivedi, "What Is Your Dinner Doing to the Climate?" *New Scientist*, September 11, 2008, http://environment.newscientist.com/article/mg19926731.700.

REASON 5: *Our World Is Not Compassionate to Animals*

Page 129, *the U.S. National Research Council recently concluded that the testing of toxic substances*: "Toxicity Testing in the 21st Century: A Vision and a Strategy," National Academy of Sciences, 2007, http://dels.nas.edu/dels/rpt_briefs/Toxicity_Testing_final.pdf; for the report from England, see "Call to End Animal Pain-Research," BBC News, August 14, 2008, http://news.bbc.co.uk/2/hi/health/7561061.stm.

Page 129, *Sharon Begley discovered that "153 out of 167 government-funded studies of bisphenol-A"*: Sharon Begley, "Just Say No — To Bad Science," *Newsweek*, 2007, http://www.newsweek.com/id/35104.

Page 130, *rent the 2005 documentary film* Earthlings: To see a preview of *Earthlings*, and get information about screenings, visit http://www.earthlings.com.

Page 131, *"The Army says it's critical to saving the lives of wounded soldiers"*: "Army Shoots Live Pigs for Medical Drill," *MSNBC*, July 18, 2008, http://www.msnbc.msn.com/id/25735344/.

Page 131, *"Newly released videos are raising questions about the military's continued use"*: "Videos Renew Debate on Military Use of Animals," *CNN*, June 5, 2009, http://www.cnn.com/2009/POLITICS/06/05/ military.animals.training.

Page 132, *"A dolphin has died after colliding with another dolphin"*: "Dolphin Dies After Aerial Collision in US," *Sydney Morning Herald*, April 29, 2008, http://www.smh.com.au/news/news/dolphin-dies-after-aerial-collision-in-us/2008/04/29/1209234842080.html.

Page 132, *"The Berlin Zoo is under pressure to explain the fate of hundreds of animals"*: Kate Connolly, "Unbearable Zoo Mystery Turns into Potboiler," *Sydney Morning Herald*, March 29, 2008, http://www.smh.com.au/news/environment/unbearable-zoo-mystery-turns-into-potboiler/2008/03/28/1206207408578.html.

Page 133, *"Senior zoo experts, staff and the RSPCA have accused the Melbourne Zoo"*: Royce Miller and Cameron Houston, "Zoo Rocked by Abuse Allegations," *The Age*, January 19, 2008, http://www.theage.com.au/news/national/zoo-rocked-by-abuse-allegations/2008/01/18/1200620212113.html.

Page 134, *"Staff at a Hamburg zoo say one of their orangutans died"*: "Orangutan Drowns in German Zoo," *De Spiegel*, July 31, 2008, http://www.spiegel.de/international/zeitgeist/0,1518,569266,00.html.

Page 134, *"Thirty-two research monkeys at a Nevada laboratory died"*: Scott Sonner, "32 Research Monkeys Die in Accident at Nevada Lab," *Asssociated Press*, August 7, 2008, http://www.foxnews.com/wires/2008Aug07/0,4670,ResearchMonkeyDeaths,00.html.

Page 134, *"A monkey, slotted to be used in a drug-product research experiment"*: Chris Halsne, "Monkey Boiled Alive at Research Lab," KIRO TV, January 31, 2008, http://www.kirotv.com/news/15189249/detail.html.

Page 136, *U.S. Department of Agriculture statistics for the fiscal year 2005 listed*: The information about this USDA report is from the "Animal Experimentation in the United States (2007)" fact sheet by *Stop Animal Exploitation Now*, http://www.all-creatures.org/saen/fact-anex-2007.html.

Page 136, *Worldwide in 2005, it was estimated that in 179 countries about 58.3 million*: Katy Taylor, N. Gordon, G. Langley, and W. Higgins, "Estimates for Worldwide Laboratory Animal Use in 2005," *Alternatives to Laboratory Animals* 36 (2008): 327–42.

Page 136, *Veterinarian Andrew Knight has estimated that 68,607,807 additional animals*: Andrew Knight, "127 Million Non-human Vertebrates Used Worldwide for Scientific Purposes in 2005," *ATLA: Alternatives to Laboratory Animals* 36, no. 5 (2008): 494–96.

Page 137, *Britain reported that experiments on animals rose to 3.2 million*: Nigel Morris, "Experiments on Animals Rose to 3.2m Last Year," *The Independent*, July 22, 2008, http://www.independent.co.uk/news/science/experiments-on-animals-rose-to-32m-last-year-873747.html.

Page 137, *In the United States . . . a marked increase in primates imported*: These numbers come from the Humane Society of the United States website, "An Introduction to Primate Issues," http://www.hsus.org/animals_in_research/general_information_on_animal_research/an_introduction_to__primate_issues.html.

Page 137, *"In all, 1,149 people were convicted in 2007 for crimes against animals"*: James Meikle, "RSPCA: 'Throwaway Society' Blamed as Animal Cruelty Convictions Rise," *The Guardian*, July 30, 2008, http://www.guardian.co.uk/uk/2008/jul/30/ukcrime.

Page 138, *the market for purebred or pedigree dogs has led to the rise of abusive "puppy mills"*: For more information, see the Humane Society of the United States website, "Puppy Mills," http://www.hsus.org/pets/issues_affecting_our_pets/get_the_facts_on_puppy_mills.

Page 138, *Renowned Australian veterinarian Paul McGreevy laments, "Pedigree dogs"*: Paul McGreevy, "Comment: We Must Breed Happier, Healthier Dogs," *New Scientist*, October 8, 2008, http://www.newscientist.com/channel/opinion/mg20026776.400-comment-we-must-breed-happier-healthier-dogs.html; for BBC coverage of the Crufts dog show, see Henry Chu, "A British Fight Over Dog-breeding Ethics Gets Pug Ugly," *Los Angeles Times*, March 5, 2009, http://articles.latimes.com/2009/mar/05/world/fg-britain-dogshow5.

Page 138, *Internationally, millions of wild animals are traded illegally*: For more information on the illegal wildlife trade, see the websites of the Humane Society of the United States, "Wildlife Trade," http://www.hsus.org/wildlife/issues_facing_wildlife/wildlife_trade, and of "Traffic," http://www.traffic.org.

Page 140, *Worldwide, as many as 300,000 cetaceans slowly meet their death*: For this information, see "Shrouded by the Sea: The Animal Welfare Implications of Cetacean Bycatch in Fisheries — a Summary Document," Whale and Dolphin Conservation Society (2008), http://www.wdcs.org/submissions_bin/wdcs_bycatchreport_2008.pdf.

Page 141, *a thirty-year study on Ram Mountain in Alberta, Canada, biologist Marco Festa-Bianchet Sherbrooke*: Lily Huang, "It's Survival of the Weak and Scrawny," *Newsweek*, January 12, 2009, http://www.newsweek.com/id/177709?from=rss. For more on this research, see Cornelia Dean, "Research Ties Human Acts to Harmful Rates of Species Evolution," *New York Times*, January 12, 2009, http://www.nytimes.com/2009/01/13/science/13fish.html?_r=2&ref=science.

Page 141, *elephants spend between 72 to 96 percent of the time chained*: For more information on animal welfare in circuses, visit www.captiveanimals.org.

Page 142, *a suit was filed against Ringling Brothers and Barnum & Bailey Circus*: David Stout, "Suit Challenges Image of Circus Elephants as Willing Performers," *New York Times*, January 31, 2009, http://www.nytimes.com/2009/02/01/us/01circus.html?_r=1&scp=1&sq=suit%20challenges%20image&st=cse.

Page 142, *a recent British study found that about 54 percent of elephants*: Craig Redmond, "The Elephant in the Cage," *The Guardian*, December 12, 2008, http://www.guardian.co.uk/commentisfree/2008/dec/12/elephants-zoos-animal-welfare.

Page 142, *Wouldn't zoos without elephants and lions . . . become lessons in compassion?*: For an editorial proposing this idea, see Lori Marino, Gay Bradshaw, and Randy Malamud, "Zoos Without Elephants: A Lesson in Compassion," *Los Angeles Times*, December 15, 2008, http://www.latimes.com/news/opinion/la-oew-marino15-2008dec15,0,1163582.story.

Page 143, *the minimum standard of care for animals . . . is established by the Animal Welfare Act (AWA)*: For more information on the AWA, see the U.S. Humane Society website, "Laws Protecting Animals in Research," http://www.hsus.org/animals_in_research/general_information_on_animal_research/laws_protecting_animals_in_research.

Page 143, *violations of the Animal Welfare Act in the United States increased more than 90 percent*: For more information on animal research, see the Stop Animal Exploitation Now! (SAEN) website, http://www.all-creatures.org/saen.

Page 143, *"Millions of birds suffer miserably each year in government, university"*: Karen Davis, "The Experimental Use of Chickens and Other Birds in Biomedical and Agricultural Research," *United Poultry Concerns*, 2003, http://www.upc-online.org/genetic/experimental.htm.

Page 144, *"The federal government should conduct a thorough review of the regulations"*: "Against Vicious Activism," editorial, *Nature* 457, February 5, 2009, http://www.nature.com/nature/journal/v457/n7230/pdf/457636a.pdf.

Page 145, *a 2008 story in the* New Scientist *looked at researchers who weep*: Andy Coghlan, "Lab Animal Carers Suffer in Silence," *New Scientist*, March 26, 2008, http://www.newscientist.com/article/mg19726493.700-lab-animal-carers-suffer-in-silence.html.

Page 146, *"Mice are lousy models for clinical studies"*: The quote by Mark Davis is from "Mouse Trap? Immunologist Calls for More Research on Humans, Not Mice," *Science Daily*, December 31, 2008, http://www.sciencedaily.com/releases/2008/12/081218122154.htm.

Page 146, *"Since President Richard Nixon declared the war on cancer"*: Andrew Knight, "Animals Needn't Die to Save Human Lives," *Seattle Times*, October 14, 2003, http://www.aknight.info/pages/publications/animal%20research%20medical/editorial_seattle_times_2003.htm.

Page 147, *The U.S. National Institutes of Health . . . promotes a children's coloring book called* The Lucky Puppy: To see this coloring book, visit http://kids.niehs.nih.gov/images/coloring/luckycolor.pdf.

Page 147, *Stuart Derbyshire and Andrew Bagshaw wrote, "We believe that animals are sufficiently different"*: "Animal Pain Is Scientifically Valid: Whether It Is Morally Acceptable Is Another Question," *Alternatives to Laboratory Animals* 36 (2008): 491.

Page 147, *Roberto Caminiti, chair of the Programme of European Neuroscience Schools, argues*: The quotes of Roberto Caminiti and Bill Crum are from Bill Crum, "It Should Be Possible to Replace Animals in Research," *Nature* 457, February 2009, http://www.nature.com/nature/journal/v457/n7230/pdf/457657b.pdf.

Page 148, *"When one empirically analyzes animal models using scientific tools"*: Niall Shanks, Ray Greek, and Jean Greek, "Are Animal Models Predictive for Humans?" *Philosophy, Ethics, and Humanities in Medicine* 4, no. 2 (January 15, 2009), http://www.peh-med.com/content/4/1/2/abstract.

Page 148, *"When it comes to adapting therapeutic interventions"*: "Mouse Trap? Immunologist Calls for More Research on Humans, Not Mice," *Science Daily*, December 31, 2008, http://www.sciencedaily.com/releases/2008/12/081218122154.htm.

Page 149, *In a paper titled "The Poor Contribution of Chimpanzee Experiments to Biomedical Progress"*: Andrew Knight, "The Poor Contribution of Chimpanzee Experiments to Biomedical Progress," *Journal of Applied Animal Welfare Science* 10, no. 4 (2007), http://lib.bioinfo.pl/pmid:17970631.

Page 149, *the U.S. National Institutes of Health and the Environmental Protection Agency announced a five-year deal*: Larry Greenemeier, "Feds Agree to Toxicity Tests that Cut Animal Testing," *Scientific American*, February 15, 2008, http://www.scientificamerican.com/article.cfm?id=feds-agree-to-toxicity-test.

Page 150, *"In previous studies, researchers showed that humans who had been paralyzed"*: Benedict Carey, "Monkeys Think, Moving Artificial Arm as Own," *New York Times*, May 29, 2008, http://www.nytimes.com/2008/05/29/science/29brain.html?_r=1&scp=1&sq=monkeys+robot+arm&st=nyt&oref=slogin.

Page 150, *The deplorable maternal-deprivation studies of Harry Harlow at the University of Wisconsin*: For more information on the current and historic use of monkeys at the University of Wisconsin, visit the website for Madison's Hidden Monkeys, http://www.madisonmonkeys.com/index.htm.

Page 151, *Psychologist Kenneth Shapiro has written extensively about the use of animal models*: For instance, see Kenneth Shapiro, *Animal Models of Human Psychology: Critique of Science, Ethics and Policy* (Seattle: Hogrefe & Huber Publishers, 1998).

Page 152, *"The monoclonal antibody TGN1412 was safe in monkeys"*: John J. Pippin, "Opposing View: Replace Animal Experiments," *USA Today*, December 15, 2008.

Page 152, *Jonathan Balcombe and his colleagues analyzed eighty published studies*:
Jonathan Balcombe, "Laboratory Routines Cause Animal Stress," *Contemporary Topics in Laboratory Animal Science* (autumn 2004), as announced in a news release by the Physicians Committee for Responsible Medicine, November 18, 2004, http://www.pcrm.org/news/release041118.html.

Page 153, *I am not interested to know whether vivisection*: Quoted in Joshua Katcher, "Vivisection Takes Front Stage in New York Times, Today," *The Discerning Brute*, May 28, 2008, http://thediscerning brute.com/2008/05/28/vivisection-takes-front-stage-in-new-york-times-today/.

Page 153, *an antivivisection movement has argued that these practices are immoral*: In 2008 the American Anti-Vivisection Society published an extremely useful historical account of the anti-vivisection movement, called "The Birth of a Movement"; to read it, visit http://www.aavs.org/images/spring2008.pdf. For more information on animal use in research and education, visit InterNiche, http://www.interniche.org.

Page 154, *Medical schools in the United States are also "swapping pigs for plastic"*: Meredith Wadman, "Medical Schools Swap Pigs for Plastic," *Nature News*, May 7, 2008, http://www.nature.com/news/2008/080507/full/453140a.html.

Page 154, *In January* 2008, *the* New York Times *reported that all American medical schools*: Nicholas Bakalar, "Killing Dogs in Training of Doctors Is to End," *New York Times*, January 1, 2008, http://www.nytimes.com/2008/01/01/health/research/01dog.html?_r=1&scp=1&sq=belloni%20dogs&st=cse&oref=slogin. For more information on dissection and its alternatives, see the American Anti-Vivisection Society (www.aavs.org), and In Defense of Animals' Dissection Campaign (http://www.idausa.org/campaigns/dissection/dissection.html), and PETA Kids (www.petakids.com/disindex.html).

Page 155, *"such a severe case of capture myopathy — a kind of muscle meltdown"*: "Bears Captured for Research More Prone to Injuries, Death," *Edmonton Journal*, August 19, 2008, http://www.canada.com/topics/news/national/story.html?id=7be8722e-083c-42ce-af35-6ecaa7f3ee36.

Page 156, *John Brusher and Jennifer Schull have developed nonlethal methods for determining*: John Brusher and Jennifer Schull, "Non-lethal Age Determination for Juvenile Goliath Grouper *Epinephelus itajara* from Southwest Florida," *Endangered Species Research* 7 (July 2009), http://www.int-res.com/articles/esr2009/7/n007p205.pdf.

Page 156, *Even a 2009 essay in the* New York Times *noted the effectiveness of noninvasive research*: Jim Robbins, "Tools that Leave Wildlife Unbothered Widen Research Horizons," *New York Times*, March 9, 2009, http://www.nytimes.com/2009/03/10/science/10wild.html?scp=1&sq=tools%20wildlife%20unbothered&st=cse.

Page 158, *Israeli scientists are using the behavior of disturbed animals in zoos*: "Bears, Gazelles and Rats Inspire New Obsessive-Compulsive Disorder

(OCD) Treatment," *Science Daily*, January 28, 2009, http://www.science daily.com/releases/2009/01/090127170708.htm.

Page 159, *injuries in rodeos are very common*: For more on rodeo injuries, mutton busting, and more, visit the website Showing Animals Respect and Kindness (SHARK), http://www.sharkonline.org, and the ASPCA, http://www.aspca.org/about-us/policy-positions/rodeo.html. For the Bud Kerby quote, see the PETA fact sheet "Rodeo: Cruelty for a Buck," http://www.peta.org/fact sheet/files/FactsheetDisplay.asp?ID=69.

Page 159, *In June 2009 in Longmont, Colorado, a twelve-year-old boy was killed when a bull*: Vanessa Miller, "Coroner: Boy Died of Ruptured Heart Valve," *The Daily Camera*, June 29, 2009, www.dailycamera.com/ci_13126842.

Page 160, *Ralph, an adolescent, twenty-two-foot-long whale shark, died mysteri-ously*: Shaila Dewan, "Death of a Shark Leaves Scientists Grasping," *New York Times*, January 13, 2007, http://www.nytimes.com/2007/01/13/science/13shark.html. For more on animal welfare in zoos, see Michael D. Lemonick, "Who Belongs in the Zoo?" *Time*, June 11, 2006, http://www.time.com/time/magazine/article/0,9171,1202920,00.html.

Page 161, *an essay in* Time *magazine even speculated whether Tatiana*: Alexandra Silver, "Did This Tiger Hold a Grudge?" *Time*, December 28, 2007, http://www.time.com/time/health/article/0,8599,1698987,00.html.

Page 162, *Stephen Zawistowski, science adviser for the American Society for the Prevention of Cruelty to Animals*: Lisa Leff and Terence Chea, "Experts Say Taunting Wasn't Only Factor in Tiger Attack," *Big Cat News*, January 18, 2008, http://bigcatnews.blogspot.com/2008/01/experts-say-taunting-wasnt-only-factor.html.

Page 163, *when I was a reader for the "Review of the Smithsonian Institution's National Zoological Park"*: For more details on this report, see Marc Bekoff, "It's Not Happening at the Zoo," *Animal Welfare Institute*, http://www.awionline.org/ht/d/ContentDetails/i/1927/pid/2505. For my January 26, 2004, reader's report on the National Zoo's review, visit the Animal Welfare Institute website, http://www.awionline.org/ht/display/ContentDetails/i/11644/pid/2505.

Page 167, *"In the past 10 years Western zoos have spent or committed"*: Georgia Mason, "It Is Cruel to Keep Elephants in Captivity," *The Independent*, December 12, 2008, http://www.independent.co.uk/opinion/commentators/georgia-mason-it-iisi-cruel-to-keep-elephants-in-captivity-1062899.html.

Page 169, *A recent study conducted by the Association of Zoos and Aquariums*: "Why Zoos & Aquariums Matter," Association of Zoos & Aquariums, 2007, http://www.aza.org/uploadedFiles/Education/why_zoos_matter.pdf.

Page 170, *In one study conducted at the Edinburgh Zoo in Scotland*: See Animalearn Fact Files, #11, Animals in Entertainment, published by the American Anti-Vivisection Society, http://www.animalearn.org/home.php.

Page 170, *the conservation camps in Chengdu, China, which Sarah Bexell and her*

*Chinese colleagues have organized*: See Sarah Bexell, "Effect of a Wildlife Conservation Camp Experience in China" (2006) and "Nurturing Humane Attitudes toward Animals" (2010); full citations are in References.

Page 173, *the results of a national survey of 157 veterinary faculty in the United States*: C. R. Heleski, A. Mertig, A. J. Zanella, "Results of a National Survey of US Veterinary College Faculty Regarding Attitudes Toward Farm Animal Welfare," *Journal of the American Veterinary Medical Association* 226, no. 9 (May 2005), http://www.cababstractsplus.org/google/abstract.asp? AcNo=20053093469.

Page 174, *Françoise Wemelsfelder stresses in her excellent work*: Françoise Wemelsfelder, "How Animals Communicate Quality of Life: The Qualitative Assessment of Behavior," *Animal Welfare* 16 (May 2007), http://www.ingentaconnect.com/content/ufaw/aw/2007/00000016/A001 02s1/art00005.

Page 175, *"Although it is true that I chose the items listed as critical to the welfare"*: Sue Savage-Rumbaugh, "Welfare of Apes in Captive Environments: Comments On, and By, a Specific Group of Apes," *Journal of Applied Animal Welfare Science* 10, no. 1 (March 2007, http:// www.informaworld.com/ smpp/content~content=a788000924~db=all~order=page. For more on Sue Savage-Rumbaugh and her bonobo studies, see Wendy Jewell, "Science Hero: Dr. Sue Savage-Rumbaugh," My Hero.com, http:// www.myhero.com/my hero/hero.asp?hero=sue_savage_rumbaugh; and the Great Ape Trust of Iowa website, http:// www.iowagreatapes.org/media/releases/ 2008/nr_10a08.php.

REASON 6: *Acting Compassionately Helps All Beings and Our World*

Page 177, *"To see animals who have been tortured all their lives"*: Hannah Wiest, "Wipe Your Paws," *Casper Star-Tribune*, September 13, 2008, http://www.trib.com/news/state-and-regional/article_3c80a45c-2590-5636-9eee-2cb44df9c865.html. For more on the Kindness Ranch, visit their website, http://kindnessranch.org.

Page 178, *In 2002, the Party for the Animals was founded in the Netherlands*: For more on Partij Voor de Dieren (Party for the Animals), visit http://www .partijvoordedieren.nl/content/view/129.

Page 179, *the European Union was considering revising and updating its regulations over the use of animals*: "Revision of Directive 86/609/EEC on the Protection of Animals Used for Experimental and Other Scientific Purposes," European Commission website, May 11, 2008, http://ec.europa.eu/ environment/chemicals/lab_animals/revision_en.htm; see also "Revised Directive 86/609/EEC on Animal Experiments," Dr. Hadwen Trust, November 5, 2008, http://www.drhadwentrust.org/news/revised-directive -86609eec-on-animal-experiments-read-the-dr-hadwen-trusts-reaction -to-new-draft. For more on Animals Count, visit their website, www.animalscount.org.

Page 179, *In July 2009, China drafted the country's first law on animal protection*: "Animal Rights on the Agenda in China," *CCTV*, June 28, 2009, http://www.cctv.com/program/newshour/20090628/102405.shtml.

Page 180, *In the small Portuguese town of Viana do Castelo . . . the mayor banned bullfighting*: "International Praise for Portuguese Mayor After Bull Ring Is Redeveloped," *League Against Cruel Sports*, January 8, 2009, http://www.league.org.uk/news_details.asp?NewsID=1133.

Page 180, *Governor Arnold Schwarzenegger signed a law that strengthened the protection of downed cows*: "Gov. Schwarzenegger Signs Law Strengthening California's Protection for Downed Cows," Humane Society of the United States press release, July 22, 2008, http://www.hsus.org/press_and_publications/press_releases/schwarzenegger_signs_law_protecting_california_downed_cows_072208.html.

Page 180, *In New Jersey, Farm Sanctuary achieved a precedent-setting victory*: "Unanimous Decision of New Jersey Supreme Court Results in Precedent-Setting Victory for Farm Animals," Farm Sanctuary press release, July 30, 2008, http://www.farmsanctuary.org/mediacenter/2008/pr_nj_decision08.html. See also the main Farm Sanctuary website, www.farmsanctuary.org.

Page 182, *"Colorado is now the first state in the country to ban the use of gestation crates"*: "Colorado Bans the Veal Crate and the Gestation Crate," Compassion in World Farming press release, May 19, 2008, http://www.ciwf.org.uk/news/factory_farming/colorado_bans_veal_crates.aspx.

Page 183, *"[Lily] Tomlin last year took up the cause of Jenny"*: Patrick Williams, "Appealing to Dallas' Wallet, Lily Tomlin Keeps Trying to Move Jenny the Elephant," *Dallas Observer*, January 28, 2009, http://www.dallasobserver.com/2009-01-29/news/never-forget.

Page 183, *"The unwanted horses seemed destined for death"*: Lyndsey Layton, "A Dramatic Rescue for Doomed Wild Horses of the West," *Washington Post*, November 18, 2008, http://www.washingtonpost.com/wp-dyn/content/article/2008/11/17/AR2008111703680.html.

Page 184, *"Spain's parliament voiced its support on Wednesday"*: Martin Roberts, "Spanish Parliament to Extend Rights to Apes," *Reuters*, June 25, 2008, http://www.reuters.com/article/scienceNews/idUSL2565863200806255?sp=true.

Page 184, *"Born Free USA . . . today congratulated the US House of Representatives"*: "US Congress Moves Swiftly on Legislation to Stop 'Pet' Primate Trade," *Reuters*, February 24, 2009, http://www.reuters.com/article/pressRelease/idUS241547+24-Feb-2009+PRN20090224.

Page 185, *"The government of Cameroon has created a new national park"*: Richard Black, "Protection Boost for Rare Gorilla," *BBC News*, November 28, 2008, http://news.bbc.co.uk/2/hi/science/nature/7754544.stm.

Page 186, *"The European Commission on Wednesday proposed a ban on seal products*": Leigh Phillips, "Brussels proposes ban on seal cruelty," *EU Observer.com*, July 23, 2008, http://euobserver.com/9/26530.

Page 193, *soldiers in Zimbabwe are being fed elephant meat for their rations*: "Zimbabwe Troops 'Eat Elephants,'" *BBC News*, January 9, 2009, http://news.bbc.co.uk/2/hi/africa/7820885.stm.

Page 194, *"If you want to protect wildlife in developing countries"*: Bryan Walsh, "Eco-Bargain: Save Animals, Reduce Poverty," *Time*, February 1, 2008, http://www.time.com/time/health/article/0,8599,1709186,00.html.

Page 197, *As Mike Tidwell points out in his essay "The Low-Carbon Diet"*: Mike Tidwell, "The Low-Carbon Diet," *Audubon*, January-February 2009, http://www.audubonmagazine.org/features0901/viewpoint.html.

Page 201, *Our stewardship of wild animals should continue*: Clive Marks, "When Extinction Becomes a Heresy," *Sydney Morning Herald*, September 27, 2008, http://www.smh.com.au/news/environment/conservation/when-extinction-becomes-a-heresy/2008/09/26/1222217517619.html?page=fullpage#contentSwap2.

Page 203, *"In July last year, a butterfly landed on my shoulder"*: Dan Southerland, "The Butterfly Effect," *Washington Post*, August 24, 2008, http://www.washingtonpost.com/wp-dyn/content/article/2008/08/15/AR2008081502356_pf.html.

Page 206, *"Human beings are wired to care . . . and it's probably our best route to happiness"*: Patricia Leigh Brown, "Even If You Can't Buy It, Happiness Is Big Business," *New York Times*, November 26, 2008, www.nytimes.com/2008/11/27/us/27happy.html?scp=3&sq=dacher&st=cse.

# REFERENCES

Many of the sources for which I've included websites can be found in the archives of my and Jane Goodall's organization, Ethologists for the Ethical Treatment of Animals (EETA; www.ethologicalethics.org). As I was writing this book, I constantly found myself thinking about the important messages of eco-psychologists like David Abram, E. N. (Géne) Anderson, Warwick Fox, and Laura Sewall: how the ways in which we sense and feel the presence of individual animals directly influences how we interact with them; how good we feel when we interact with animals and nature in peaceful, kind, and benevolent ways; and how these good feelings motivate us to do more for the world at large. Detailed information about numerous topics in ethology, cognitive ethology, and human-animal interactions can be found in my other books *Animals Matter, The Emotional Lives of Animals, Wild Justice: The Moral Lives of Animals* (with Jessica Pierce), the *Encyclopedia of Animal Behavior*, the *Encyclopedia of Human-Animal Relationships: A Global Exploration of Our Connections with Other Animals*, and the *Encyclopedia of Animal Rights and Animal Welfare* (second edition). A chronology of events related to animal protection can also be found in my *Encyclopedia of Human-Animal Relationships* and my *Encyclopedia of Animal Rights and Animal Welfare*.

Books with information about nonanimal alternatives in research and animal protection organizations include my *Encyclopedia of Animal Rights and Animal Welfare* and *Animals Matter*, Amy Bount Achor's *Animal Rights: A Beginner's Guide*, Nick Jukes and Mihnea Chiuia's *From Guinea Pig to Computer Mouse: Alternative Methods for a Humane Education*, Jonathan Balcombe's *The Use of Animals in Higher Education: Problems, Alternatives, and Recommendations*, and *Why Dissection? Animal Use in Education* by Lynette Hart and her colleagues. A web search for "animal protection organizations" will generate a very useful list of organizations around the world.

Abram, David. *The Spell of the Sensuous: Perception and Language in a More-Than-Human World*. New York: Pantheon Books, 1996.

Adams, Carol. *The Sexual Politics of Meat: A Feminist Vegetarian Critical Theory*, 10th ed. New York: Continuum, 1999.

Allen, Colin, and Marc Bekoff. *Species of Mind*. Cambridge, MA: MIT Press, 1997.

Allen, Karen, et al. "Presence of Human Friends and Pet Dogs as Moderators of Autonomic Responses to Stress in Women." *Journal of Personality and Social Psychology* 61 (1991): 582–89.

Anderson, Allen, and Linda Anderson. *Rescued: Saving Animals from Disaster.* Novato, CA: New World Library, 2006.

Anderson, E. N. *Ecologies of the Heart: Emotion, Belief, and the Environment.* New York: Oxford University Press, 1996.

Anderson, Virginia DeJohn. *Creatures of Empire: How Domestic Animals Transformed Early America.* New York: Oxford University Press, 2004.

Animal Welfare Information Center, http://awic.nal.usda.gov. Run by the U.S. Department of Agriculture, the *AWIC Bulletin* provides current information on animal welfare to investigators, technicians, administrators, exhibitors, and the public.

Appleby, Michael C., Joy A. Mench, and B. O. Hughes. *Poultry Behaviour and Welfare.* Cambridge, MA: CABI Publishing, 2004.

Archer, J. *The Nature of Grief: The Evolution and Psychology of Reactions to Loss.* New York: Routledge, 1999.

Arluke, Arnold, and Clinton Sanders, eds. *Between the Species: A Reader in Human-Animal Relationships.* Upper Saddle River, NJ: Pearson Higher Education, Allyn & Bacon, 2008.

Balcombe, Jonathan. *The Use of Animals in Education: Problems, Alternatives, and Recommendations.* Washington, DC: Humane Society of the United States, 2000.

———. *Pleasurable Kingdom: Animals and the Nature of Feeling Good.* London: Macmillan, 2006.

Balcombe, Jonathan P., Neal D. Barnard, and Chad Sandusky. "Laboratory Routines Cause Animal Stress." *Contemporary Topics* (American Association for Laboratory Science) 43 (2004): 42–51.

Baldwin, Ann, and Marc Bekoff. "Too Stressed to Work." *New Scientist* (June 2, 2007): 24.

Bates, L. A., and R. W. Byrne. "Creative or Created: Using Anecdotes to Investigate Animal Cognition." *Methods* 42 (2007): 12–21.

Bateson, P. "Assessment of Pain in Animals." *Animal Behaviour* 42 (1991): 827–39.

Baur, Gene. *Farm Sanctuary: Changing Hearts and Minds About Animals and Food.* New York: Touchstone, 2008.

Bearzi, M., and C. B. Stanford. *Beautiful Minds: The Parallel Lives of Great Apes and Dolphins.* Cambridge, MA: Harvard University Press, 2008.

Beck, Benjamin B. "Chimpanzee Orphans: Sanctuaries, Reintroduction, and Cognition." In *The Mind of the Chimpanzee: Ecological and Experimental Perspectives,* edited by E. Lonsdorf, S. Ross, and T. Matsuzawa. Chicago: University of Chicago Press, 2010.

———. "Marking, Trapping, and Manipulating Animals: Some Methodological and Ethical Considerations." In *Wildlife Mammals as Research Models: In the Laboratory and Field*, edited by K. A. L. Bayne and M. D. Kreger, 31–47. Greenbelt, MD: Scientists Center for Animal Welfare, 1995.

Bekoff, Marc. "Play Signals as Punctuation: The Structure of Social Play in Canids." *Behaviour* 132 (1995): 419–29.

———. "Animal Emotions: Exploring Passionate Natures." *BioScience* 50 (2000): 861–70.

———, ed. *The Smile of a Dolphin: Remarkable Accounts of Animal Emotions.* Washington, DC: Random House/Discovery Books, 2000.

———. *Strolling with Our Kin: Speaking for and Respecting Voiceless Animals.* New York: Lantern Books, 2000.

———. *Minding Animals: Awareness, Emotions, and Heart.* New York: Oxford University Press, 2002.

———, ed. *Encyclopedia of Animal Behavior.* Westport, CT: Greenwood Publishing Group, 2004.

———. "Wild Justice and Fair Play: Cooperation, Forgiveness, and Morality in Animals." *Biology & Philosophy* 19 (2004): 489–520.

———. "Animal Emotions and Animal Sentience and Why They Matter: Blending 'Science Sense' with Common Sense, Compassion and Heart." In *Animals, Ethics, and Trade*, edited by J. Turner and J. D'Silva, 27–40. London: Earthscan Publishing, 2006.

———. "Animal Passions and Beastly Virtues: Cognitive Ethology as the Unifying Science for Understanding the Subjective, Emotional, Empathic, and Moral Lives of Animals." *Zygon: Journal of Religion and Science* 41 (2006): 71–104.

———. *Animal Passions and Beastly Virtues: Reflections on Redecorating Nature.* Philadelphia: Temple University Press, 2006.

———. "The Public Lives of Animals: A Troubled Scientist, Pissy Baboons, Angry Elephants, and Happy Hounds." *Journal of Consciousness Studies* 13 (2006): 115–31.

———. *Animals Matter: A Biologist Explains Why We Should Treat Animals With Compassion and Respect.* Boston: Shambhala, 2007.

———. *The Emotional Lives of Animals: A Leading Scientist Explores Animal Joy, Sorrow, and Empathy — and Why They Matter.* Novato, CA: New World Library, 2007.

———, ed. *Encyclopedia of Human-Animal Relationships: A Global Exploration of Our Connections with Other Animals.* Westport, CT: Greenwood Publishing Group, 2007.

———. "Why 'Good Welfare' Isn't 'Good Enough': Minding Animals and Increasing Our Compassionate Footprint." *Annual Review of Biomedical Sciences* 10 (2008): T1–T14.

———, ed. *Encyclopedia of Animal Rights and Animal Welfare*, 2nd ed. Westport, CT: Greenwood Publishing Group, 2009.

Bekoff, Marc, and Colin Allen. "Cognitive Ethology: Slayers, Skeptics, and Proponents." In *Anthropomorphism, Anecdote, and Animals: The Emperor's New Clothes,* edited by R. W. Mitchell, N. Thompson, and L. Miles, 313–34. Albany, NY: SUNY Press, 1997.

Bekoff, Marc, Colin Allen, and Gordon M. Burghardt, eds. *The Cognitive Animal: Empirical and Theoretical Perspectives on Animal Cognition.* Cambridge, MA: MIT Press, 2002.

Bekoff, Marc, and John A. Byers, eds. *Animal Play: Evolutionary, Comparative, and Ecological Approaches.* New York: Cambridge University Press, 1998.

Bekoff, Marc, and Dale Jamieson. "Reflective Ethology, Applied Philosophy, and the Moral Status of Animals." *Perspectives in Ethology* 9 (1991): 1–47.

———. "Ethics and the Study of Carnivores: Doing Science While Respecting Animals." In *Carnivore Behavior, Ecology, and Evolution,* edited by J. Gittleman, 16–45. Ithaca, NY: Cornell University Press, 1996.

———, eds. *Readings in Animal Cognition.* Cambridge, MA: MIT Press, 1996.

Bekoff, Marc, and Jessica Pierce. *Wild Justice: The Moral Lives of Animals.* Chicago: University of Chicago Press, 2009.

Bentham, Jeremy. *An Introduction to the Principles of Morals and Legislation.* New York: Hafner Press, 1789/1948.

Berry, Thomas. *The Great Work: Our Way Into the Future.* New York: Bell Tower, 1999.

———. "An interview with Thomas Berry." *Wild Earth* (summer 2000): 93–97.

Beston, Henry. *The Outermost House.* New York: Ballantine Books, 1928/1956.

Bexell, Sarah M. "Effect of a Wildlife Conservation Camp Experience in China on Student Knowledge of Animals, Care, Propensity for Environmental Stewardship, and Compassionate Behavior Toward Animals." PhD diss., Georgia State University, 2006.

Bexell, Sarah M., Olga S. Jarrett, Luo Lan, Hu Yan, and Estelle A. Sandhaus. "Observing Panda Play: Implications for Zoo Programming and Conservation Efforts." *Curator* 50 (2007): 287–97.

Bexell, Sarah M., Olga S. Jarrett, Xu Ping, and Feng Rui Xi. "Nurturing Humane Attitudes toward Animals: An Educational Camp Experience in China." *Encounter* (2010): 1–3.

Bradshaw, G. A., A. N. Schore, J. L. Brown, J. H. Poole, and C. Moss. "Elephant Breakdown." *Nature* 433 (2005): 807.

Bradshaw, G. A., and A. N. Schore. "How Elephants Are Opening Doors: Developmental Neuroethology, Attachment, and Social Context." *Ethology* 133 (2007): 426–36.

Brakes, Philippa, A. Butterworth, M. Simmonds, and P. Lymbery. *Troubled Waters: A Review of the Welfare Implications of Modern Whaling Activities.* London: World Society for the Protection of Animals, 2004. http://www.wdcs.org/submissions_bin/troubledwaters.pdf.

Burns, J. G., A. Saravanan, and F. H. Rodd. "Rearing Environment Affects the Brain Size of Guppies: Lab-Reared Guppies Have Smaller Brains than Wild-Caught Guppies." *Ethology* 115 (2009): 122–33.

Carbone, Larry. *What Animals Want: Expertise and Advocacy in Laboratory Animal Welfare Policy.* New York: Oxford University Press, 2004.

Chinese Animal Protection Network, http://www.capn.ngo.con/en.asp. This is the first Chinese network for animal protection.

Clubb, R., M. Rowcliffe, P. Lee, K. U. Mar, C. Moss, and G. Mason. "Compromised Survivorship in Zoo Elephants." *Science* 322 (2008): 1649.

Coetzee, J. M. *The Lives of Animals.* Princeton, NJ: Princeton University Press, 2001.

Croke, Vicki. *The Modern Ark: The Story of Zoos: Past, Present, and Future.* New York: Scribners, 1997.

Darwin, Charles. *The Descent of Man and Selection in Relation to Sex.* New York: Random House, 1871/1936.

———. *The Expression of the Emotions in Man and Animals,* 3rd ed. New York: Oxford University Press, 1872/1998. The complete works of Darwin can be found at http://darwin-online.org.uk.

Davis, Karen. *More Than a Meal: The Turkey in History, Myth, Ritual, and Reality.* New York: Lantern Books, 2001.

———. *The Holocaust and the Henmaid's Tale: A Case for Comparing Atrocities.* New York: Lantern Books, 2005.

Dawn, Karen. *Thanking the Monkey: Rethinking the Way We Treat Animals.* New York: HarperCollins, 2008.

DeGrazia, David. "Moral Vegetarianism from a Very Broad Basis." In *Encyclopedia of Animal Rights and Animal Welfare,* 2nd ed., edited by Marc Bekoff. Westport, CT: Greenwood Publishing Group, 2009.

Doty, Mark. *Dog Years.* New York: HarperCollins, 2007.

Douglas-Hamilton, Iain, S. Bhalla, G. Wittemyer, and F. Vollrath. "Behavioural Reactions of Elephants Towards a Dying and Deceased Matriarch." *Applied Animal Behaviour Science* 100 (2006): 87–102.

Dudzinski, Kathleen, and Toni Frohoff. *Dolphin Mysteries: Unlocking the Secrets of Communication.* New Haven, CT: Yale University Press, 2008.

Duncan, Ian J. H. "Poultry Welfare: Science or Subjectivity?" *British Poultry Science* 43 (2002): 643–52.

Ehrlich, Paul. *A World of Wounds: Ecologists and the Human Dilemma.* Oldendorf/Luhe, Germany: Ecology Institute, 1997.

Eisner, Gail A. *Slaughterhouse.* New York: Prometheus, 1997.

Finsen, L., and S. Finsen. *The Animal Rights Movement in America: From Compassion to Respect.* New York: Twayne Publishers, 1994.

Forthman, D., L. F. Kane, D. Hancocks, and P. F. Waldau, eds. *An Elephant in the Room: The Science and Well-Being of Elephants in Captivity.*

North Grafton, MA: Tufts Center for Animals and Public Policy, Tufts University, 2009.

Fox, Michael W. *Bringing Life to Ethics: Global Bioethics for a Humane Society*. Albany, NY: SUNY Press, 2001.

―――. *Eating with Conscience*. Troutdale, OR: New Sage Press, 1997.

Fox, W. *Toward a Transpersonal Ecology: Developing New Foundations for Environmentalism*. Foxhole, England: Green Books Ltd, 1995.

Francione, Gary L. *Introduction to Animal Rights: Your Child or the Dog?* Philadelphia: Temple University Press, 2000.

―――. *Animals as Persons: Essays On the Abolition of Animal Exploitation*. New York: Columbia University Press, 2008.

Franklin, Adrian. *Animals and Modern Cultures: A Sociology of Human-Animal Relations in Modernity*. London: Sage, 1999.

Fraser, David. *Understanding Animal Welfare: The Science in Its Cultural Context*. Sussex, England: Wiley-Blackwell, 2008.

Garner, R. "The Economics and Politics of Animal Exploitation." In *Political Animals: Animal Protection Politics in Britain and the United States*. New York: St. Martin's Press, 1998.

Gilbert, F.F., and N. Gofton. "Terminal Dives in Mink, Muskrat and Beaver." *Physiology & Behavior* 28 (1982): 835–40.

Goodall, Jane. *Through a Window*. Boston: Houghton-Mifflin, 1990.

Goodall, Jane, and Marc Bekoff. *The Ten Trusts: What We Must Do to Care for the Animals We Love*. San Francisco: HarperCollins, 2002.

Greek, C.R., and J.S. Greek. *Sacred Cows and Golden Geese: The Human Cost of Experiments on Animals*. New York: Continuum, 2000.

―――. *Specious Science: How Evolution and Genetics Explain Why Medical Research on Animals Kills Humans*. New York: Continuum, 2002.

Green People, http://www.greenpeople.org/animalrights.htm. This website provides links to organizations in the United States by state and to organizations around the world.

Greive, B.T. *Priceless: The Vanishing Beauty of a Fragile Planet*. Riverside, NJ: Andrews McMeel Publishing, 2003.

Griffin, Donald R. *The Question of Animal Awareness: Evolutionary Continuity of Mental Experience*. New York: Rockefeller University Press, 1976/1981.

―――. *Animal Minds*. Chicago: University of Chicago Press, 1992.

Group for the Education of Animal-Related Issues (GEARI), http://www.geari.org. A nonprofit education organization.

Hadidian, John. *Wild Neighbors: The Humane Approach to Living With Wildlife*. Washington, DC: Humane Society Press, 2007.

Hall, Lee. *Capers in the Churchyard: Animal Rights Advocacy in the Age of Terror*. Darien, CT: Nectar Bat Press, 2006.

Hancocks, David. *A Different Nature: The Paradoxical World of Zoos and Their Uncertain Future*. Berkeley: University of California Press, 2002.

Hatkoff, Amy. *The Inner World of Farm Animals: Their Amazing Intellectual, Emotional, and Social Capacities*. New York: Stewart, Tabori & Chang, 2009.

Heinrich, Bernd. *Mind of the Raven: Investigations and Adventures with Wolf-Birds*. New York: Cliff Street Books, 1999.

His Holiness the Dalai Lama. *The Path to Tranquility: Daily Wisdom*. Compiled and edited by Renuka Singh. New York: Viking Arkana, 1999.

———. "Understanding Our Fundamental Nature." In *Visions of Compassion: Western Scientists and Tibetan Buddhists Examine Human Nature*, 66–80. New York: Oxford University Press, 2002.

Horowitz, Alexandra C., and Marc Bekoff. "Naturalizing Anthropomorphism: Behavioral Prompts to Our Humanizing of Animals." *Anthrozoös* 20 (2007): 23–36.

International Society for Anthrozoology, www.isaz.net. This organization studies human-nonhuman interactions and publishes the journal *Anthrozoös*.

Irvine, Leslie. *If You Tame Me: Understanding Our Connections with Animals*. Philadelphia: Temple University Press, 2004.

———. *Filling the Ark*. Philadelphia: Temple University Press, 2009.

Jamieson, Dale. "Against Zoos." In *In Defense of Animals*, edited by Peter Singer, 108–17. New York: Basil Blackwell, 1985.

———. *Ethics and the Environment*. New York: Cambridge University Press, 2008.

Kellert, Stephen, and J. Berry. "Attitudes, Knowledge and Behaviors Toward Wildlife As Affected By Gender." *Wildlife Society Bulletin* 15 (1997): 363–71.

Kelsey, Elin. *Watching Giants: The Secret Lives of Whales*. Berkeley: University of California Press, 2009.

Keltner, Dacher. *Born to Be Good: The Science of a Meaningful Life*. New York: W. W. Norton & Company, 2009.

Knight, Andrew. "Non-animal Methodologies Within Biomedical Research and Toxicity Testing." *Alternatives to Animal Experimentation* 25 (2008): 213–31. http://www.animalconsultants.org/portfolio/animal_experimentation_non-animal_methodologies_knight_2008_altex.htm.

Kumar, Satish. "Simplicity for Christmas and Always." *Resurgence* (November/December 2000): 3.

Lawrence, Elizabeth A. *Rodeo: An Anthropologist Looks at the Wild and the Tame*. Knoxville: University of Tennessee Press, 1982.

———. *Hoofbeats and Society: Studies of Human-Horse Interactions*. Bloomington: Indiana University Press, 1985.

Louv, Richard. *Last Child in the Woods: Saving Our Children from Nature Deficit Disorder*. Chapel Hill, NC: Algonquin Books, 2005.

Mallonée, Jay S. *Timber: A Perfect Life*. Whitehall, MT: New Perceptions Press, 2007.

Mallonée, Jay S., and Paul Joslin. "Traumatic Stress Disorder Observed in an

Adult Wild Captive Wolf." *Journal of Applied Animal Welfare Science* 7 (2004): 107–26.

Marino, Lori, R. C. Conner, R. E. Fordyce, L. M. Herman, P. R. Hof, et al. "Cetaceans Have Complex Brains for Complex Cognition." *PLoS Biology* 5, no. 5 (2007).

Masson, Jeffrey, and Susan McCarthy. *When Elephants Weep: The Emotional Lives of Animals.* New York: Delacorte Press, 1995.

McMillan, Frank D., with Kathryn Lance. *Unlocking the Animal Mind: How Your Pet's Feelings Hold the Key to His Health and Happiness.* Emmaus, PA: Rodale, 2004.

Midgley, Mary. *Animals and Why They Matter.* Athens: University of Georgia Press, 1983.

Midkiff, Ken. *The Meat You Eat.* New York: St. Martin's Griffin, 2004.

Miller, Henry. *Big Sur and the Oranges of Hieronymus Bosch.* New York: New Directions, 1957.

Moss, Cynthia. *Elephant Memories: Thirteen Years in the Life of an Elephant Family.* Chicago: University of Chicago Press, 2000.

Newkirk, Ingrid. *Making Kind Choices: Everyday Ways to Enhance Your Life Through Earth- and Animal-Friendly Living.* New York: St. Martin's Griffin, 2005.

Niman, Nicolette H. *Righteous Porkchop: Finding a Life and Good Food Beyond Factory Farms.* New York: Collins Living, 2009.

Ogorzaly, Michael A. *When Bulls Cry: The Case Against Bullfighting.* Bloomington, IN: AuthorHouse, 2006.

Olmert, Meg Daley. *Made for Each Other: The Biology of the Human-Animal Bond.* New York: De Capo Press, 2009.

Orlans, Barbara F. "The Injustice of Excluding Laboratory Rats, Mice, and Birds from the Animal Welfare Act." *Kennedy Institute of Ethics Journal* 10 (2000): 229–38.

Peterson, Dale. *Eating Apes.* Berkeley: University of California Press, 2003.

Phelps, Norm. *The Great Compassion: Buddhism and Animal Rights.* New York: Lantern Books, 2004.

———. *The Longest Struggle: Animal Advocacy from Pythagoras to PETA.* New York: Lantern Books, 2007.

Pickover, Michelle. *Animal Rights in South Africa.* Capetown, South Africa: Double Storey, 2005.

Pollan, Michael. *The Omnivore's Dilemma: A Natural History of Four Meals.* New York: Penguin, 2006.

———. *In Defense of Food: An Eater's Manifesto.* New York: Penguin, 2008.

Poole, Joyce. *Coming of Age with Elephants: A Memoir.* New York: Hyperion, 1996.

———. "An Exploration of a Commonality Between Ourselves and Elephants." *Etica & Animali* 9, no. 98 (1998): 85–110.

Poulsen, Else. *Smiling Bears: A Zookeeper Explores the Behavior and Emotional Lives of Bears*. Vancouver, British Columbia: Greystone Books, 2009.

Rachels, James. *Created from Animals: The Moral Implications of Darwinism*. New York: Oxford University Press, 1990.

Reardon, Lynn. *Beyond the Homestretch: What I've Learned from Saving Racehorses*. Novato, CA: New World Library, 2009.

Regan, Tom. *The Case for Animal Rights*. Berkeley: University of California Press, 1983.

———. *Empty Cages: Facing the Challenge of Animal Rights*. New York: Rowman & Littlefield, 2004.

Ridley, Mark. *The Origins of Virtue: Human Instincts and the Evolution of Cooperation*. New York: Viking, 1996.

Rilling, James K., D.A. Gutman, T.R. Zeh, G. Pagnoni, G.S. Berns, and C.D. Kitts. "A Neural Basis for Cooperation." *Neuron* 36 (2002): 395–405.

Rollin, Bernard E. *The Unheeded Cry: Animal Consciousness, Animal Pain, and Science*. New York: Oxford University Press, 1989.

Ryder, Richard D. "Speciesism." In *Encyclopedia of Animal Rights and Animal Welfare*, edited by Marc Bekoff, 320. Westport, CT: Greenwood Publishing Group, 1998.

Salem, Deborah J., and Andrew N. Rowan, eds. *The State of the Animals IV, 2007*. Washington, DC: Humane Society Press, 2007.

Scharper, Stephen. *Redeeming the Time*. New York: Continuum, 1997.

Scully, Matthew. *Dominion: The Power of Man, the Suffering of Animals*. New York: St. Martin's Press, 2002.

Sewall, Laura. *Sight and Sensibility: The Ecopsychology of Perception*. New York: Jeremy P. Tarcher/Putnam, 1999.

"Shrouded by the Sea: The Animal Welfare Implications of Cetacean Bycatch in Fisheries — a Summary Document." Whale and Dolphin Conservation Society (2008), http://www.wdcs.org/submissions_bin/wdcs_bycatchreport_2008.pdf.

Singer, Peter. *Animal Liberation*, 2nd ed. New York: New York Review of Books, 1990.

Singer, Peter, and Jim Mason. *The Way We Eat: Why Our Food Choices Matter*. Emmaus, PA: Rodale, 2006.

Skutch, Alexander. *The Minds of Birds*. College Station, TX: Texas A&M University Press, 1996.

Slobodchikoff, C.N., B.S. Perla, and J.L. Verdolin. *Prairie Dogs: Communication and Community in an Animal Society*. Cambridge, MA: Harvard University Press, 2009.

Smith, Ethan, with G. Dauncey. *Building an Ark: 101 Solutions to Animal Suffering*. Gabriola Island, British Columbia, Canada: New Society Publishers, 2007.

Sneddon, Lynne U. "The Evidence for Pain in Fish: The Use of Morphine as an Analgesic." *Applied Animal Behaviour Science* 83 (2003): 153–62.

Solisti, Kate, and Michael Tobias, eds. *Kinship with Animals*. Tulsa, OK: Council Oaks Books, 2006.

Steiner, Gary. *Animals and the Moral Community*. New York: Columbia University Press, 2008.

Taussig, Nick. *Gorilla Guerrilla*. London: Revolver Books, 2008.

Taylor, Katy, N. Gordon, G. Langley, and W. Higgins. "Estimates for Worldwide Laboratory Animal Use in 2005." *Alternatives to Laboratory Animals* 36 (2008): 327–42.

Tobias, Michael, and Jane Morrison. *Sanctuary: Global Oases of Innocence*. San Francisco: Council Oak Books, 2008.

Trungpa, Chögyam. *Shambhala: The Sacred Path of the Warrior*. Boston: Shambhala, 1988.

Turner, Jackie, and Joyce D'Silva, eds. *Animals, Ethics, and Trade*. London: EarthScan Publishing, 2006.

Unti, Bernard, and Andrew Rowan. "A Social History of Post War Animal Protection." In *The State of the Animals*, edited by Deborah Salem and Andrew Rowan. Washington, DC: Humane Society Press, 2001. http://www.hsus.org/press_and_publications/humane_bookshelf/the_state_of_the_animals_2001.html.

Van Dernoot, L., and C. Burk. *Trauma Stewardship: An Everyday Guide to Caring for Self While Caring for Others*. San Francisco: Berrett-Koehler Publishers, 2009.

Waldau, Paul, and Kimberley Patton, eds. *A Communion of Subjects: Animals in Religion, Science, and Ethics*. New York: Columbia University Press, 2006.

Weil, Zoe. *Above All, Be Kind: Raising a Humane Child in Challenging Times*. Gabiola Island, British Columbia, Canada: New Society Publishers, 2003.

Wemelsfelder, Françoise, and Alistair B. Lawrence. "Qualitative Assessment of Animal Behaviour as an On-Farm Welfare-Monitoring Tool." *Acta Agriculturae Scandinavica* 30 (2001): S21–S25.

White, Thomas I. *In Defense of Dolphins: The New Moral Frontier*. Malden, MA: Blackwell Publishing, 2007.

Williams, Erin, and Margo DeMello. *Why Animals Matter: The Case for Animal Protection*. Amherst, NY: Prometheus Books, 2007.

Williams, Terry Tempest. *Finding Beauty in a Broken World*. New York: Vintage, 2009.

Wise, Steven M. *Rattling the Cage: Toward Legal Rights for Animals*. Cambridge, MA: Perseus Publishing, 2000.

———. "The Evolution of Animal Law Since 1950." In *The State of the Animals II*, edited by Deborah Salem and Andrew Rowan. Washington, DC: Humane Society Press, 2003. http://www.hsus.org/press_and_publications/humane_bookshelf/the_state_of_the_animals_ii_2003.html

Woodroffe, R., S. Thirgood, and A. Rabinowitz, eds. *People and Wildlife, Conflict or Coexistence?* Cambridge, MA: Cambridge University Press, 2005.

WordPress.com, Animal Protection Organizations, http://wordpress.com/tag/
    animal-protection-organizations. This blog focuses on animal news, politics,
    and organizations.

World Animal.Net, http://www.worldanimal.net. The world's largest network
    of animal protection societies with consultative status at the United Nations.

Zahn-Waxler, C., M. Radke-Yarrow, E. Wagner, and M. Chapman. "Develop-
    ment of Concern for Others." *Developmental Psychology* 28 (1992): 126–36.

# INDEX

# ABOUT THE AUTHOR

*Marc and Bessie, a rescued cow, at Farm Sanctuary, Orland, California.*

MARC BEKOFF is Professor Emeritus of Ecology and Evolutionary Biology at the University of Colorado, a Fellow of the Animal Behavior Society, and a former Guggenheim Fellow. In 2009 he became a faculty member of the Humane Society University and a scholar-in-residence at the University of Denver's Institute of Human-Animal Connection. In 2000 he was awarded the Exemplar Award from the Animal Behavior Society for major long-term contributions to the field of animal behavior. Marc is also an ambassador for Jane Goodall's Roots & Shoots program, in which he works with students of all ages, senior citizens, and prisoners. Marc has published more than two hundred scientific and popular essays and twenty-two books, including *Minding Animals, The Ten Trusts* (with Jane Goodall), *The Emotional Lives of Animals, Animals Matter, Animals at Play: Rules of the Game* (an award-winning children's book), *Wild Justice: The Moral Lives of Animals* (with Jessica Pierce), the *Encyclopedia of Human-Animal Relationships*, the *Encyclopedia of Animal Behavior*, and two editions of the *Encyclopedia of Animal Rights and Animal Welfare*. In 2005 Marc was presented with the Bank One Faculty Community Service Award for the work he has done with children, senior citizens, and prisoners. In 1986 he became the first American to win his age-class at the Tour du Var bicycle race (also called the Master's/age-graded Tour de France). Among Marc's hobbies are cycling, skiing, hiking, and reading spy novels of varying quality.

His websites are www.marcbekoff.com
and, with Jane Goodall, www.ethologicalethics.org.